A COUNTRY STOREKEEPER IN PENNSYLVANIA

{ A }

COUNTRY STOREKEEPER

IN PENNSYLVANIA

CREATING ECONOMIC NETWORKS
IN EARLY AMERICA,
1790–1807

DIANE E. WENGER

THE PENNSYLVANIA STATE UNIVERSITY PRESS
UNIVERSITY PARK, PENNSYLVANIA

Library of Congress Cataloging-in-Publication Data

Wenger, Diane E., 1948–
A country storekeeper in Pennsylvania : creating economic networks in early America /
Diane E. Wenger.
p.   cm.
Summary: "Examines the role that country storekeeper Samuel Rex of Schaefferstown,
Pennsylvania, played in the society and economy of the mid-Atlantic region from 1790 to
1807. Studies consumption patterns of one typical Pennsylvania-German community"—
Provided by publisher.
Includes bibliographical references and index.
ISBN 978-0-271-03413-3 (pbk : alk. paper)
1. Rex, Samuel, d. 1835.
2. General stores—Pennsylvania—Schaefferstown—History—18th century.
3. Merchants—Pennsylvania—Schaefferstown—History—18th century.
4. Business networks—Pennsylvania—Schaefferstown—History—18th century.
5. Schaefferstown (Pa.)—Commerce—History—18th century.
6. Schaefferstown (Pa.)—Economic conditions—18th century.
7. Schaefferstown (Pa.)—History—18th century.
I. Title.

HF5429.5.S35W46 2008
381'.1092—dc22
2008017894

The Pennsylvania State University Press is a member of
the Association of American University Presses.

It is the policy of
The Pennsylvania State University Press to use
acid-free paper. This book is printed on stock that meets
the minimum requirements
of American National Standard for Information Sciences—
Permanence of Paper for Printed Library Material,
ANSI Z39.48–1992.

CONTENTS

FIGURES AND TABLES

PREFACE AND ACKNOWLEDGMENTS

In 1970 my husband and I bought and began to restore an old log house in Schaefferstown, a small village in eastern Lebanon County, Pennsylvania. One day, while removing the crumbling plaster from the walls of a second-floor bedroom, I paused to look out the window. Although the window frame was an old one, its panes were new, and they provided a clear view of Main Street. Unlike the modern glass through which I peered, old glass is uneven and sometimes produces a distorted image. I imagined that one piece of eighteenth-century glass remained, and that this imperfect pane had somehow captured the scenes it had looked upon two centuries ago. If only one could gaze through such glass, I mused, and see back to 1800, when the street was nothing more than a dusty road, lined with log houses. Who lived here? What was life like in Schaefferstown then?

Fast-forward to 1993. I had returned to school and was working on my master's degree in American studies at Penn State Harrisburg and I needed to find a nineteenth-century document for a class project. I recalled that some Schaefferstown store ledgers had recently become available, and I decided that one of these would make an adequate, if not very exciting, study. It was a choice that proved far more interesting and more fruitful than I anticipated. In fact, through Samuel Rex's store ledgers and related documents, I found that window back to the past that I had longed for, and I gained the tools that enabled me to visit Schaefferstown and beyond in the early years of the Republic.

Along the way I received help and encouragement from a number of persons who made this work possible, and I am pleased to thank them here. Robert C. Bucher generously lent me a Rex daybook from his personal collection for my initial research paper in 1993, and thus set me on the path that made this project possible. Orpha M. Lewis gave me permission to make a copy of the Leon E. Lewis microfilm collection for my own use. As I continued my research, the directors of Historic Schaefferstown, Inc., allowed me free access to their archives and to the Gemberling-Rex House. Cynthia Falk, a fellow student of Pennsylvania German culture, provided numerous leads on sources and ongoing encouragement, as did Howard Applegate, my good friend and former colleague at Lebanon Valley College. My advisor at the University of Delaware, Cathy Matson, helped me in countless ways to plan the research and write the dissertation that evolved into this book. She and the other members of my committee, J. Ritchie Garrison, Peter Kolchin, and Rosalind Remer, offered many insightful comments that guided me as I revised the dissertation for publication. Jim Dibert offered a number of useful suggestions for revision after reading the chapter on the iron community. Alan Keyser and Steve Longenecker provided crucial information and advice on Pennsylvania Germans' material life and religion, respectively. Schaefferstown resident and good friend Barbara Smith shared many Schaefferstown photographs and documents. Dr. Robert Kline was generous with his Schaefferstown papers and his knowledge of local history. Numerous conversations with Charlie Bergengren about eighteenth-century tavern life and the Gemberling-Rex House architecture increased my understanding of the building Samuel Rex made his home.

My research was made easier with the help of many very capable librarians, especially Donna Miller at Lebanon Valley College and the staff of the Joseph Downs Collection. Penn State Press editors Peter Potter and Sanford G. Thatcher guided me through the revision and contract stage of the manuscript, and readers for the Press provided helpful recommendations for revision that made this a much better work than it could ever have been otherwise. Any errors that remain are my own.

Portions of several chapters of this book first appeared in an article entitled "Delivering the Goods: The Country Storekeeper and Inland Commerce in the Mid-Atlantic," *Pennsylvania Magazine of History and Biography* 129 (January 2005): 45–72. I use them here with the kind permission of the Historical Society of Pennsylvania.

Finally, I need to thank my family. My mother, Doris M. West, inspired me with her love of history, and as a volunteer at the Lebanon County Historical Society she assisted my research in many ways. My three grown children, Ethan, Seth, and Laura, probably got tired of hearing about Samuel Rex a long time ago, but they never once showed it. Most important, I am grateful to my husband, Lynn, a banker by profession but a fellow historian at heart, for his patience, encouragement, and love.

Mom, Ethan, Seth, Laura, and Lynn: this book is for you.

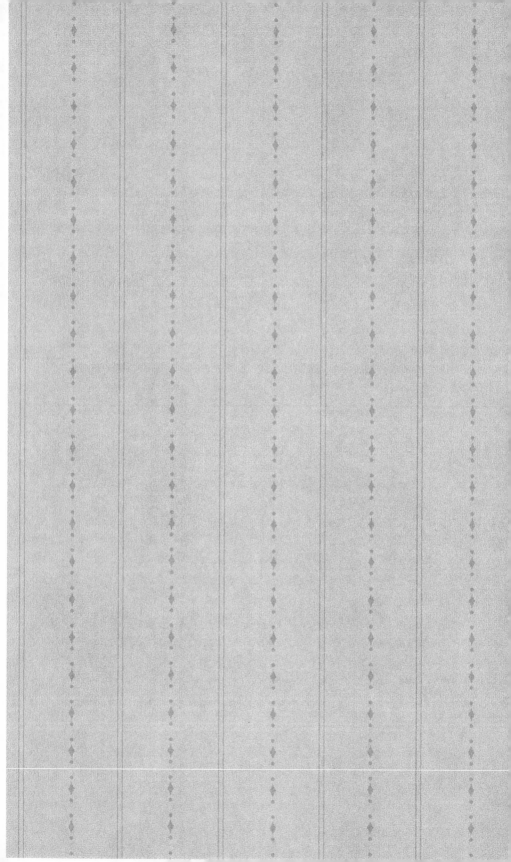

INTRODUCTION:
A COUNTRY STOREKEEPER AND HIS NETWORK OF RELATIONSHIPS

SCHAEFFERSTOWN IS A SMALL PENNSYLVANIA German village located about seventy-five miles northwest of Philadelphia. Founded in 1758, it is noteworthy for its European-style town square, its early water system, and its many Germanic buildings. These include two eighteenth-century taverns: the Franklin House, built by town founder Alexander Schaeffer, and the Gemberling-Rex House, a *Fachwerk* (half-timbered) building that retains a number of early and significant architectural features. Besides their original function as eighteenth-century taverns, what these two buildings have in common is the man who operated a country store in the former and lived in the latter from about 1802 until his death in 1835—storekeeper Samuel Rex.

Rex himself was not unique. Hundreds of men—and some women—operated general stores in early America. When the Duc de la Rochefoucauld-Liancourt toured the United States in the 1790s, he observed, "There is no point . . . however remote, even in the woods, in which one store, and frequently more, may not be found."[1] Nor is the survival of Rex's store and home particularly remarkable. What sets Rex apart is the large number of documents that survive from his business and permit a close analysis of one country storekeeper and his role in the economy and society of the Mid-Atlantic region.

Rex's business was far more complicated than his rural location would suggest. His customers extended from Schaefferstown out into the countryside to farms and iron furnaces, and from there to the merchant community in Philadelphia, and the deals that he negotiated in each of these places created an interconnected network of relations that linked rural and urban producers and consumers with each other and with the Atlantic world of goods. The purpose of this study is to locate Rex's role in each node of this network, and to analyze how customers in each place used and were affected by his services.[2]

The idea of a network of relationships is not new. Darret and Anita Rutman introduced the concept in the 1970s and demonstrated its utility in *A Place in Time: Middlesex County, Virginia, 1650–1750.* The Rutmans explain that this approach enables researchers to see a geographic neighborhood not as an isolated locale but as part of a much larger set of relationships that link the local community to the broader society. Likewise, in *Community and Social Change in America,* Thomas Bender describes trade in colonial America as "bounded by networks of personal relationships."[3]

While my analysis of Rex's network offers insights into rural south-central Pennsylvania and country-urban trade in the late eighteenth and early nineteenth centuries, it also has implications beyond local and regional history. This study calls into question one of the most powerful historical models for this period—a sudden, disruptive market revolution and its assumption of a community-oriented eighteenth century giving way, amid struggle and disharmony, to a market-oriented nineteenth century.[4] It demonstrates that a more fitting paradigm for understanding early America is a blended society in which market and community interests existed simultaneously. Despite profound differences among the communities that Rex dealt with, residents in all three regions blended traditional, community-based negotiations with impersonal, market-driven deals. When it came to doing business, early Americans in the late eighteenth and early nineteenth centuries melded community and market relations.

Rex's network also reveals the important role that the rural storekeeper played in the economy and society of early America. When I set out to study Rex, I expected to find him selling, as Charles Sellers suggests was the case in all country stores, "a limited range of high-utility commodities."[5] I soon discovered that Rex sold far more than the necessities of rural life. Alongside tobacco, molasses, powder, and shot, Rex's store offered such nonessentials as sling glasses, Tenerife wine, and twilled velvet. My initial misconceptions about Rex and his customers are hardly surprising, given a pervasive nostalgia for rural America. Despite evidence to the contrary, frontier myths continue to evoke images of sturdy yeomen who raised all their own food, dressed in homespun, and obtained other modest necessities by bartering with neighbors.[6] Likewise, literature on general stores has contributed to misunderstandings about life in early America.[7]

Writers alternately celebrate the country store as a gathering place where locals played checkers, swapped stories, and exchanged gossip, or vilify the storekeeper as a cheat and swindler, but most downplay the store's important commercial functions and its place in the local and national economy. As Thomas Schlereth points out for a later era, "paeans are sung to its legendary front porch, its inspirational cracker barrel, and its hospitable potbellied stove rather than its innovative merchandising displays, special bargain packaging, or widespread use of national-brand advertising."[8]

Although nostalgic depictions of the store and negative tales of predatory storekeepers seem to be diametrically opposed, the two readings have a common thread. Underlying both views is the distinction between community and market not unlike Ferdinand Tönnies's classic *Gemeinschaft und Gesellschaft* opposition.[9] In this construct, the intimate social relations characteristic of a community are disrupted and even destroyed by the impersonal, coldly calculating, mercenary market economy; depending on one's interpretation, the storekeeper symbolizes either the warm, personal community or the disruptive forces of the competitive market.

While the supposed transformation from community-knit to market-driven storekeeping also involved changes and technological improvements often characterized as a "transportation revolution,"[10] many historians follow Tönnies's lead and see the phenomenon in social relations. Paul G. E. Clemens explains that community implies personally negotiated exchanges, often of goods and labor, conducted according to local custom; such exchanges met immediate needs and conserved assets for the next generation. At the other extreme, market exchanges are portrayed as part of a more distant world and often include taking risks to make profits. Prices are set by supply and demand; wage labor rather than neighborly exchange of service is common; and goods are produced with a view toward selling them for profit.[11]

The tensions between community and market emerged in the early 1970s as part of the new social history. Historians who wrote in the community studies genre mourned "the world we have lost," in Peter Laslett's famous phrase, and the destruction of community cohesion by encroaching capitalistic relationships.[12] Most community studies addressed these market forces obliquely, but Paul Boyer and Stephen Nissenbaum, in *Salem Possessed: The Social Origins of Witchcraft*, explicitly linked the witchcraft hysteria of the late seventeenth century to anxiety over New England's changing economy.

While the first community studies focused on New England, a few historians looked to Pennsylvania.[13] In *Best Poor Man's Country: A Geographical Study of Early Southeastern Pennsylvania,* James T. Lemon stressed that early settlers in this region of Pennsylvania were classically "liberal"; "they placed individual freedom and material gain over that of public interest . . . [they] planned for themselves much more than they did for their communities." He noted correctly that Pennsylvanians were part of two economic systems: the subsistence (or household) economy and the Atlantic business world; linking rural residents to this world was a chain of credit—a network—that included backcountry storekeepers.[14]

James A. Henretta refuted Lemon's argument, and his response opened the scholarly debate on America's "transition to capitalism."[15] Henretta reasoned that farmers strongly resisted market involvement and favored a safety-first *mentalité* that would secure their estates for their children, and he specifically cited storekeepers as one of the problems farmers faced. He explained that, from the seventeenth to the early nineteenth century, there were increasingly antagonistic social relations and a growing class gap between farmers and middlemen, including rural merchants, who frequently appropriated a share of farmers' profits in the form of monetary liens. While these liens were sometimes imposed for good reason, more often "the farm population—especially those of its members who were young or landless—paid a disproportionate price for access to the productive system because bankers, speculators, and merchants were able to use their political and economic power to set the terms of exchange in order to gain a greater share of the growing wealth of the society than was warranted by their entrepreneurial contribution."[16] Ironically, while Henretta was challenging Lemon's work on Pennsylvania, the resulting debate focused on New England and clouded scholarly understanding of the Mid-Atlantic region. Although Pennsylvania, with its staple wheat crop, was quite different from New England and its mixed economy, both regions became subject to the same broad assumptions. In fact, the transition-to-capitalism theory is an especially poor fit for the Mid-Atlantic region, where eighteenth-century farmers grew wheat and other products using new technologies, were dependent on world prices and long-distance markets, and lived within age-old social relations. Indeed, the Rex study is important simply for its geographic focus on Pennsylvania, since the rural Mid-Atlantic region has been woefully neglected in comparison to New England and the Chesapeake.[17]

On one side of the transition debate are "social" historians who take a neo-Marxist view and see early America in transition (from an unspecified economic state) to capitalism. This transition involved a struggle between farmers and middlemen who sought to appropriate farmers' livelihood and turn them into dependent wage workers. On the opposing side are "market" or "economic" historians who view farmers as enterprising protocapitalists and capitalism as a natural development of an expanding economy.[18] A number of historians have addressed the market/community question, but Winifred Rothenberg and Christopher Clark have emerged as the foremost spokespersons for the two positions. In *From Market Places to Market Economy: The Transformation of Rural Massachusetts, 1750 to 1850,* Rothenberg challenges social historians' concept of a "moral economy," in which farmers resisted the market, and argues persuasively that this theory speaks more to historians' own political ideology than to that of eighteenth-century farmers. Using neoclassical economic models, she charts the convergence of local and regional crop prices and wages to determine when a market economy (as opposed to the market as a place of exchange) began to change the nature of agriculture in Massachusetts. Rothenberg is more interested in farmers' behavior than in their mindsets; she points out that they were increasingly willing to travel greater distances to sell crops and buy consumer goods, and that they showed other signs of market orientation as early as 1750.[19]

Clark interprets farmers' actions differently. In *The Roots of Rural Capitalism: Western Massachusetts, 1780–1860,* he concludes that farmers sold crops (a true "surplus" rather than goods produced specifically for sale) only after they had met their families' needs. When economic changes forced farmers to take on new kinds of work, raise different crops, and deal with outside markets, they did so reluctantly, while still clinging to their old values. In Clark's analysis, storekeepers did not actively seek out country produce; they were forced to take crops and goods in payment because cash-poor customers had no other means of payment. For Clark, relationships between storekeepers and their customers were antagonistic rather than complementary; local commodity exchanges and the market cash nexus were "competing ethics of exchange."[20] As we will see, the evidence from the Rex store complicates Clark's reading.

Debates on the transition to capitalism have lost their early vigor, but the question of how rural residents responded to new market forces has not yet been settled. More recently, historians have rephrased the question, seeking evidence of an early nineteenth-century "market revolution." Following the lead of Charles Sellers, some see the rise of the modern market economy as the cause of political, religious, and social changes of unprecedented magnitude.[21] The concepts of "transition to capitalism" and "market revolution" are related, but,

Clark warns, they are not interchangeable: "Adaptation to dependence on markets entailed changes in the practices of production and consumption, [but] it did not necessarily bring about changes in social relations. . . . The transition to capitalism was, on the other hand, essentially a shift in social relations, particularly the growth of wage labor."[22]

Although the focus of the discussion has shifted, Hal Barron comments that the "expansion of the market economy in the rural Northeast during the nineteenth century has become the *ur* debate for the field [of rural history]—its conceptual paradigm." As Barron notes, this debate has social and political implications as well as academic relevance. Farming was the primary occupation in early America; a Jeffersonian reverence for agrarian life and individual freedom remains ingrained in the American character. Furthermore, many present-day Americans are deeply concerned about suburban sprawl, disappearing farmland, and a fragile environment.[23] Related to this is a suspicion of big business; as Americans recoil from accounting scandals and corruption among CEOs that toppled businesses and sent stocks plummeting early in the twenty-first century, the evils of unbridled capitalism seem more apparent than ever, and nostalgia for the values of a simpler rural time likewise grows apace.

A market revolution is a compelling, and perhaps a comforting, way of understanding early America, but this model has fostered a simplistic interpretation of the past. It has become common to characterize the eighteenth century as a time of traditional community-based exchanges and the nineteenth as an era dominated by impersonal market and long-distance exchanges. In a similar way, the transition-to-capitalism debate overlooks the fact that participating in the market and providing for one's family are not inherently antithetical practices. The theory of a sharp disjuncture between old and new ignores the fact that market-based and traditional community transactions existed simultaneously in both the eighteenth and the early nineteenth centuries.

Some historians, however, suggest an alternative to the transition-to-capitalism and market-revolution models, a more nuanced and, as this study suggests, a more accurate way of understanding this era is a blend of market and community *mentalités*. Daniel Vickers argues that farmers strove for competency or "comfortable independence" and that this concept arrived in America with the first immigrants and endured until industrialization. Farmers who were motivated by achieving competency were neither averse to the market nor immersed in it; they used market opportunities to meet their household needs, not to accumulate wealth. The point at which a person reached competency

varied according to individual needs and desires. Sally McMurry stresses that
the idea of competency could have satisfyingly moral overtones. She determined that New York dairy farmers and their wives produced cheese and sold
poultry to provide "necessaries and conveniences of life without superfluity."[24]

In a similarly conciliatory mode, some scholars argue that the economy of
early America was a blend of market and community. Clemens notes that such
factors as distance from urban centers, growing conditions, and cultural con-
siderations affected farmers' interactions with markets. Rather than a community-oriented eighteenth century giving way to a market-oriented nineteenth
century, he sees the Mid-Atlantic region at this time as a place where market
and community transactions took place simultaneously and market relations
were "embedded in community life."[25] Richard Lyman Bushman likewise
advises that historians abandon the notion of a sudden and dramatic turning
point and instead perceive the change from the eighteenth to nineteenth century as evolutionary. He argues that eighteenth-century farms were neither
subsistence nor commercial enterprises but a "composite" of both, a blending
of economies in which crops were produced for use and for sale with no distinction between the two—even in New England, home to communal villages.[26]
Naomi R. Lamoreaux also argues for a more nuanced understanding of business relations in the early Republic. She finds that the behavior of farmers and
merchants was remarkably similar. Both used single-entry bookkeeping and
seldom charged interest; both routinely hired family members and forgave debts
owed by relatives; and both relied on the support of a community of their
peers. As the century wore on, Lamoreaux notes, these similarities decreased.[27]

Two recent studies of New York also address the market-versus-community
paradigm. Martin Bruegel's *Farm, Shop, Landing: The Rise of a Market Society in
the Hudson Valley, 1780–1860* eschews the notion (implicit in Rothenberg's work)
of the market as an inexorable force and focuses on the strategies that often
struggling farmers used to provide for their families. Bruegel concludes that
Hudson Valley farmers "straddled two worlds that historians and ethnologists
have often tended to view as incompatible." As part of their striving for competency, these farmers worked at crafts and participated in community networks
of exchange; they also sent products to distant markets in order to obtain cash
and goods they could not produce or obtain locally. Rather than seeing con-
frontation between farmers and storekeepers, Bruegel finds mutuality of interest; two "logics of exchange" came together at the country store. Thomas
S. Wermuth agrees that, in the Hudson River valley, "long-distance and local

exchange networks were not mutually exclusive." Wermuth finds that, even by the mid-nineteenth century, the economy was "transitional . . . not yet wholly capitalistic nor truly communal. Kin, community, and neighborhood networks still exerted power . . . but did so within the framework of a market economy that had existed since the earliest days of settlement."[28]

A few years ago, Joyce Appleby summed up historians' "vexed" efforts to describe America's economic development and called for scholars to redirect their attention to the economic agency of ordinary people. Hal Barron concurs. What, he asks Clark, were the relationships between storekeepers and customers, outside of business deals? What did longer trips to market signify to Rothenberg's farmers?[29] Reconstructing Rex's network puts individual economic actors back in the picture and fills in the gap identified by Appleby and Barron.

Related to the developing market economy is the idea of a "consumer revolution"—a rise in consumption parallel to the "Industrial Revolution" that produced an increased quantity of goods.[30] Store records provide an ideal opportunity to probe consumer habits, as Ann Smart Martin, Elizabeth Perkins, and others have demonstrated. In fact, after studying a Kentucky storekeeper's books, Perkins concluded that "consumption and community grew up together in the backcountry."[31] The present study provides insight into consumption and production among the Pennsylvania Germans, the largest European ethnic minority in early America, and suggests that, with a few exceptions, ethnicity was not a driving factor when it came to choosing consumer goods. Recent studies suggest that factors such as gentility and status, rather than the desire to appear more fashionably English, moved Pennsylvania Germans in their consumer choices, and this was true of Rex's customers in Schaefferstown.[32]

One issue related to consumption that needs to be better understood is how goods reached early America's consumers.[33] Again, Rex's papers help to answer this question by presenting detailed evidence of wagonloads of goods that he hauled between Schaefferstown and Philadelphia. Moreover, his method of moving the goods—hiring local farmers, craftsmen, and laborers to drive the wagons—provides new insight into labor and transportation in this period. Rex's regular shipments to and from the city also reveal that, contrary to some assertions, the weight of the load and the distance to market were not barriers to trade.[34] Rex's trade in the city demonstrates that he patronized many different merchants and stores to get the right mix of products, but that he also maintained a close relationship with select wet and dry goods dealers who served as his agents.

Even as they adopted new fashions and customs, Pennsylvania Germans (in Schaefferstown and elsewhere) did not forsake their ethnic heritage. In fact, they retained their language and other distinctive traits well into the twentieth century. This folk culture is particularly evident in examples of Pennsylvania German decorative arts; today these are sought actively by collectors and bring prices that would astonish their makers.[35] Because Pennsylvania Germans retained their language and culture (even as they embraced consumer goods and American notions of liberty), the services of storekeepers, ministers, and other educated people were particularly useful in helping them deal with an English-speaking majority. Scholars label those who served this function "culture brokers," a term that fits Rex particularly well. As a third-generation Pennsylvania German who was raised in the Chestnut Hill area of Germantown (where English and German influence commingled early on), Rex was fluent in both languages, and he was at home in both the Pennsylvania German community in Schaefferstown and the English-speaking commercial and legal worlds.[36]

Rex's papers also provide insight into an aspect of Pennsylvania German society that remains largely unexplored—the role of its women—by demonstrating their economic contributions as producers and consumers. As was true in other regions of early America, male customers outnumbered females at the Rex store. But, although they may have shopped less frequently than men, Schaefferstown-area women contributed to the household and regional economy by producing and selling goods—especially butter—at the store. While women made the butter, the male head of the household received the store credit in his name; still, all members of the household benefited from the consumer products the family purchased with butter sales.[37]

The second segment of Rex's network was a small group of Pennsylvania ironmasters and their workers. The ironmasters regularly purchased large quantities of meat and other necessities for their employees, and the workers used Rex's store as an auxiliary company store. This interdependence between ironmasters and storekeeper and the level of purchases made by the workers suggest that the usual understanding of the iron plantations as self-contained and isolated is inaccurate. There have been many studies of the technological, social, and economic aspects of the Pennsylvania iron industry, but locating the workers' place in Rex's network shows the iron community in a different, more personal light, by highlighting their individual economic activities and choices.[38]

If the rural Mid-Atlantic has been neglected by scholars, there is no shortage of works on Philadelphia, the most distant part of Rex's network.[39] Although it focuses on a slightly earlier period, the most useful of these works, relative to the country-city trade, is Thomas M. Doerflinger, *A Vigorous Spirit of Enterprise: Merchants and Economic Development in Revolutionary America.* The Rex study builds on and adds to Doerflinger's analysis. Rex's trade in the city clearly demonstrates the mutuality of transactions between country storekeepers and city merchants that Doerflinger mentions, and it reveals something new: a storekeeper-agent relationship not previously identified in literature on domestic trade.[40]

There also have been numerous studies of the career path of city merchants and wealthy businessmen, but there are fewer comparable studies of country storekeepers.[41] The pattern of New England storekeepers establishing factories is also well known.[42] Some storekeepers, however, increased agricultural production and home manufactures rather than establishing factories. Rex followed this model; he spent his post-storekeeping years managing tenants on his farms, selling the grain they raised, lending money at interest, and working as a justice of the peace. By investing in farming, Rex and others engaged in a form of capitalistic enterprise that, as Joyce Appleby notes, has largely escaped the scrutiny of historians who study this period.[43]

The sources for this study truly constitute an embarrassment of riches. The Rex family was active in storekeeping and other businesses in Schaefferstown for nearly a century, and they preserved a collection of business, personal, and legal papers that spans two centuries.[44] The volume of papers from Samuel Rex's business alone is impressive. Some forty-four of his estimated forty-eight daybooks survive, along with three ledgers, two receipt books, an 1807 store inventory, his estate records, and letters, bills, and receipts from more than one hundred Philadelphia merchants. Legal documents that Rex wrote for his clients offer further insight into and context for his business, as do the account books of his brother and nephews who followed him in storekeeping.

Rex ran his store from December 1790 to May 1807, but I have chosen three periods for close analysis: 1791, his first full year as a storekeeper; 1798, a midpoint in his career and the year that the federal government mandated that all buildings be assessed for the direct tax; and May 1806 to May 1807, Rex's final year in business. Since a primary objective was to understand how local customers used the store for commodity exchanges, I analyzed the credits in store books to determine the means his customers used to pay for goods and services and the commodities they sold at the store. I entered credits from Rex's daybooks for the three key years and from his ledger 5 (1798 to 1806) into databases, and I constructed linked databases of property owners and their holdings in 1798 to determine how customers' occupations and relative wealth related to their store credits. I also analyzed Rex's purchases in the city, drawing on Philadelphia merchants' bills and receipts from 1790 to 1801. Because bills and receipts for the years after 1801 apparently have not survived, I relied on Rex's receipt book for expenditures in Philadelphia after 1801. The receipt book entries are not itemized, so I could not quantify these purchases, but I was able to determine the amount that he spent at each business, and I could usually discern the general category of goods these merchants sold by consulting Philadelphia city directories.

Chapter 1 focuses on Schaefferstown and its inhabitants. It addresses the religious and political climate of the town as well as the material life and relative wealth of the farmers and tradesmen who lived in and around the village. I also look at the town's earlier storekeepers and the services and goods they offered, as well as at the fragility of these businesses and the competition that Rex faced when he set up his store.

Chapter 2 assesses the economic climate of the early Republic, the emergence of south-central Pennsylvania as a diverse region of relative prosperity, and Schaefferstown's particularly good conditions for business by 1790. I explain Rex's store operation, analyze local customers' choices as reflections of their ethnicity, and detail how store sales reflected agricultural cycles and folk customs. I also compare customers' sales of manufactured and farm products at the store, explain how farmers benefited to a greater degree than craftsmen from these sales, and discuss the services and goods both groups sought in exchange for their products. The chapter ends with a brief discussion of Rex as a culture broker and his need to be a friend and neighbor while also running a profitable business.

Chapter 3 turns to the iron-producing community, beginning with an overview of the regional iron plantations and the ironmasters who did business with Rex. I describe the services that the ironmasters and their employees expected from Rex, the use of iron as currency, and the relationship Rex had with the managers at the furnaces. The concluding sections analyze how customers in both Schaefferstown and the iron community paid their bills, detail Rex's method of recovering delinquent payments, and discuss his need to balance both community and market priorities in these local transactions.

Chapter 4 follows Rex on a shopping trip to Philadelphia and compares Philadelphia stores, their furnishings, and their business practices with those in the countryside. I discuss his teamsters (the local farmers and craftsmen he hired to drive his goods), and analyze the relationship between country storekeepers and city merchants, especially the small group of merchants who worked closely with Rex as his agents.

Chapter 5 describes Rex's post-storekeeping years and his economic activities after selling the store to his younger brother. The chapter includes an analysis of Rex's home and its furnishings as a reflection of his place in the community, and concludes with an examination of the changing business climate in Schaefferstown as the nineteenth century wore on.

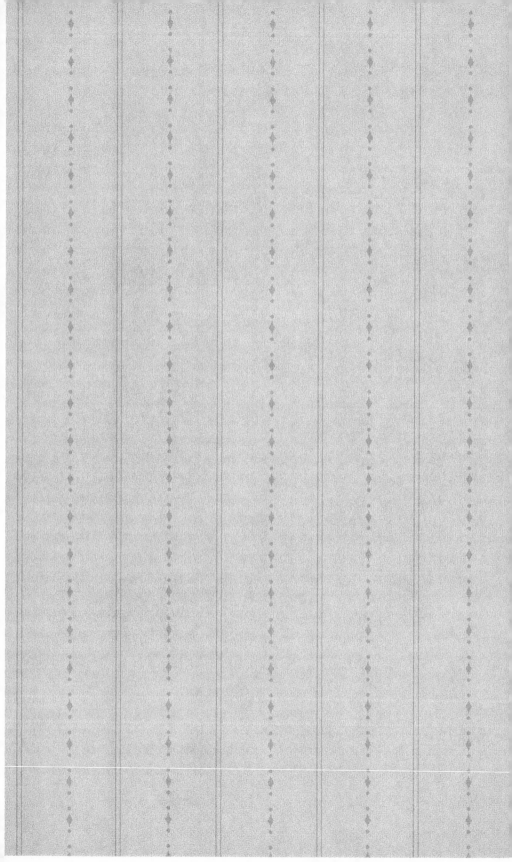

CHAPTER ONE

BEYOND "WILD FOREST PEOPLE":
SCHAEFFERSTOWN, PENNSYLVANIA

ON A HOT SUNDAY AFTERNOON in August 1763, a "numerous gathering" crowded the Lutheran church in Heidelberg (later to be known as Schaefferstown), Pennsylvania, to hear visiting minister Henry Melchior Muhlenberg conduct services. Muhlenberg wrote in his journal that his listeners were attentive that sultry day, but his overall impression was not favorable. The well-traveled, well-educated minister perceived Heidelberg inhabitants as far from genteel, writing, "The novelty [of the text he had chosen] makes people attentive and the application makes it impressive, so that at least something sticks that will give these wild forest people something to meditate on." In later entries, the Lutheran patriarch was less critical of the Schaefferstown flock, at least some of whom he found "awakened" and "hungry for grace."[1]

When Muhlenberg visited the "wild forest people," the village was just five years old; the people and place undoubtedly seemed primitive compared to more sophisticated towns that Muhlenberg had seen. But Schaefferstown and its inhabitants were not as crude or as isolated from the larger world as Muhlenberg's words imply. Even in 1763 the town's storekeepers were selling imported goods, buying local products, and offering other commercial services, and the village was well on its way to becoming a busy market center. Although Schaefferstown people would retain much of their German culture, in the next few decades they would also display a taste for consumer goods and acquire some of the trappings of refinement, complicating the primitive image sketched by Muhlenberg.

A View of Schaefferstown

The first European settlers had reached the area that would become Schaefferstown by the early eighteenth century, but the town was not founded until
1758, when Alexander Schaeffer laid out a formal grid of streets and building
lots (see figs. 1 and 2).[2] The settlement was located at the intersection of two
major roads; one ran east to west, from Harris's Ferry (Harrisburg) and Hummelstown to Ephrata via the Cornwall Iron Furnace, and the other ran north to
south, connected Conrad Weiser's settlement at Tulpehocken with Lancaster,
and passed by Elizabeth Furnace. Because of its prominent location, businesses
were soon established in Schaefferstown to cater to travelers and residents alike.
In 1761, when Nicholas Heniek advertised that a post rider would take mail each
Monday between Lancaster and Lebanon, he listed tavern keeper Paul Gamber-
ling (Gemberling) in "Heidelberg Town" as one of the regular stops.[3]

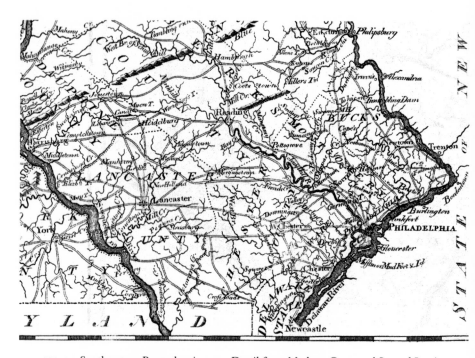

FIG. 1. Southeastern Pennsylvania, 1795. Detail from Mathew Carey and Samuel Lewis,
"State of Pennsylvania," *Carey's American Atlas* (Philadelphia: Mathew Carey, 1795). The
central position of Schaefferstown ("Heidelburg") at the intersection of major through-
ways is evident, as are the routes Rex might have taken to Philadelphia. The map also
helps situate Rex's business geographically. Map courtesy of David Rumsey Cartography
Associates.

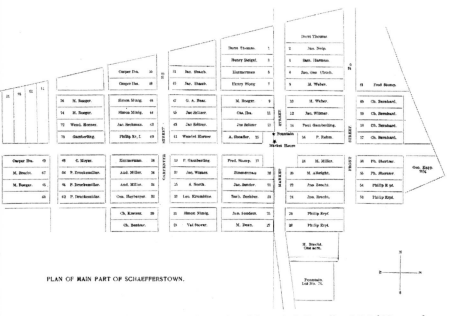

PLAN OF MAIN PART OF SCHAEFFERSTOWN.

FIG. 2.   Plan of Schaefferstown, 1758. Reproduced from A. S. Brendle, *A Brief History of Schaefferstown* (York, Pa.: Dispatch Publishing, 1901).

Schaeffer arranged for a public market house to be built on the town square, revealing that he planned the village to be an exchange center, but the hoped-for market never materialized. The townspeople kept the market house in repair, but A. S. Brendle, writing around 1900, knew "of no particular use ever made of the market house, except during the annual cherry fairs." By the mid-nineteenth century the market house had outlived its usefulness, and residents removed it.[4] Stephanie Grauman Wolf describes a similar pattern in Germantown, where the village erected and maintained "for generations" a market house that they did not use. Still, as Wolf notes, the very presence of such a building is significant, for it symbolizes the market orientation of the town and "a community's ability to accumulate a surplus."[5] The public waterworks is another indication of Schaeffer's aspirations for Schaefferstown. He installed a system of underground wooden pipes to channel mountain spring water from an enclosed reservoir at one end of Market Street to two "fountains" (troughs) on the town square.[6]

If the town's market house did not fulfill its intended function of enabling the distribution and exchange of local goods, the town's private businesses did. Although there were a number of craftsmen working and selling their products there, Schaefferstown, like other rural towns in Pennsylvania, was predominantly a service center, its businesses focused on collecting and selling produce rather than manufacturing. In this era the few industries that existed, notably mills and ironworks, were located in the countryside near the natural resources they relied upon, rather than in towns. James T. Lemon notes that in market towns, "merchants, tavernkeepers, and public officials, not industrialists, were the key figures," and Schaefferstown was no exception.[7] In 1798 and 1802 Samuel Rex administered a fund to repair the market house, and in 1820 his brother Abraham, also a storekeeper, headed the movement to rebuild it.[8] In 1799 tavern keepers Anthony Seyfert and James Huston arbitrated a dispute among fifteen town residents who claimed a $250 reward offered for the apprehension of the murderers of a local man.[9] Some store- and tavern keepers were involved in political and legal work; Seyfert was the Dauphin County coroner before moving to Schaefferstown; Huston, like a number of other local businessmen, including Rex, would go on to become a justice of the peace. Storekeepers and innkeepers were also among the market-savvy men who might be called on to prepare a household inventory following a death in the community.

As a village rather than a borough, Schaefferstown's administrative unit was (and still is) Heidelberg Township, a political division encompassing Schaefferstown, a few hamlets, and rural regions.[10] In the eighteenth and nineteenth centuries, Heidelberg Township also included the villages of Myerstown and Newmanstown. In 1779 Schaefferstown, with about three hundred residents, was the largest of the three settlements, while Newmanstown had about a hundred residents, and Myerstown had only eighty-four.[11] Originally in Lancaster County, Heidelberg Township became part of Dauphin County when it was split off in 1786; since 1813 it has been a division of Lebanon County.[12]

A comparison of Schaefferstown with the larger settlements of Reading (to the east) and Lancaster (to the south) offers further insight into the character and commercial climate of the small village. In 1779 Schaefferstown had at least two shopkeepers to serve three hundred residents, while Lancaster had an estimated population of 3,618 and twenty-two shopkeepers, and Reading (in 1773) had about fifteen hundred residents and nine shopkeepers.[13] Significantly, although the three places differed dramatically in size, their percentage of storekeepers was the same, six-tenths of 1 percent (.006) of the total population. On the other hand, Schaefferstown never grew large enough for specialty businesses to develop. Its storekeepers handled a general selection of merchandise, and they would continue to do so into the mid-twentieth century, while Lancaster businesses were already specializing by the mid-eighteenth century.[14]

There were also differences in the type of crafts produced in Schaefferstown compared to larger centers. The 1779 and 1782 tax lists for Schaefferstown included a weaver, a nail smith, a shoemaker, a saddler, various other smiths, a brewer, and a tanner.[15] The town of Reading had a similar array of workers, suggesting that it was somewhere between small town and large city in this respect.[16] By contrast, Lancaster artisans were producing luxury and big-ticket items; they worked in silver, pewter, and copper and crafted high chests, musical instruments, and even fire engines, in addition to plying more homely trades.[17]

The three places also differed in ethnic and religious makeup, even though all were located in a region where Pennsylvania Germans were the majority. Schaefferstown had two churches, the German Lutheran and the German Reformed. Reading and Lancaster, by contrast, had more diverse populations that included Anglicans, Quakers, Mennonites, Catholics, and, in the case of Lancaster, Moravians, as well as German Lutheran and Reformed congregations.[18]

As Lancaster and Reading grew into boroughs and then cities, Schaefferstown lagged behind. The Berks-Dauphin Turnpike (1817), the Schuylkill and Susquehanna Canal (later known as the Union Canal, begun in 1793 but not completed until 1827), and, most significantly, the railroad all missed Schaefferstown.[19] Political power also bypassed the town; the closest Schaefferstown came to the excitement of a court session were hearings held by justices of the peace, shooting matches, the annual Battalion Day, and the Cherry Fair, a midsummer "promiscuous gathering for merrymaking."[20]

Language, Religion, and Politics in *Schaeffersschteddel*

The first settlers of Schaefferstown arrived in the third wave of German immigration, which occurred between 1717 and 1775.[21] Third-wave migrants left Europe when the region that would become Germany was in transition from feudalism and subsistence farming to capitalism, and farmland was growing increasingly scarce because of partible inheritance.[22] In the transition-to-capitalism debate, some historians, James T. Lemon and Stephanie Grauman Wolf among them, stress the market orientation and entrepreneurialism of those who immigrated in this later period; Scott Swank notes they "were further along the path to middle class than those left behind."[23] Aaron Fogleman, however, argues that such an assertion cannot be proved. He points out that the motivation of those third-wave immigrants simply differed from that of earlier arrivals. Unlike seventeenth-century Germans who sought religious freedom, eighteenth-century immigrants were pulled to America by opportunities for economic advancement and abundant land.[24]

Fogleman further explains that by the early years of American nationhood Pennsylvania Germans had adopted a dual identity. "Being German in 1790 meant participating in American public affairs," he writes, "but speaking and reading German, going to a German church, marrying a German, and living with other Germans." Steven M. Nolt observes that when confronting the mainstream political and religious cultures, Pennsylvania Germans resisted assimilation and change and spurned the evangelical movement and English-speaking public schools in order to maintain their linguistic and cultural purity. Indeed, Nolt postulates that Pennsylvania Germans used the rhetoric of constitutional liberties to support their rights as good Americans to maintain their Germanic culture.[25]

The Schaefferstown community clearly shared the desire for economic opportunity and the bifurcated identity described by Nolt and Fogleman. Its people were part of a traditional ethnic culture, evidenced by language, food, decorative arts, religion, and architecture, but they did not shun Anglo-American ways. Even as they fostered a traditional community-centered culture and resisted total assimilation, they also produced goods for distant markets and sought (with some exceptions) the same imported goods as their non-German counterparts.

One reason why Pennsylvania Germans retained such a distinctive culture may have to do with their habit of ethnic clustering. They tended to come to America in entire village groups and settle in lands already occupied by German speakers; once settled, they stayed put, and so they and their descendents clung to Old World customs for decades.[26] Theophile Cazenove noted this tendency when he traveled through Myerstown, just north of Schaefferstown, in 1794, and commented on the old world clothing residents wore. "It seemed to me I saw people coming out of church in Westphalia, so much have these farmers kept their ancestors' costume."[27]

Like the clothing Cazenove described, language was a cultural marker that endured for generations in Schaefferstown and other Pennsylvania German settlements. In formal situations such as church and school, standard (High) German was used, but area residents conversed with each other informally in a dialect called Pennsylvania German, Pennsylvania Dutch, or simply Dutch. Muhlenberg commented disparagingly on this patois in 1772: "The old Germans, who are otherwise discerning, spoil the English language and in time produce a third language, which is neither English nor German."[28] Muhlenberg's scorn notwithstanding, Pennsylvania Germans continued to speak the dialect well into the twentieth century, and it persists among certain groups today.[29]

Schoolmasters at the Schaefferstown Lutheran church school taught classes in German, but at the apparently more progressive Reformed church school, by the early nineteenth century, parents could choose to have their children instructed in either English or German.[30] The advent of state-run public schools in 1834 (with teaching in English) marked the beginning of the end for the church schools.[31] German survived much longer in worship services, and the transition to English was long and difficult for some Schaefferstown people. German was used exclusively at the Reformed church until 1871, when the congregation began using English and German on alternating Sundays. The changeover was not without problems, and in 1893 language issues divided the congregation. When the church consistory showed little interest in the English services, the congregation elected a "second set of consistory men."[32] By the mid-nineteenth century Schaefferstown Lutherans were also using English and German alternately at Sunday afternoon services. In 1894 the Lutheran church council debated whether to initiate English preaching on Sunday mornings but "declared [it] inexpedient on account of the old members who do not understand the English language."[33] As late as 1918 the Lutheran council balked at a suggestion to hold two English services for every one in German; by "common consent it was decided that we make no more mention about it and let the matter die out."[34]

Nolt explains that Lutheran and Reformed congregations "often shared meetinghouses and lived within a common Pennsylvania German cultural context that often meant more than dogmatic differences."[35] This was the case in Schaefferstown, where the two groups shared a union church for the first few years of settlement and a common union Sunday school well into the nineteenth century. A similar community spirit shows in the way the town established its burial ground. Alexander Schaeffer deeded two parcels of land for a cemetery to the two congregations, to be held in common. The cemetery was located on a hill north of the town rather than next to an individual church so that it could be shared by all, yet it was sectioned off into separate congregational areas. It is not clear whether burial in the cemetery was restricted to church members early on, but in the early decades of the nineteenth century a section was set aside for burial of strangers and paupers, suggesting an openness and tolerance that extended beyond the Pennsylvania German community.[36]

At the same time, there was sometimes dissension within congregations. In the 1760s, during the religious awakening that was occurring throughout the colonies, Schaefferstown Lutherans were divided. According to Muhlenberg, one faction began to follow a "schooled, but wrong-headed so-called ortho- dox Lutheran preacher, who was given to strong drink," and built their own separate church, a wooden building. To counter this, "faithful and well-to-do" members of the congregation who stayed loyal to regular pastor J. Nicholas Kurtz decided in 1765 to build a church of "massive stones in the center of the village," presumably to provide the community with tangible and substantial evidence of their faith (see fig. 3). This plan backfired to some extent. The "wrong-headed" preacher tried to lure people away from the Kurtz faction by suggesting they would have to help pay for the expensive new structure. The trouble continued; the objectionable preacher moved away in 1769, but the sep- arated Lutherans soon took up with "another unconverted, entirely disorderly preacher," Peter Mischler.[37] Muhlenberg implies that class differences may have been involved in the schism. Among the "somewhat prosperous" mem- bers who built the church were innkeeper Philip Erpff, who owned one of the highest-valued buildings in town, and George Schwengel, who owned two hun- dred acres of land and was the overseer of the poor.[38] Another man of substance, ironmaster Henry William Stiegel, who lived a few miles from Schaefferstown at Elizabeth Furnace but who was a frequent visitor to and benefactor of the Schaefferstown Lutheran Church, was concerned enough about the schism to urge Henry Muhlenberg to send a regular minister (rather than an itinerant) who could devote more time to the area churches.[39]

Controversy over religion also surfaced on two occasions when Jacob Albright, a German Methodist and founder of the Evangelical Association, preached in Schaefferstown. Albright was a former Lutheran who converted to Methodism and felt called to take the denomination's message to German speak- ers.[40] On October 8, 1796, while the Reformed congregation was dedicating a new church building, Albright mounted a pile of wood at the entrance to the market house and addressed the assembled crowd. Met with "a furious attack . . . by a godless mob," he was saved from injury only when a local man seized him bodily and carried him to safety. In 1799 Albright came back to preach

FIG. 3. German Lutheran Church, East Main Street. This early photo shows the church as it would have looked in Samuel Rex's day, with doors on three sides and steeple on the west end. The Lutherans erected this limestone building with sandstone quoins in 1765 to show congregational solidarity after a splinter group separated and formed a new church. In 1884 the congregation remodeled this building extensively by extending the building eighteen feet to the west, moving the steeple to the east end, and installing modern pews, altar, and pulpit. Photo courtesy of Historic Schaefferstown, Inc.

during an autumn fair, and again he was attacked; this assault left him "bruised and bleeding, and with garments torn from his body." Despite the marked resistance to the rising evangelical movement, Albright made converts, including farmer Jacob Bricker, a member of the Reformed church in Schaefferstown, who offered his house to Albright for services.[41]

Just as they sometimes differed over religion, the people of Schaefferstown were also divided over their politics. Nolt explains that after the Revolution, Pennsylvania Germans, officially as "American" as any other residents of the new Republic, had to grapple with the idea of citizenship and equality. Over time they divided into two camps: one group, with Federalist leanings, upheld the traditional deference to those in authority and translated this into a respect for government and those in power. The other group took the opposite path. They were suspicious of state power and regarded it as a threat to the individual liberties guaranteed them as citizens; they favored the Republican Party. These differing views separated clergymen and their congregations and caused cleavages among members of congregations. They played out publicly in attitudes toward the 1798 direct tax, passed by Congress under President John Adams, a Federalist. This tax on buildings, land, and slaves was intended to raise revenue for expanding the military in preparation for war with France. It was a regressive tax: although owners of more expensive houses paid at a higher rate than owners of small properties, improved land (such as the farms owned by most Pennsylvania Germans) was taxed at a higher rate than unimproved land. Suspicious and resentful of the tax, the party that levied it, and the men who assessed their properties, some Pennsylvania Germans in Berks, Bucks, Northampton, and Montgomery counties protested vehemently, in what has become known as Fries's Rebellion.[42]

Disgust with the tax spread across the state, and disgruntled Germans, including some in towns quite close to Schaefferstown, erected liberty poles in protest. In Lebanon (seven miles away) residents erected two poles; in Jonestown, some fifteen miles distant, the liberty pole looked "at least a hundred feet high." In Myerstown (part of Heidelberg Township and only a few miles from Schaefferstown), the pole "flew a large flag with the motto, 'THE UNITED STATES OF AMERICA, FREE, SOVEREIGN, AND INDEPENDENT.'"[43]

In some areas residents threatened assessors when they tried to estimate the size and value of properties and tally the number of windows. (The tax was popularly known as the "window" or "glass" tax.) Feelings ran particularly high among Pennsylvania Germans in counties where tax assessors were

English-speaking Quakers or Moravians (whose pacifist beliefs had precluded their participation in the Revolution, making them seem unpatriotic to those Pennsylvania Germans who had fought in the war), but the situation was complicated when tax assessors were themselves Pennsylvania Germans. This was the case in Heidelberg Township, where the assessors were local farmers Henry Weiss and Mathias Bittner. When Weiss and Bittner assessed the buildings in Myerstown, they surely understood what the liberty pole there stood for, but it is not clear that township residents resented them personally.

Still, tensions continued to build among Pennsylvania Germans throughout the state. On the heels of Fries's Rebellion came the 1799 gubernatorial election, in which Pennsylvania Germans "exhibited more acrimony, malice, and indecency than was ever known on any former occasion."[44] The candidates for governor were James Ross, a Federalist, and Thomas McKean, a Republican. For Pennsylvania Germans the issue was not ethnicity, since neither candidate was German, but political philosophy.[45] Many saw the election as a way to retaliate for the much-despised tax. To counter the growing tide of Pennsylvania Germans who supported the Republicans, Federalists circulated handbills claiming that only a vote for Ross would remove the taint of Fries's Rebellion from the Germans' reputation; otherwise they would be "as cursed as the Irish."[46] In August 1799 fourteen Schaefferstown men, including Samuel Rex and tax collectors Weiss and Bittner, were invited by "friends of James Ross" to Jacob Greenawalt's tavern in Hummels Town, "in order to concert the most proper measures to promote his [Ross's] election. As it is of infinite importance to have a large and respectable meeting on that day and as we know you to be the friends of your country, firmly attached to its Constitution and government and consequently interested in the election of Mr. Ross we take the liberty earnestly to request that you will make a point of attending and bringing with you as many of your neighbors as are disposed to unite with us in this great and important work." Most recipients of this letter were relatively wealthy farmers or influential businessmen who were expected to favor the Federalists. The only craftsman on the list was saddler John Reidel (Reydel).[47]

On Election Day most Pennsylvania Germans supported McKean, who won by a slim majority, with 53.29 percent of the vote; Pennsylvania German votes made up more than half of McKean's support.[48] In Heidelberg Township voters also favored McKean, who garnered 109 votes to Ross's 42.[49] In addition to rank in the community, geography may have played a role in the way township residents thought and voted. Heidelberg Township was part of Dauphin

County at the time, and Dauphin went Democratic (2,042 to 1,054). But Heidelberg Township's southern border abuts Lancaster County, and Lancaster was a
Federalist stronghold, where voters chose Ross over McKean, 3,258 to 2,258.[50]

Federalists were clearly in the minority in Heidelberg Township, but there
is no evidence that being identified with the Federalist Party affected one's
community standing negatively. Local people continued to patronize Rex, even
if they differed politically. In fact, being a Federalist might have helped Rex in
some venues, particularly when he dealt with ironmasters Robert Coleman
and George Ege, both staunch Federalists.[51]

Property, Occupation, and Rank

Schaefferstown's ethnic origins are apparent in its architecture, which displays
what Charles Bergengren describes as "a late medieval mentalité."[52] Early buildings were one or two stories high and were built of hewn logs, Fachwerk, or
limestone. Typically, house roofs were steep, sometimes covered with red clay
tiles or thatched with rye straw, and they often had a distinctive "kick" upward
at the eaves. These buildings caught the attention of traveler Johann Schoepf,
who observed that a chimney protruding from the center of a roof was a sure
sign of a German home, since the English used end chimneys.[53] Schoepf referred to a building plan that was common in Schaefferstown and other Pennsylvania German regions: the Flurkuchen, or hall kitchen dwelling.[54] This was
a one- or two-story house with a center fireplace and three rooms on the first
floor: the Kich (kitchen), the Kammer (bedroom), and the Stup (parlor or, literally, "stove room").[55] Germans were also known for using iron stoves for heating; in the earliest houses this was accomplished by a five-plate jamb stove fed
from the kitchen hearth, with its box projecting into and heating the parlor.
By the end of the eighteenth century Germans in Schaefferstown and elsewhere built houses to accommodate freestanding ten-plate stoves rather than
jamb stoves.

House plans did not vary from the village to the countryside. Still, farmers,
who were more prosperous in terms of land ownership than townsfolk (most
of whom were craftsmen), lived in houses that were valued more highly than
those in the village. Farmers were also more likely to own larger houses, to
own a house built of stone, and even to apply fashionable clapboards on their
dwellings.[56] In 1798 the average house in Schaefferstown was assessed at $268,

while the average farmhouse was assessed at $434. (See fig. 4 for a comparison of house and property value by occupation.)

In 1798 the average Heidelberg Township farmstead comprised 160 acres; a farm this size would have been small enough to be tended by the farmer, his family, and one or two other laborers, yet large enough for commercial production.[57] Besides family members, farmers used indentured servants, hired hands who worked on an annual or daily basis, and tenant workers.[58] A few township farmers used slaves. In 1771 seven area residents owned eight "Negroes" who ranged in age from fifteen to forty; in 1780 only four residents still owned slaves.[59] Not all farmers needed or could afford hired help. David Gromer lived in a 20 × 18-foot one-story log house north of Schaefferstown. His house was "old and in bad order" and worth only $101, and his farm included a small log barn and thirty acres of "poor gravel land" assessed at an additional $150.[60] Christian Ley of Myerstown, by contrast, could have hired as many workers as he needed. Ley's "well finished" 40 × 32-foot two-story limestone house was valued

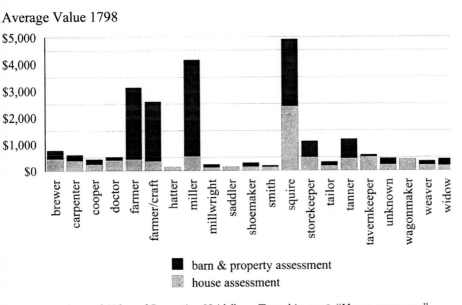

Average Value 1798

FIG. 4. Assessed Value of Properties, Heidelberg Township, 1798. "House assessment" shows the average value from schedule I of the federal direct tax (houses more than $100 in value and properties of two acres or fewer). "Barn & property assessment" shows the average value from properties on schedule II (barns, mills, land holdings of more than two acres, and houses valued at less than $100). Farmers who had craft shops on their property are listed as farmer/craft. The squire is local justice of the peace Henry Schaeffer, to whom Rex accorded this courtesy title.

at $1,500, and his 660-acre plantation contained three tenant houses, for a total assessment of $15,482.[61]

Though farmers varied in wealth, large farms were said to characterize Pennsylvania German settlements in general—and to indicate their focus on agricultural production for the market. In 1743, when Lewis Evans traveled through Tulpehocken, a few miles north of Schaefferstown, he was impressed by the Pennsylvania Germans there, "who have fine plantations, raise great quantity [sic] of wheat, and manufacture it into fine flour."[62] Benjamin Rush wrote that Pennsylvania German farms stood out "by the superior size of their barns," and he lauded Germans for the "fertility of their fields; [and] the luxuriance of their meadows." Rush also approved of the entrepreneurship of the region's residents; he noted that Germans "sell their most profitable grain, which is wheat; and eat that which is less profitable, but more nourishing, that is rye or Indian corn."[63] However, while German farmers produced abundant crops and lived in houses that were more fashionable and more highly valued than those in town, the rural landscape may not have been particularly tidy. Theophile Cazenove, a more critical observer, was appalled by area farmers' "slovenliness," lack of refinement, and indifference to the appearance of their properties, even when they could easily afford improvements. But even Cazenove was impressed by the "excellent ground and the charm of the country," though he bemoaned the "total lack of education of the farmers."[64]

Another indication of the importance of grain production in the region was the prominence of mills and the men who owned them. The seven millers in Heidelberg Township owned houses that were assessed on average at just over $544, but their real wealth was in their mills and other commercial buildings, which ranged in value from $520 to $5,700. Michael Miller of Millbach owned the most valuable of these properties; his complex included a house, gristmill, barn, stillhouse, and sawmill worth a total of $6,900.[65]

Millers and farmers were the wealthiest township residents because of their substantial investments in property and equipment; people who worked at crafts or operated smaller businesses varied in their situations. In 1798 the largest and most highly valued buildings in Schaefferstown housed businesses. Henry Schaeffer's hotel (fig. 5) was a 40 × 36-foot limestone pile; Philip Erpff's inn was 36 × 26 feet and also built of limestone; John Kapp's tavern was a 40 × 24-foot *Fachwerk* building. These holdings were assessed at $1,200, $450, and $700, respectively. In its size and in the number and finish of its buildings, the property of the town tanner, John Kline (Klein), valued at $600, also offered visible proof of his success. Tanners had to choose the location of these structures carefully; they required a source of fresh water and ample space for the vats used to process animal hides.[66] Kline's tanyard at the edge of town took up six lots and included a stream and a 30 × 18-foot log tanning house. His dwelling house (27 × 22 feet) and log barn (40 × 18 feet) sat on another two-lot parcel. Moreover, the house was one of the few log homes in town to be covered in weatherboards, suggesting an attempt on Kline's part to display his status and wealth, even though the tax assessors termed the house "in good order [but] not well finished."[67] Another town businessman, brewer Jacob Phillipi, ranked just below the tanner. Phillippi lived in a one-story log house (26 × 20 feet) but he owned a limestone brew house and barn, all set on three town lots, for a total assessment of $450.[68] Wagon maker Peter Riem Jr. also did relatively well for himself. He had an 18 × 24-foot shop and lived in a 24 × 28-foot two-story

FIG. 5. Schaeffer Hotel (the Franklin House), Market Square. This rare photograph, with the town band in the foreground, shows the hotel (building on the right) before a third story and mansard roof were added in 1884. Customers entering the building through the center door would find the bar on one side of the hall and the store on the other. The building on the left is Abraham Rex's store, built in 1815. Photo courtesy of Historic Schaefferstown, Inc.

log house on two town lots; assessors tallied his holdings at $400. Carpenter Philip Boyer's wealth was almost entirely in his land; his log house and barn were not in good repair, but they stood on four town lots, for a total value of $300. Coopers' products were in constant demand since storekeepers, brewers, millers, and distillers (among others) needed a steady supply of barrels for storage. The average value of property owned by Schaefferstown's four coopers was just over $250, putting them above some other craftsmen, though one of their number, Peter Lydig, owned only a small parcel of land worth $16, with no improvements on it.

Smiths' dwellings varied in size and value. Philip Brecht had a log locksmith shop so small that tax assessors did not record its dimensions, but he also owned two lots and a 22 × 20-foot one-story house in "middling order." John Dissinger had a "small smith shop" of unstated dimensions, and Christian Seiler worked in a log smithy that was 12 × 13 feet, but both men lived in houses valued at $105 and in "bad order." Some craftsmen did not own any property. Hatter Christian Gerret (Garret) rented his shop from Samuel Rex, while shoemaker James Maddoch (Murdoch) and nail smith John Sweitzer rented buildings (or rooms in buildings?) from widowed women, who most probably relied on such rentals for much of their income. By contrast, a few craftsmen were landlords; weaver George Strickler, for example, owned three town lots and two houses. He lived and worked in a two-story log building (28 feet square), and he obtained additional income from renting out a smaller, one-story house.

As this description suggests, rural craftsmen who worked in utilitarian trades rarely achieved high economic status; indeed, as a group they were among the lowest-assessed taxpayers, ranking just above farm laborers. They had some options, however. To improve their situation, some craftsmen moved to another area or bought land to farm.[69] Those who could afford a horse and wagon might expand the area in which they sold their products or haul goods for extra money. Some men opened taverns to supplement their incomes. Others relocated to places where there were more opportunities; John Flower rented his house and pottery shop while he lived in Heidelberg Township, but eventually he was able to move to Westmoreland County and purchase his own land.[70]

Many scholars argue that early Americans combined craft work with farming. Johanna Miller Lewis suggests that southern backcountry craftsmen had to work at farming until the region became populated enough to support full-time craft production. Winifred Rothenberg writes that even in densely settled New

England, craftsmen kept farms as a hedge against "the vicissitudes of commerce." Martin Bruegel has found that New York State farmers needed a backup occupation. Likewise, Fogleman claims that many eighteenth-century Pennsylvania Germans combined farming with a craft.[71]

However, Scott Swank alleges that there was little overlap between craft production and farming among Pennsylvania Germans because both were demanding, full-time jobs, and this seems to have been true in Heidelberg Township.[72] Almost all craftsmen lived in villages, not on farms; they sometimes had a few acres outside town for a wood lot or garden, but they did not possess enough land to do meaningful farming. Nor does it seem that township farmers made crafts for sale, even though a few farmsteads (seven out a total of 162 in the entire township) included craft shops among their ancillary buildings. Peter Sheetz, for example, had a blacksmith shop on his farm, but he rented it, along with a tenant house, to John Neip. John Bullman operated a smith shop on his 160-acre farm, but tax assessors noted explicitly that he used it only for his own work. There was a turner's shop on John Phillipi's 168-acre plantation, but whether he operated it commercially is not known. Four other local residents, with holdings that ranged from one to two hundred acres, had weaver shops among their farm buildings, but it does not seem that these farmers were weaving on a large scale; they neither purchased related tools nor sold woven products at the Rex store, but they did sell their farm produce to Rex.[73] In Chester County, during this same time period, farmer Caleb Brinton hired George Henthorn to help with the hay harvest and do the family's weaving.[74] Perhaps these Heidelberg Township farmers were using their shops for a similar purpose.

Furthermore, as we will see in the next chapter, when it came to selling goods to the store, farmers generally sold farm produce and craftsmen sold craft products, not vice versa. Because Rex's market for farm produce was greater than his need for crafts, the already wealthier farmers enjoyed more opportunities to sell their products to the store and had no need to expand into craft production, while most craftsmen did not have sufficient land to raise extra produce or livestock for sale to the store.

"A Late Medieval *Mentalité*" with Ties to the Market

Regardless of their economic standing, Schaefferstown-area farmers and townspeople were part of several economies. At the most basic level was the household economy, followed closely by a community economy where individuals traded goods and services with one another.[75] But Schaefferstown folk, like rural inhabitants in other regions, could not rely solely on their own production or that of their neighbors. There were some items—necessary or highly desirable— that could not be produced on local farms or in craft shops. And although Cazenove criticized Pennsylvania Germans for lacking gentility and Muhlenberg sniffed at their rude ways, at least some Schaefferstown-area people, including craftsmen, sought rather luxurious accoutrements for themselves and their homes. Despite their generally lower economic standing, cooper Peter Moore brewed his tea in an imported teapot and carpenter Benjamin Mace carried a silver watch.[76]

The probate inventories of selected residents provide further insight into their material lives—and their consumer needs.[77] Peter Sheetz Sr., who died in 1795, lived in a 38 × 30-foot limestone house on a 444-acre plantation just outside Schaefferstown; in addition to owning extensive property, Sheetz was also one of Schaefferstown's few slave owners.[78] (In 1798 the farm, by then owned by his son, Peter Jr., was assessed at $10,502, making it the third-most-valuable property in the township.) Sheetz's barns were full, and he had many head of livestock. His large two-story dwelling seems to have been furnished sparsely in contrast to his vast array of farm equipment. He owned two chests, four tables, six Windsor chairs, a kitchen dresser, a pair of looking glasses, an armchair, four bedsteads, and two ten-plated stoves, as well as a selection of books. Kitchen utensils included two coffee mills and a pot, assorted teaware, and a copper teakettle; he also had a bag of salt, a barrel of vinegar, and small amounts of pepper and allspice. Among Sheetz's possessions are items hinting at his status and wealth. His eight-day house clock (valued at £10, it was his most expensive possession) and his gold pocket watch (worth £6) symbolized his prosperity, which would have been clear to anyone who visited his house or saw him check his showy timepiece. The gold watch is particularly significant, since his equally well-to-do neighbor, Henry Schaeffer, made do with a silver one. Altogether Sheetz's personal property was worth £1,726. (The difference in currencies between the 1795 probate inventory and the 1798 property assessment is the result of the new dollar-and-cents monetary system adopted in 1792.)[79]

Much of Jacob Umbenhend's wealth also lay in his real estate—a 143-acre farm valued at $3,067 in 1798. Although he had an extensive investment in livestock, including a half share in a stud horse worth £45, Umbenhend lived more modestly than Sheetz. When he died in 1811, his house was furnished with eleven chairs, one table, a clothes press, a chest, and six beds and bedsteads. He owned eight delft plates, which, although old-fashioned by the early nineteenth century, he and his wife may have used along with their "twenty pair teaware" to entertain friends. Unlike many of his peers, he did not own an expensive house clock, but his total inventory was still valued at a substantial sum, £1,737.[80]

Farmer Henry Mock, who also died in 1811, was less affluent. He lived in a 30 × 30-foot two-story log house that was "old and in bad order"; he farmed sixty acres of "good dry limestone land"; and in 1798 his farm was valued at $1,330. But at least one window of his shabby dwelling was curtained, and he slept snug in a bed hung with curtains on rods (a nicety that the haughty Cazenove claimed Germans had little use for).[81] Mock owned four beds and bedsteads, a ten-plate stove, a house clock, a kitchen dresser, and three chests; he also left behind books valued at a total of £6 10s., making his small library more valuable than even his stove and bedstead, valued at £6 each; altogether his estate was worth £485.

The inventory of farmer Jacob Smith, who died in 1792, was recorded room by room, enabling us to step across his threshold for a closer look at everyday life in late eighteenth-century Schaefferstown.[82] Smith's front room downstairs was probably the best room in the house. It contained a small oval table, a walnut dining table, three chairs, and an eight-day clock (at £7 10s., his most expensive household item), but household chores and personal hygiene were also conducted in this space, as shown by a spinning wheel, reel, looking glass, whetstone, and razor. The kitchen held a pine worktable and a dresser containing tin, pewter, and copper; in addition to cooking implements, Smith stored saws, a hammer, and a steelyard (scales) here. The kitchen fireplace contained a crane, iron pots, and a frying pan.

On the second floor, an oak bedstead and straw tick occupied the space at the top of the stairs. Smith's wearing apparel and linens were stored in a walnut clothes press in the front room, which also held his prayer book, gun, and buckskin. In a second-floor back room was a pine corner cupboard and an old oak bedstead with straw mattress. In the garret were flax, yarn, a wool wheel, a dough trough, and baskets; provisions stored here included salt, grain, smoked meat, and a chest filled with dried peaches and apples. The cellar held empty barrels, vinegar, a copper kettle, a milk churn, and four stilling tubs. (Smith no longer distilled his own grain and fruit; "Long the Stiller" had twenty-eight gallons of Smith's whiskey ready to deliver.) A two-story springhouse held tubs and sundries. Livestock included two sheep, three horses, a cow, heifer, and calf, three hives of bees, and some swine; among his farm equipment were a plow, a wagon, and a windmill. Smith had been a tanner earlier in life; his tanyard still held a wheelbarrow, knife, and hooks. The inventory does not list the farm's value, but with personal property valued at only £132, Smith seems to have lived rather meanly, despite the tall clock in his parlor.

Town dweller Martin Albrecht (whose occupation is unknown) lived adjacent to the market square in a 26 × 22-foot one-story "bad old house" made of *Fachwerk* and valued at $200. The small barn next to the dwelling housed his cow and two hogs. Albrecht's most expensive possession was his house clock (£7 10s.), but he heated the house with a stove and pipe worth nearly that much—£6. His other household furniture included a table, two cupboards, four chests, and two beds and bedsteads. Perhaps Albrecht and his family (he had six children, one born a month after he died) used the chests as seating, because there are no chairs in his inventory.[83] When he died in December 1799, the total value of Albrecht's household inventory was just under £66. While his tangible effects were meager, he left his family with other assets: three bonds on interest worth more than £127.

Schaefferstown residents who were most closely linked to commerce and the market boasted a more varied array of goods, though not necessarily more wealth. Innkeeper Philip Erpff, who died in 1802, lived in the center-hallway two-story building with attached kitchen ell shown in figure 6. Erpff left behind an estate worth more than £648, but more than half of this (£330) consisted of bonds due him for outstanding loans. He had few livestock (only two cows and two hogs), but his clothing and textiles, worth some £43, included eleven window curtains. (Window curtains rarely appear in township inventories, so Erpff's ownership of eleven is impressive.) His most expensive household furnishings were two beds (one hung with curtains) at £8 each, a ten-plate stove worth £6, and a clock and case worth £5; there was also a third bed, twenty chairs, three chests, six tables, and a large walnut clothes press. He had imported "queens ware" (cream-colored tableware), wine glasses, and tea canisters in his cupboard, and more utilitarian pewter and tin in the kitchen dresser. His silver included his sleeve buttons, knee and shoe buckles, some old teaspoons, and a sugar tongs.

This small sampling shows the varying lifestyles in the Schaefferstown area, and it also demonstrates that people of all occupations and incomes were furnishing their homes, seasoning their food, and dressing themselves with goods that were not produced locally. How did these "wild forest people" get a new razor, a set of teaware, silver buttons, or a Lutheran hymnal to use in their new church? They might choose to make the long ride into Lancaster or Philadelphia to shop, but they could save themselves time and trouble by patronizing a local storekeeper with city connections.

Stores in Early Schaefferstown

Schaefferstown residents would have had no problem finding a place to buy the goods they could not make for themselves, since stores were an important feature in the village from its earliest days. A survey of the town's early businesses reveals important points about everyday life in early Schaefferstown and about keeping a store in rural America; it also provides the context for Samuel Rex's arrival in town.

Schaefferstown stores often operated in conjunction with a tavern, a common plan in many rural areas.[84] All the town storekeepers stocked a wide selection

FIG. 6. Philip Erpff Tavern, South Market Street. Erpff erected his limestone center-passage house about the time Schaeffer laid out the town. Used as a combination residence and commercial building from the time it was built, the structure was heated by corner fireplaces on the north side and by a stove on the south side of the building, where the tavern and store were located. Abraham Rex bought the building for his home in 1834; it remained in the hands of his descendents until the mid-twentieth century. Photo by author, 2007.

of general merchandise, much of it imported from the West Indies and Europe, and all accepted local commodities in exchange for store goods. That is, to help pay for their purchases, farmers brought produce to the store, and craftsmen sold what they made; even town dwellers occasionally traded pork or butter for store credit. The experience of some of Schaefferstown's early storekeepers also shows that there were difficulties associated with running a store; while it may have been relatively easy to set oneself up in business, it was not so easy to succeed.

Town founder Alexander Schaeffer was himself a storekeeper; when he laid out the town he reserved a prime lot for a large hotel building, the King George, later renamed the Franklin House.[85] The two-story limestone structure was built on a center-passage plan, with a taproom on one side of the hall and a store on the other.[86] Its cellar consists of "six arched groin vaults, supported by short square columns, and lit by large flaring windows to the north and south."[87] Kept cool by the vaults, the cellar would have been useful for storing liquor and other supplies for the tavern and store.

Schaeffer identified one of his customers as "der alt Eirisch von der Forness wo den Winter in die Schtubb gesaagt" (the old Irisher from the furnace who urinated in the stove room in the winter), revealing both the means by which he heated his building and the vexing problems that could be caused by one's customers. In his dual-purpose building Schaeffer dispensed drinks, served meals, rented rooms, and sold goods ranging from ABC books to saddles and spices. Customers paid for purchases with a mixture of cash and goods; one customer even knitted new feet in a pair of Schaeffer's stockings to pay a bill. The tavern was also a place where customers could borrow cash and pay debts to each other, but sometimes these roles were reversed. At least once Schaeffer borrowed money from a customer.[88] Schaeffer was an entrepreneur; in 1758, he owned more than seven hundred acres of land, including his hundred-acre farmstead on the edge of town. He also earned income from the annual ground rents he collected from people who had bought lots in Schaefferstown, and when he died in 1786, he left a sizable estate. (Schaeffer's son Henry inherited the hotel and rented it to tenants, including, from 1795 to 1807, Samuel Rex. Henry's son, Henry Jr., ran the store from 1815 to 1816.)[89]

Drawn by the village's felicitous location, other storekeepers, some backed by outside investors, soon followed Schaeffer's lead. In 1759 Benjamin Nathan set up a store in Philip Erpff's tavern on South Market Street. In June 1759 Nathan advertised his extensive inventory and varied payment options in Christopher Sauer's German newspaper:

From him may be bought cheaply various wares of woolen and linen fabrics, calico, fine linen, all sorts of files, augers, sickles, all kinds of accessories for saddlers, nails, sewing needles, pins, alum, dye wood, tea, coffee, sugar. All kinds of spices, coarse and fine hats . . . buttons, silver pocket watches, and many other silver items, along with an assortment of all kinds of other goods that are necessary in the country which are too numerous to list here. He will accept as payment anything that people may have, namely butter, tallow, 6 pence a pound, wax, flaxseed, all grains. Also linen rags, old silver, coffee, etc. N.B. If people need money he will also give a portion of payment in hard cash for such wares.[90]

Sometime before 1763 Nathan moved out of his rented space. Along with his brother, Lyon, he purchased a stone structure across the street from Erpff's inn (fig. 7) and opened a new store there. That same year the Nathans sold their new building to a group of Philadelphia merchants and Lancaster businessman Joseph Simon. Benjamin Nathan continued to run the store, but now

FIG. 7. Simon-Nathan Store, South Market Street. Joseph Simon and Benjamin Nathan had their store in the south side of this large limestone building—the three-bay section on the left, which dates to the 1750s. A nineteenth-century owner doubled the size of the structure with the three-bay section on the north. Photo by author, 2007.

he did so in partnership with Simon.[91] They advertised in *Der wöchentliche philadelphische Staatsbote* in 1764: "Joseph Simon and Benjamin Nathan have for sale in the newly founded store in Heidelberg, in Lancaster County, for cash or short credit, an important assortment of merchandise, just received by the last ships from London and suitable th[r]oughout for the Germans: Fine Broad cloth of all colors, Rattinets, Kerseys, half-linens, flannels . . . all kinds of iron ware . . . window glass, gunpowder and shot . . . and numerous articles too tedious to mention."[92]

In August 1769 the Nathans announced that they were continuing to keep store in Heidelberg.[93] Simon was no longer listed as a partner, but he apparently kept an interest in the business. By 1773 the joint venture had gone bad. Probably Simon was feeling the effect of the imperial crisis on his investments, but he was also dissatisfied with Nathan's management. Along with his son-in-law, Lancaster storekeeper Levy Andrew Levy, Simon sued Nathan for back debts and charged him with theft and intemperance. Nathan apparently had no assets to fall back on; the lawsuit cost him most of his belongings, and he was left with only his devotional needs—a prayer shawl, prayer book, grindstone, and knife for kosher slaughtering.[94]

Money problems also caused the downfall of Frederick Stump, who ran his store-tavern on the southwest corner of the town square from 1759 to 1766. The notice he placed in the Germantown *Pennsylvanische Berichte* in November 1759 emphasized his wide selection and willingness to buy local goods— along with the fact that he was open on Saturday. "Frederick Stump, in Heidelberg Township in Lancaster County makes known that he has for sale powder, lead and all kinds of peddler-ware, which only late came from England. Also shoe-leather, and he also buys flax-seed, butter and all kinds of other things that people have, and gives the highest price for the same . . . he can also be dealt with on Saturday."[95] The reference to being open on a day when the town's Jewish storekeepers closed for their Sabbath indicates that competition was keen among the town's storekeepers—so keen, perhaps, that even with innovative advertising, Stump did not prosper. Perhaps three stores were simply too many for the small town to support, or it may be that the depression that followed the Seven Years' War hit Stump particularly hard. In 1763 he mortgaged the store property. He also sold off his land in the northern part of the county, where he had established the village of Stumpstown, but in the end, he could not avoid foreclosure. In May 1766 the county sheriff seized Stump's store and sold it to Mathias Bush of Philadelphia, who held the mortgage.[96]

Heidelberg Township storekeeper Bernard Jacobs also experienced financial problems.[97] In 1762 Jacobs lost his store on the Millbach Creek, northeast of Schaefferstown, after the Lancaster partnership of Bush, Gratz, Levy, Franks, and Simon sued him for the astonishing sum of £2,126 16s. 6d.[98] Remarkably, Jacobs rebounded from the loss and retained his community standing. His neighbors must have perceived that the bankruptcy was not due to dishonesty, for the congregation of the Millcreek church later hired Jacobs to oversee their fundraising lottery. He subsequently opened a store in Schaefferstown that remained in operation for about twenty years. Jacobs is noteworthy for more than his resilience; he was an itinerant *mohel* (ritual circumciser) who performed thirty-three circumcisions for the widely scattered Jewish community in Philadelphia, Reading, York, Easton, and Lancaster between 1757 and 1790.[99] Although this is an average of just one ceremony a year, one has to admire Jacobs's diligence. Moreover, as Eileen Hoover observes, "Schaefferstown must have indeed been a successful trading center to hold such a cosmopolitan man for so long."[100]

In 1789 Lewis Kreider set up still another store in Schaefferstown.[101] Kreider would be only a minor footnote in the history of the town's early storekeepers, except for one fact: he was responsible for bringing Samuel Rex to Schaefferstown. It seems that when Kreider was in Philadelphia buying merchandise to furnish his store, he hired the twenty-three-year-old Rex as his clerk. Rex, who was working as a clerk or scrivener in the city, agreed to move to Schaefferstown to "tend store from the 23rd of November 1789 for one year for the sum of £30 specie and he [Kreider] paying my washing, mending and boarding."[102]

An advertisement in the *Lancaster Journal* in August 1798 describes the necessary qualifications for a store clerk in this region: "Wanted. A Young Man who can speak the English and German languages, of good character and recommendations, to attend a store in Lancaster Borough."[103] Samuel Rex seems to have met these qualifications and more. He was the grandson of a German-speaking immigrant, and he had grown up in Chestnut Hill, a small, predominantly German village north of Philadelphia, so he was fluent in German and familiar with the culture.[104] He was also proficient in English, the language he used for bookkeeping, scrivening, and correspondence, including his letters to his family. Furthermore, he knew the storekeeping business through his father, Abraham Rex Sr., who kept the most prosperous of the many "great stores" in Chestnut Hill. Great stores were exchange centers for the region. Farmers sold their produce at these places to avoid the ten-mile trip over bad roads into

Philadelphia, and city merchants periodically came to the stores to buy farm goods.[105] This means not only that Rex grew up in a storekeeping family but that he had the opportunity to make valuable contacts with city merchants who did business with his father. Moreover, Kreider certainly thought that Rex had "good character" and was trustworthy, because he sent him ahead to Schaefferstown with several wagonloads of valuable goods and money to pay the men who drove the teams. Kreider's brief but detailed instructions to his new clerk offer insight about setting up a new store and show what Rex could expect when he arrived:

> Pay Mr. John Hinkle at Heidelberg £5 . . . Mr. Barnard Wolf at Heidelberg £4.13 . . . Mr. Christian Geisse at Heidelberg £3.12; deduct paid Hinkle at Philada 30/. Put the rum, sugar, molasses and oil in the cellar and the rest of the things upp in the store. Hurry the carpenter, and if any house furniture comes tell them I'll pay them when I come upp. If the man should not give you possession of the house call at Mr. Boyers and unload there until I come. Don't let the carters go farther than ten miles until you rec. the permit for wine. Be careful & don't leave the teams by no means.[106]

This brief note shows that Kreider had shopped so extensively that it took three wagons (driven by Hinkle, Wolf, and Geisse, who were paid rather handsomely) to haul the heavy goods. Moreover, this was a new venture for Kreider, whose store space was not yet furnished. Still, Kreider was known well enough in the village to be confident that residents would trust him to pay later for his furniture. Rex, however, was a stranger, and if the owner would not let him into the store building, he would have to tarry at Boyer's tavern until Kreider arrived. Storekeeping also involved a certain amount of red tape, including obtaining a license to sell wine, and it entailed risks, as we see in Kreider's instruction to Rex to stay with the wagons and protect the merchandise.

Once established in Schaefferstown, Rex's duties as clerk included waiting on customers and recording transactions in the daybook when Kreider was away. None of Kreider's daybooks survive, but his correspondence reveals that Rex sometimes kept the store records. In February 1795, after leaving Schaefferstown, he wrote to ask for Rex's support in a disagreement with potter Peter Newman over a store bill: "You certainly know as much about the Books at that time as I do and know the[y] were kept regular."[107] Rex may also have done quite a bit of manual labor, moving heavy barrels and crates, loading goods into customers' wagons, and perhaps putting up security shutters. As one student of country stores has noted, such tasks could result in physical injury.[108] Although there is no way to know for certain whether he hurt himself in the store, Rex did require the attention of a physician while working for Kreider. His expenses during his first year in Schaefferstown included a doctor's bill of £1 19s. 4d.[109]

Kreider paid Rex's wages partly in cash and partly with store goods, and the goods that Rex took in payment provide more clues about his work—and perhaps about his aspirations for the future. Some choices are rather mundane; he chose six yards of linen (enough to have two shirts made), silk handkerchiefs, and a pair each of boots and buckles. A charge for two panes of glass may have been to replace store windows that he had broken. However, he also selected a silver watch, hinting at a desire to become a businessman of status—someone who needed a timepiece to regulate a busy schedule.[110]

Kreider's Schaefferstown store was short lived. When Rex's contract expired in November 1790, Kreider relocated to Jonestown, where he opened a new store and tavern and made two unsuccessful bids for public office.[111] Because he left town so soon, Kreider did not have time to collect all the bills that his customers owed him or to pay Rex all of his wages. It was not until May 1793 that he paid the last installment to Rex, and it took even longer to receive payment from former customers. In 1795 Kreider wrote to Rex that he "drew out about eighty accounts against sundry people in and about Shaffers Town," meaning that he took legal action to try to recover what they owed him.[112] In 1799 Kreider was still having money problems; when he could not pay his debt to fellow Jonestown shopkeeper Martin Meily, Meily sued him.[113] Kreider's experience emphasizes that even in a vigorous economy, storekeepers encountered financial difficulties.

When Kreider moved on, Rex stayed in Schaefferstown and went into business for himself. He opened his store in a rented room in Henry Valentine's tavern on the southwest corner of the town square, the same building where Frederick Stump had operated his tavern.[114] Unlike some early Schaefferstown storekeepers, Rex did not turn to city merchants for financing. Rather, he tapped into his family network by borrowing £25 and purchasing twenty-four pairs of Germantown stockings from his father.[115]

As a relative newcomer in the village, Rex faced competition from at least two long-established storekeepers, as well as from the inn- and tavern keepers who sold goods. One competitor was longtime resident Philip Erpff, who took over the store after his tenant, Benjamin Nathan, moved out.[116] Erpff's receipt book shows that from May 1774 to April 1776, and from May 1787 to May 1798, he purchased groceries and dry goods in amounts ranging from £3 to £57 in Philadelphia. (The gap in Erpff's receipt book during the Revolutionary years is one of the few concrete clues about the effect of the war on Schaefferstown.)[117] Erpff's shop was small; his bills for Philadelphia merchandise were substantially lower than Rex's in the same years, so he probably was not much of a threat to Rex's business. Rather, the two men were friends who sold each other store inventory and helped each other by hauling goods; in his will Erpff even named Rex one of the executors of his estate.[118]

More serious competition came from the Kapp family, longtime residents who had kept a sizable store and tavern on the town square for at least a decade before Rex's arrival.[119] (The Kapp store and tavern were in separate buildings, making them an exception to the usual tavern/store combination.)[120] When Andreas Kapp died in 1797, assessors valued the store inventory at £775; his household goods and outstanding loans totaled £1,065.[121] Clearly, the Kapp store was much more substantial than Erpff's, and even larger than Rex's, whose store inventory in 1807 was worth £675.[122] There is scant evidence of trade between Rex and the Kapps—once, in 1800, John Kapp purchased "velvet &c."—and no hint of friendship. Regardless of his familiarity with goods and prices, Rex was not one of the men who inventoried Andreas's estate in 1797. Moreover, when Andreas's son George took over the family store, he competed with Rex not only for store customers but as a fellow justice of the peace. (Rex was commissioned a justice in 1799, and George Kapp received his appointment one year later.) The Kapp family store was in operation until at least 1815.[123]

Although Rex's store was not the only option for Schaefferstown folk, the level of trade was sufficient to sustain more than one business. Customers arriving on the town square could have chosen to shop at either Kapp's or Rex's store; how many preferred to deal with Kapp is not known, but, as we will see in Chapter 2, enough people chose Rex to keep his business thriving.

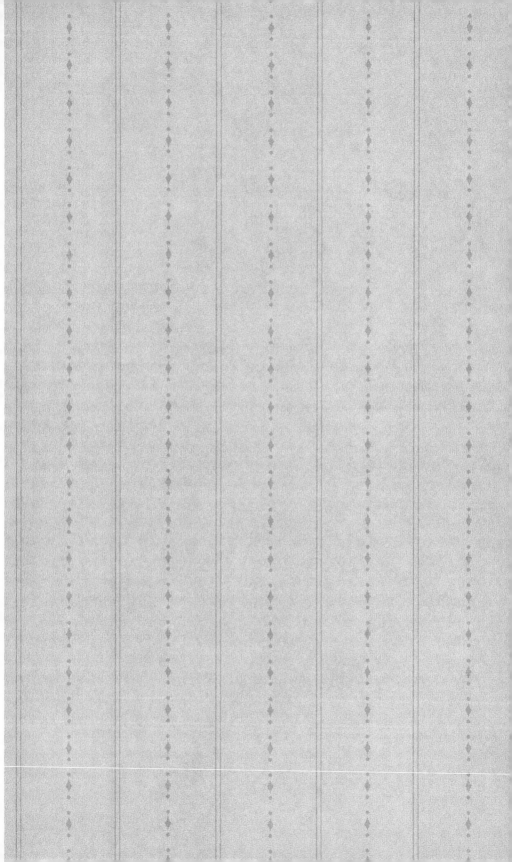

CHAPTER TWO

··

THE REX STORE AND ITS LOCAL CUSTOMERS

YEARS AFTER HE HAD RETIRED FROM STOREKEEPING, Samuel Rex, in a reflective moment, opened his ledger and wrote, "Monday, November 30, AD 1789. Samuel Rex first arrived in Sheafferstown, from Germantown, and in December 1790, he commenced storekeeping for himself which he continued until May 1807, being about sixteen and a half years."[1] When Rex penned this entry he was looking back on a long and profitable career. But, as the experiences of some other area storekeepers show, success was not a given. Storekeepers took physical and financial risks driving fragile goods over rough and dangerous roads. They had to assess accurately a customer's creditworthiness or risk not getting paid. Rex once explained that Michael Valentine and sons failed at storekeeping because they lacked good judgment. "When they got goods home they had a great run . . . that is they trusted anybody and everybody that never intended to pay."[2]

Storekeepers also needed to be knowledgeable about a wide variety of goods, and they had to buy the right amount of each but not pay too much. They were at the mercy of urban wholesalers who expected prompt payment, and they faced ruin if the economy soured. When European suppliers called in accounts of Philadelphia merchants or when crop failures hit nearby farmers, storekeepers felt the rippling effects from above and below them on the distribution chain. Even getting the capital to start a store could be problematic; Rex was supposed to begin working for Kreider on November 23, but Kreider was temporarily "disappointed about cash" to buy his dry goods, and so he was forced to delay the store opening one week.[3]

Fortunately for Rex, he had the right combination of education and experience (combined, perhaps, with a bit of luck) to make good as a storekeeper. He also had picked a felicitous time and place to open his store.

Doing Business in the Early Republic

When Rex set up business in 1790, the United States had just ratified the new Constitution and the commercial economy was recovering its vigor after the depression of the previous decade.[4] Under the Articles of Confederation (1781 to 1789), during a time that some historians term America's "critical period," the nation suffered from high unemployment, increased bankruptcies, and an unfavorable balance of trade that many saw as a threat to America's moral health.[5] The recovery began in 1789–90, when the devastation of the Napoleonic Wars increased European demand for food and Alexander Hamilton proposed a plan to restore the nation's fiscal soundness that bolstered producers' confidence. By 1791 American commerce was flourishing; in the nation's busiest port, Philadelphia, merchants filled their ships with cargoes bound for Europe and the West Indies and placed large orders with their overseas suppliers. In 1792, after years of dealing with a confusing variety of foreign and domestic currencies and the inflationary revolutionary money, the United States adopted its own decimal system of coinage. Newly established state and local banks began to circulate currency freely and thus contributed to the increasing prosperity and rising interest in speculative ventures. At the same time, transportation developments—including the construction of turnpikes and canals and, soon enough, steam engines—resulted in improved travel, shipping, and communication within the new nation. America doubled its physical size, thanks to the Louisiana Purchase in 1803, and its population grew from four million in 1790 to twelve million by 1830.

Although Rex could not have known it, this was an era when the essentials of a much later industrial capitalism, "a flexible currency, banking, corporations, new transportation systems, industrialism, and pervasive consumerism," had their genesis.[6] These changes did not happen immediately, though, and despite the rising economic climate business customs remained traditional in many ways. Increasingly sophisticated credit instruments and communication methods would ultimately change the nature of business, but Rex and his trading partners in both the city and countryside conducted business on a face-to-face basis with people they knew, or knew of, and whose circumstances they under-stood.[7] Although there were banks in Philadelphia in Rex's day, in Schaeffers-town, Rex (and other relatively wealthy men) provided the banking services. Canals and railways would ultimately revolutionize and reduce the cost of trans-portation, but these developments came too late to benefit Rex, and he had to be content with overland hauling.

For now, however, it was a good time to be a country storekeeper, and Rex had also chosen a good place—the rich limestone farm country of south-central Pennsylvania. Although this region did not sustain battle damage during the Revolution, its farmers saw the market for their grain fall in the economic slump following the war. After 1789, as exports to Europe increased, Schaefferstown-area farmers resumed sales of grain to local merchant-millers and carried other crops directly to Philadelphia. Traveler Theophile Cazenove observed that farmers in the region had "all become rich, through the high prices of grains since the French Revolution."[8] Increased trade in the port of Philadelphia and reviving markets for hinterlands produce made rural Pennsylvania in 1790 an ideal place to do business.

Building the Business

As a stranger in town, Rex probably had to work to become accepted into the close-knit rural community, but he helped that process along by attending the local German Lutheran church and, even more so, by marrying a local woman, Anna Maria (Mary) Valentine, the daughter of his landlord, innkeeper Henry Valentine. The couple married in December 1791; Mary was thirty-four and Samuel was twenty-five.[9]

When his father-in-law died in November 1792, Rex bought the Valentine inn and for a few years kept store there while his brother-in-law, Michael Val-entine, operated the tavern side of the business.[10] Then, in March 1795, Rex and Valentine moved their joint operation across Main Street to the large hotel built by Schaeffer half a century earlier.[11] The move allowed the men to estab-lish themselves in a property that may have been too costly or unavailable for purchase but was within their reach as tenants. Renting a store building was not unusual, as this ad from the February 1787 *Pennsylvania Gazette* shows:

To be LETT for one year or longer . . . a LARGE and convenient STORE ROOM, in a stone messuage, situate in the town of Lebanon in Dauphin county, adjoining to the center of the said town, with a good cellar under the same, and also a Store-house adjoining the said messuage; the store-room fronts on the two principal streets in the said town, which lies in an opulent part of the country, on the great road leading from Reading to Harrisburg. The premises have been occupied for three years past by storekeepers, and was leased for £42.10 per annum.[12]

Even if they were tenants, not owners, the move to the Schaeffer hotel was a step up for Rex and Valentine, for it was the most imposing structure on the square. Although the frame and brick Valentine tavern had two stables and was relatively large (36 × 22 feet), it was only one story and in poor condition (or "bad order," according to the tax assessors who valued it at $300). By contrast, the Schaeffer hotel was in good repair and worth $1,200. The hotel also had an adjoining kitchen and a large cellar, along with a barn and stables with ample space for food preparation, storage of spirits and groceries, and accommodation of teams.[13] All of this marked such a momentous change in circumstances for Rex and his business that he started a fresh daybook and labeled it "Number 1," even though it was at least his third book since he had arrived in Schaefferstown five years earlier.[14]

Michael Valentine is not listed as an occupant or owner of any other dwelling in 1798, so it is likely that he and his wife (who was expecting their first child) moved into the second floor of the Schaeffer hotel, a space they probably shared with overnight guests.[15] It is not clear whether the Rexes also lived in this building or whether they had rooms in one of his other properties. Rex still owned the old Valentine inn, but he was leasing it to Jacob Gass, a carpenter, and John Kely (or Kaley), a dyer.[16] And he had recently purchased still another property, the former Gemberling tavern adjacent to the northeast corner of the town square (fig. 8), but he rented this place to Anthony Seyfert, who kept the tavern, and to Christian Garret, a hatter who had his shop in a small building on the grounds.[17] No matter which property they made their home, the Rexes were probably crowded in with a number of other people, but Rex was increasing his status and protecting his business interests all the same. By buying these key buildings he prevented rival storekeepers from moving in (Seyfert lent cash and sold "sundries" at the tavern, but these were modest sales that did not compete with Rex's array of goods and services), and he gained prestige by owning and/or doing business in three properties on the busy town square.[18]

The rentals also gave Rex additional income and provided him with a cushion against slow times. He earned further income from scrivening and legal work, charging fees for writing and filing legal documents and for his services as a justice of the peace.[19] Operating supplemental businesses was common among rural storekeepers. Harrisburg storekeeper John Harris owned a mill and ferry; William Polk of St. George's, Delaware, owned a farm and gristmill in addition to his store; and Jeremiah Brown of Little Britain Township, Lancaster County, was proprietor of both a store and a mill.[20]

Rex was now established in his new location inside the commodious hotel, but his move begs the question, how would a first-time visitor find his business? That is, how would a stranger in town know that there was a store inside the large hotel? Unlike purpose-built, gable-front store buildings, stores combined with taverns did not advertise their function by form.[21] Did a window

FIG. 8. Gemberling-Rex House. Dating to c. 1758, this building is a rare example of *Fachwerk* (half-timbered) construction. Early on, the exterior was plastered and painted in a red-and-black diaper-work pattern to resemble brick. It was a tavern until 1802, when Rex and his wife moved in and made it their residence; it stayed in the hands of Rex descendents until 1974. It is now a house museum operated by Historic Schaefferstown, Inc. Photo by author, 2007.

display alert the traveler to the presence of a store, or was there a sign board to signal that store goods were available within? Henry Valentine had "a sign for an inn" among his possessions when he died, but a store sign is not listed in the extant probate inventories of any of the town's storekeepers, so these questions remain unanswered.[22] It may well be that stores were so frequently located in the larger taverns and hotels in rural areas that there was no need to advertise their presence.

Regardless of exterior configuration, Rex's new space probably had some standard features. Stores typically included two rooms, a public selling space and a private counting room in the rear where the storekeeper updated his account books; here Rex might have conferred with his customers on matters requiring more privacy than the store allowed. In Virginia only the counting room was heated, but in the colder northern states heat was essential in both areas. Rex bought a ten-plate stove from Henry Valentine in 1791; if he moved it with him to the Schaeffer hotel, it would easily have warmed more than one room.[23] (There was a second heat source in the building as well. Henry Schaeffer's 1803 probate inventory shows that he owned a stove that was in the possession of Michael Valentine, who may have used it in the tavern or in his rooms on the second floor.)[24] The salesroom was typically furnished with display shelves and a counter for cutting yard goods, counting out money, and weighing groceries. The counter also served as a barrier between the customers and valuable merchandise.[25] Some stores had built-in pigeonholes for small items.[26] Certain storekeepers kept all merchandise on prominent display, since, as one retailer stressed, advertising visibly was "a matter very *essential to promote the Sales,* as every Article is expected to be *in view.*" The exception was white goods, which were stored in trunks and bandboxes to preserve "their clear Whiteness" in the often grimy store atmosphere and to prevent damage from sunlight.[27] Other storekeepers preferred to keep breakables packed away until a customer expressed interest in them.[28]

"Suitable Throughout for the Germans"—Goods, Services, and Customers at the Store

Rex's predecessors Benjamin Nathan and Joseph Simon advertised goods specifically stocked for a German clientele. A. G. Roeber explains that in colonial America

German-speakers exhibited a marked preference for small amounts of pewter and avoidance of English tinware in eating utensils; German-American stoneware and finer porcelain shows a marked preference for red, yellow and green as the basic colors for use in the home. . . . German shopkeepers found, too, that German women favored certain styles of bonnets and specific colors for clothes. Michael Hillegas complained to an English supplier that in contacting German shopkeepers he could not be rid of a large quantity of "the Calico; believe they might have gone off if instead of Green Ground they had been blew."[29]

It is possible that German preferences may have changed after the colonial era, but Rex's stock contained only two categories of goods that seem to have been specifically targeted toward German customers: textiles and printed materials, and evidence for the textiles is scant. That is, Rex sold German stripe and German lawn, but these were only two of many different textiles he stocked, and they were not recurring items. Furthermore, it is quite likely that the designation "German" was generic, rather than a positive indication of place of origin.[30] It is possible, of course, that customers might have revealed ethnic preferences in ways other than by purchasing German-made products. For example, as Roeber notes, Germans loved bright colors and design, so they might be expected to have bought exceptionally colorful dishes and textiles from Rex. But Rex did not consistently list the color of textiles that customers bought, and he seldom recorded the color of the dishes that he sold, so this question remains unresolved.[31]

More telling is Rex's assortment of German-language books. These were mostly devotional and educational titles for home, church, and school use.[32] His inventory included German Reformed and Lutheran hymnals, some with flowered covers (see fig. 9), along with prayer books by Habermann, Starck, and Zollikofer,[33] German ABC primers,[34] and almanacs.[35] Rex also stocked similar books printed in English. When he recorded a book sale he did not always specify its language, but his purchases in Philadelphia show that he stocked far more German than English publications.[36] In 1807, when Rex sold his inventory to his brother, the transaction included ninety-one books, and only seven were identified as English.[37]

Analysis of Rex's book sales in three key years provides insight into the reading habits of his Pennsylvania German and non-German customers. In 1791 Rex sold fifteen books to thirteen different customers. Nine psalm books, prayer

FIG. 9. German Hymnals with Flowered Covers. Hymnals such as these were part of the German devotional books that Rex sold in his store. Photo courtesy of Alan Keyser.

books, and other religious texts and five almanacs went to local, German-speaking customers. Christian Armstrong, a Schaefferstown craftsman, bought an (English-language) "assistant book."[38] In 1798 Rex sold twenty-two books, of which three were almanacs, four were educational or instructional, and the remaining fifteen were religious texts.[39] The almanacs went to basket weaver David Kramer, ironmaster Henry Grubb, and Mrs. Wilson, a local woman who sold mittens to Rex, showing that people of all ranks used these popular guides.[40] Furnace manager Rudolph Kelker and farmer Philip Mock bought (English-language) copies of *Schoolmaster's Assistants.* Farmer Christian Schultz bought two ABC books. Ironworker Barney Mutz bought a Bible, miller John Shenk bought a testament, a traveler from Reamstown bought a psalm book, the widow Schaeffer bought the English prayer book, and the rest of the (presumably German) religious books were purchased by local farmers and saddler John Reydel.

In 1806–7 Rex sold thirty-one books to twenty-eight customers; twenty books were secular and eleven were religious. Ironworkers Samuel Cooper, Arthur Daley, and Patrick Bradley bought an English hymnal and almanacs, and Jacob Dennis and Julia Wellamoyer, whose surnames also suggest that they lived or worked at a furnace, bought a testament and almanacs (no language stated). The rest of the purchases were made by Pennsylvania German customers: the widow Houser and blacksmith Peter Lydig bought psalters, and carpenter Philip Boyer bought an almanac. Local farmers bought the remaining twelve almanacs, four psalters, three psalm books, two ABCs, and one history book.

Almanacs, religious texts, and schoolbooks formed the bulk of Rex's inventory, but he occasionally sold other types of literature. In January 1807 Schaefferstown resident John Smith (who was German, despite his anglicized name) purchased a recently published account of a murder trial.[41] Not only was the subject matter a departure for Rex, but Smith's purchase was one of the rare occasions when a German speaker sought an English-language text. Besides Smith, in the three years surveyed, only two other German-speaking customers bought English-language books.

Then there is the strange case of *Robinson Crusoe*. Between 1790 and 1794 Rex bought (in three separate purchases) two dozen copies of this "clerically-approved, all-time American favorite,"[42] but it seems to have been a slow-moving item, at least among his regular customers. In 1804 Rex recorded the sale, on credit, of one "Robinson Crusoe book" to ironworker John Peters, but there are no other sales of *Crusoe* listed in his extant daybooks.[43] Perhaps this type of reading appealed more to travelers, who paid cash, than to the locals who regularly charged their purchases (and who may not have been able to read enough English to enjoy *Robinson Crusoe*). The book must have attracted buyers—otherwise Rex would not have purchased additional copies—but the identity of the readers is a mystery.

In addition to his mostly religious and educational store inventory, Rex bought books in Philadelphia that were clearly intended for his own use.[44] On a few occasions he recorded in his daybooks loans that he made of these and other books from his personal library. In almost every instance these loans were to people outside the local Pennsylvania German community. Three furnace managers and one ironmaster borrowed Rex's copies of Boyle's *Voyages,* Parsons's *The Girl of the Mountains,*[45] and *Arabian Nights,* all choices that show these readers shared Rex's taste for adventure.[46] Rex also lent books, including the legal handbook *Conductor Generalis,*[47] to the town doctor and to his fellow justices of the peace, professionals in the community who were his intellectual and social peers.[48] Rex's only loan of a book to someone who was not a professional or a resident of an iron furnace community occurred on March 8, 1819, when he lent his two-volume German-English and English-German dictionary to Barbara Sherk.[49] While nothing more is known about Sherk, Rex's ownership of the dictionary—and Sherk's desire to use it—are reminders of the difficulties German speakers sometimes had in dealing with the mainstream Anglophone community.

In summary, two facts emerge from this brief look at the Schaefferstown book trade: German-speaking farmers were Rex's biggest book buyers (similar books appear in their probate inventories), and Schaefferstown's Pennsylvania Germans and ironworkers alike preferred religious subjects, educational books, and almanacs to novels. The Schaefferstonians' preference for such literature is confirmed by the author of *Bibliotheca Americana,* who wrote in 1789, "German books ... sell in parts inhabited by the Dutch, but principally books of devotion and school books. They have very few men of literature among them here. When a Dutchman is not at prayers, he is either at work or asleep." German traveler Johann Schoepf likewise expressed his disdain for Pennsylvania Germans and their reading choices. Schoepf complained that such farmers spoke a "miserable, broken fustian salmagundy of English and German" and had libraries comprising only "the Almanack, and Song-book, a small 'Garden of Paradise,' Habermann ... and the Bible." Historian Robert E. Cazden notes that Pennsylvania German farmers, though criticized for their "alien ways and clannishness," were "no more narrow intellectually than members of their class who remained in Europe," but he also points to a "small but heterogeneous" group of German-American readers who enjoyed a much wider variety of literature.[50]

In Rex's community, too, there was a group of readers whose interests were broader than those of most Pennsylvania German farmers and craftsmen and the workers at the iron sites. With the exception of ironmaster George Ege, whose rank was higher than Rex's, these men—doctors and justices of the peace—were on a social and professional level with Rex; they had the same taste in light reading and they shared his interest in educating themselves on legal issues.

Apart from German books and the occasional German cloth, Rex, unlike his predecessors, did not stock goods that were particularly targeted to Germans. Cary Carson and Cynthia Falk argue that increasing status and a desire to move from "folk to formal," rather than an effort to discard one's ethnic identity in favor of a more fashionable one (i.e., looking less German and more British), prompted early Americans' decisions about consumer goods and home improvements.[51] Rex's store offerings support this argument. For the most part, Rex's German-speaking customers selected goods from the same assortment as his non-German-speaking customers, and some of their purchases, such as tea equipage, suggest leanings toward gentility and increased status that coexisted with ethnic culture. That is, while they used and wore store-bought objects that showed their sense of mainstream fashion, Schaefferstown-area people—even those who, like Samuel Rex, were fluent in English and closely connected to the city market—continued to display their ethnicity in a number of ways. This is demonstrated by the way they organized their homes and their fondness for cast-iron stoves; by the way they slept (under heavy bags stuffed with goose feathers rather than beneath blankets); by their traditional foodways; and by their painted furniture (decorated dower chests, dressers, desks, even tall clocks). As their book purchases show, when they read their prayers, sang hymns, consulted an almanac, and taught their children, they almost always did so in German. When they wished to remember a special event such as a marriage or birth they often commissioned an artist to produce a colorful, hand-lettered, decorated certificate known as a *Fraktur*. For example, Samuel's brother Abraham, also a storekeeper with Philadelphia connections and fluent in English, owned a traditional illustrated *Taufschein* (birth certificate) commemorating his first child's birth in 1804.[52]

If German cloth was an occasional offering at the store, Rex offered a wide range of other fabrics; when he initially stocked his store, in fact, his greatest expenditure was for cloth.[53] Such a substantial investment in textiles was typical; Thomas Doerflinger found that from 1750 to 1790, 70 percent of storekeepers' purchases went to textiles. Spirited competition among Europe's dry goods exporters in the late eighteenth century brought textile prices down, and the affordability of cloth was reflected in the buying patterns of country storekeepers.[54]

Adrienne Hood suggests that in Chester County, Pennsylvania, producers did not grow enough flax or raise enough sheep to meet their clothing and household textile requirements, and so they had to purchase additional cloth. Carole Shammas's research (much of it based on Massachusetts records) showed that few people "wore or put on their tables and beds [what] had been spun at home."[55] However, it is not clear that this was true of the Pennsylvania Germans of south-central Pennsylvania, whose use of homespun lasted well into the nineteenth century. According to their household inventories, south-central farmers typically grew enough flax and raised enough sheep for their household use. Among Pennsylvania Germans the custom was for women to spin the yarn from flax, wool, or even store-bought cotton (imported from the South) and to take the yarn to a professional (male) weaver who wove it into cloth. A number of weavers worked in the Schaefferstown area, at least some of whom probably produced fine cloth. Ellen J. Gehret and Alan G. Keyser, who researched Pennsylvania German textiles, concluded that "some farmers considered certain weavers capable of producing only tow and common linen," but others were more skilled and made "fine tablecloths and woolen coverlets."[56]

In Schaefferstown, too, people grew flax and raised sheep for wool, and they used the services of local weavers for certain textiles. But they also purchased imported cloth at the Rex store. In this they were not unique. When Doer-flinger investigated cloth use in the Mid-Atlantic region, he concluded that even the thriftiest people, including Germans and Quakers, preferred imported tex-tiles over homespun.[57] As Hood puts it, "No matter how much local weavers expanded their capacity, they could not provide the silks, chintzes, and increas-ingly elaborate printed fabrics available from abroad."[58] Rex's customers bought small amounts of cloth for repairs and mending, and they also purchased yard goods in large amounts specifically for clothing and bed hangings. Typical pur-chases included "cloth for a great coat," "poplin for a petticoat," and "thickset for trousers," as well as the notions needed to complete the project. In August 1802 Schaefferstown's young women may have needed outfits for a special occasion, because five of them came to Rex for chintz and calico in six- to seven-yard lengths. This was enough to sew a traditional Pennsylvania Ger-man petticoat and matching short gown, if that was their preference, but it would also have served to make a more fashionable one-piece dress.[59]

The desirability of imported cloth for certain uses is best illustrated by the fact that Rex's customers traded homespun for imported yard goods. (Eliza-beth Perkins found this was also true in Kentucky, where women wove linen so they could exchange it at the store for nankeen.)[60] In March 1801, when John Stookey needed fourteen and a half yards of furniture cotton to dress his bed, he paid the store bill (4s. 8d.) with flax linen. Even weavers sometimes preferred purchased cloth. H. M. Shultz, a weaver in Tulpehocken, wrote to Rex in May 1801, asking him to send "black striped Ankeen . . . sufficient for a jacket. I wear a large jacket, therefore be so kind to send a full pattern."[61]

By the same token John Flower, who made his living making redware, was not always content with his own clay pots; in July 1798 he purchased an im-ported sugar bowl from Rex.[62] At 2s. 6d., the sugar bowl cost as much as Flower charged for a large cream pot, and considerably more than most of his wares. But, displayed on Flower's table or in his kitchen dresser, the sugar bowl, like Shultz's jacket, would have been tangible evidence of his good taste and mate-rial success.

When craftsmen such as Flower and Shultz needed components or tools for their businesses, they were quite likely to find them at the Rex store—rather than keeping their own parts or components inventory or patronizing other craftsmen. Johanna Miller Lewis describes a system in rural North Carolina in which artisans bought from storekeepers the raw materials and components that were too labor intensive to make for themselves.[63] This arrangement was also common in Schaefferstown and serves as additional evidence of the rural village's connection to distant markets. Flower, for example, bought red lead for his glazes by the barrel at the Rex store. Rex also stocked stirrups and other components for saddlery and the logwood, verdigreen (verdigris?), copperas, madder, and indigo used by hatters and professional dyers. Weavers could even buy weavers' reeds (small pieces of wood that fit onto the beater of a loom to produce the pattern).[64] Rather than use the services of a local smith, cabinetmakers routinely purchased imported hinges and escutcheons from Rex. Even the town doctor saved time by buying Godfrey's Cordial, a patent medicine, at the store.[65]

Despite all the goods packed into Rex's store, there were some rural necessities that he did not sell. The absence of certain products is significant because it tells us about the goods that customers made or raised for themselves or obtained through other networks. The North Carolina store records that Lewis studied, for example, do not show pottery, furniture, or silver sales, suggesting that people bought these items directly from crafts shops.[66] Rex's records reveal that in an area celebrated for grain production, he rarely sold wheat or flour, although he occasionally served as broker by buying grain for an ironmaster. He only rarely sold candles, something that his customers seemingly would have needed in large supplies. Apparently people either made their own candles or bought them from a chandler. Nor were beer, cider, fresh fruits, vegetables, guns, or furniture part of Rex's offerings. Local residents grew their own produce or traded with a neighbor for it; they obtained beer from a brewer (or made their own small beer); and they had their grain ground into flour at one of the gristmills along Mill and Hammer creeks. If they had no grain, they bought flour from the miller, who retained as his "custom" a portion of flour from each bushel of grain he milled.[67] They visited specific craftsmen for guns, and when they needed a new piece of furniture they called on a joiner or cabinetmaker and "bespoke" (custom-ordered) the piece. In the case of an exceptional piece, such as a tall clock, they may have had to travel to a larger place such as Reading or Lancaster.[68]

The Rex store was also a place to obtain banking services; customers could borrow cash or pay third-party debts by using their accounts at the Rex store.[69] When William Gayda was "in a pinch for to get hay" for his cow, he knew just where to go for assistance. He wrote to Rex, explaining that John McClane had a stack of hay to sell, but that he had no money to pay McClane. "He [McClane] told me that if I would let him have goods at your store, that would do him the same service," Gayda wrote. "The price of the hay is five dollars; if you would let him have that amount on my account, you would oblige me in the highest degree." Gayda's problems were quickly solved through a series of store exchanges. McClane presented Gayda's letter to Rex, and Rex gave McClane goods worth £1 17s. 6d. ($5) on Gayda's account.[70] Store accounts also allowed craftsmen to charge supplies directly to their own clients. In a typical exchange, in February 1798 tailor James Huston bought all the materials he needed for the coat he was making for Michael Baker and charged the cost directly to Baker's account at the Rex store.[71]

The varied products, services, and sights that were offered at the country store enticed some customers to congregate and linger there. Elizabeth Nutt, a storekeeper in Burlington, New Jersey, complained that her store was so full of people that she could hardly think.[72] News of the arrival of goods, especially when they came from Philadelphia, was another reason for customers to visit the store. A fresh keg of raisins would sell out rapidly, but Rex had runs on other items, too, as when on two days in January 1798 seven different customers all purchased "small books."[73] Rex's legal and writing services also brought in customers who needed a will or deed written, or who wanted to initiate a lawsuit. Sometimes a special event, such as the "inquisition" that Rex held, in his capacity as a justice of the peace, on November 17, 1802, might also draw spectators.[74]

Much of the lure of the store came from its communication functions. At the Rex store customers could receive or send mail; in May 1802 farmer Christian Swalley charged on his store account the price of "postage for two letters to Lancaster."[75] Even if residents were not lucky enough to find a letter waiting at the store, they could still hear the latest news from the post rider, carters passing through, or from the storekeeper himself, who gathered information from other customers and business contacts. In July 1799, for example, during the quasi-war between France and England, furnace clerk John Fletcher wrote to Rex the "glorious news of the French being defeated on all quarter."[76] Rex also posted informative broadsides, including, in 1802, the notice that tickets for a Harrisburg church lottery were on sale.[77]

At times it was more solemn business that brought customers into the store. Bereaved families bought linen for a shroud, stockings for the corpse, black silk mourning handkerchiefs, and supplies for the funeral meal. Such purchases reveal mourning customs as well as the refreshments that were typical at these events. When Joseph Bombarger died in August 1803, his heirs bought eight gallons of Lisbon wine, four gallons of spirits, six pounds of coffee, twelve pounds of sugar, six pounds of loaf sugar, twelve pounds of rice, and two nutmegs. This was a typical purchase; apparently rice pudding was a favorite dish to serve after the funeral.[78]

Like modern-day rental centers, the store was also a place to find goods needed only temporarily. The Bombarger heirs bought three new pieces of glass and tableware for the funeral, but they borrowed twenty others. As a community service, Rex lent funeral tableware free of charge. Exchanges of goods and merchandise between storekeepers and customers show community sharing and a high level of mutuality,[79] but Rex's mutuality had its limits. When a dish lent to Widow McCalley's estate was "broke at funeral," Rex charged the estate 4s. 3d.[80]

Funerals were not the only occasions on which Rex made short-term loans of goods. If a regular customer purchased molasses or liquor and forgot to bring his own jug or bottle, Rex lent one at no charge, but he required that strangers pay for their containers. When tavern keeper Anthony Seyfert needed extra glassware temporarily (probably for a special event being held in the tavern), Rex lent it to him. Some loans seem to have come from Rex's own possessions rather than store stock, as when Rex lent a small pistol to Henry Stroam and a greatcoat to George Ulrich that he urged "be returned with first opportunity."[81]

By extending these courtesies Rex built up goodwill among steady customers, but, like long-term credit, loans could not be allowed to go on indefinitely, if one was to run a profitable business. Rex therefore kept careful records so that he could convert a loan into a debit on the customer's account if the item was not returned on time. While loans helped Rex foster good community relations, as a businessman working on a close margin he could ill afford to give away store goods, let alone his own pistol and coat.

Rex logged loans of personal goods in his store daybooks, showing that businessmen in this period did not distinguish sharply between commercial and community transactions. The store's place in the community is further revealed in the way sales and services followed the agricultural calendar and local customs. For Pennsylvania Germans, the first of April was the beginning of the farm year; it was "business day," when debts were settled and farmers and hired men commenced new contracts, and it was "flitting" (moving) day, when leases expired and tenants moved into new homes.[82] In late March 1800, as Seyfert prepared to move out of the tavern he was renting from Rex, he sold some of the furnishings. Rex facilitated the sales by making loans to the purchasers so they could pay Seyfert; he lent William Dunbar 18s. 9d. to pay for a bedstead and he gave John Stevenson cash to pay Seyfert the 4s. 8d. he owed him. At the same time, Rex eased the way for Frederick Garret, his next tenant, to open his tavern business with a loan of £9 16s. 9d. This deal worked to Rex's advantage because when Garret moved in on April 1, he bought supplies from Rex. Garret may have been sprucing up the tavern; besides spirits and glasses, he bought flowered paper [wallpaper?] and brass locks, perhaps to secure his valuable liquor supply.[83]

As spring and summer wore on, farmers bought watering pots, scythes, and rakes for their gardens. Warm weather meant an increased supply of cream so housewives could make butter to sell to Rex. In November—*Schlachtmonat,* or butchering month—customers bought new knives and laid in salt and seasonings; those who had raised extra hogs might now discuss the price that Rex was willing to pay for pork.[84] With the coming of winter, Rex also saw a rise in sales of flannel and blankets. By January customers were buying new almanacs, those farm essentials that provided rural families with calendars, weather forecasts, and advice about "moon planting" according to signs of the zodiac.[85]

But despite its many attractions, the store sometimes lost customers to competitors. On June 29, 1799, the day before the Cherry Fair, innkeepers Michael Valentine and Anthony Seyfert loaded up at the Rex store on ham and glassware in anticipation of increased business. Rex himself had no customers the day of the fair. He may have been closed, but quite possibly fairgoers chose to attend the festival or patronize a local tavern rather than shop. While the Rex store was idle, across the street Seyfert was busy tallying the bills for townsmen who were celebrating the fair by downing pints of wine.[86]

Like all country stores, Rex's store operated at an uneven tempo.[87] Days on which there was only one sale, or none at all, were common; if his store was as full of people as Elizabeth Nutt's was, they didn't always make purchases. But Rex also had busy days when a steady stream of customers kept the storekeeper hopping. His first year, as he established his business, was particularly slow. From January to November 1791 he made sales an average of only sixteen days each month, with an average of eight customers a day. By 1798 he was recording sales an average of twenty-three days a month, with about ten sales a day; and by his last year in business he was open an average of twenty-four days each month, with twelve customers daily. Other stores of the period had comparable trade. Storekeepers in Christiana Bridge, Delaware, and Greensburg, Pennsylvania, saw from seven to seventeen customers daily, while William Polk served about nine customers a day in his Delaware store.[88]

In the early years as Rex scrambled for a share of the trade, he did business nearly every day of the week and on some holidays. Some cities, including Lancaster, banned Sunday trade, but townships such as Heidelberg rarely had such prohibitions.[89] As Rex's success grew, he often closed the store on Sunday, but even during his final twelve months in the store he sold merchandise on seven different Sundays. He was usually busy on December 24, and, whether through lack of trade or because he closed shop, he usually had no sales on Christmas, a holiday that he and his customers celebrated, though with less fanfare than would be common later in the century. On Christmas Day in 1797 and 1801, however, Rex made a few sales, and unlike city merchants he did business as usual each Independence Day.[90]

Most of Rex's regular customers lived within a few miles of the store. Although he had competition from taverns and other stores in the village, in 1798 fifty-eight out of a total sixty-eight heads of household in Schaefferstown (85 percent) had accounts at the Rex store. Rex also counted as customers sixty-one (25 percent) of the 244 property owners and tenants who lived in Heidelberg Township but outside Schaefferstown, Myerstown, and Newmanstown. (Residents of the latter two towns sometimes patronized the Rex store, but there were stores in their own hometowns that they could frequent more easily.) And he had eighteen regular customers out of a total of forty-nine property owners in adjacent Elizabeth Township in Lancaster County.[91]

Other customers came from a distance, including some travelers who visited Schaefferstown often enough to establish accounts. As a way of identifying these less familiar people, Rex included a notation about their hometowns in his daybook entry. Most did not come as far as William Mendenhall, who hailed from Wilmington, Delaware, or John Barr, who lived in Cumberland County, but Rex logged sales on credit for customers from Lebanon, Lititz, Womelsdorf, Reamstown, Muddy Creek, and "the Swamp," all located five to fifteen miles away.

Over time Rex's customer base grew. From 1791 to 1798 the town's population increased slowly, but Rex more than doubled his regular customer accounts as he continued to attract business from throughout the region. By his last year in the store, 1806–7, the number of customers leveled off, even as the town continued to grow. This contraction probably reflects Rex's cutting back as he prepared to sell the store, but it may also indicate that as Schaefferstown expanded, new storekeepers siphoned off some of Rex's customers.[92] Table 1 compares Rex's customer base with the total population.

The Rex store attracted customers of varying ethnicities, ranks, and ages. Rex would have conducted transactions in German to accommodate local people,

Table 1   Rex Customers Compared to Total Population

	Customer Accounts	Schaefferstown Estimated Population	Customers as Percentage of Population	Heidelberg Township Estimated Population	Customers as Percentage of Population
1782	118	336 (56 households)	35	2,084 (342 households, 32 freemen)	5.6
1798	352	408 (68 households)	86	2,148 (358 households)	16
1806	390	600 (100 households)	65		

Sources: Tax lists for 1782, 1798, in Egle, Pennsylvania Archives, ser. 3:17; U.S. direct tax, 1798, Heidelberg Township, Dauphin County, schedule I; Scott, Geographical Dictionary of the United States.

but he would have drawn on his English skills to wait on strangers and iron furnace workers, who were a diverse lot. African Americans, including Peter Sheetz's enslaved "black man" and workers from the iron furnaces, stopped at the store regularly.[93] Hired men and women (including "Indian Kate," who worked for one of the town widows) and "girls" and "boys" (whether this means children or specifically hired help is not clear) also were customers. Rex carefully noted in his daybook when a child or servant came to the store, but once he recorded their identities he trusted them to charge goods on a parent's or employer's account.

Both women and men used the Rex store, but males outnumbered females both in number of accounts and purchases. Most women who had store accounts were widows or, less frequently, single women. Married women usually did not have store accounts, but the wives of some ironmasters and iron furnace supervisors charged goods in their own names because of their high economic and social standing. At first glance, one might assume that males outnumbered females, simply because Rex listed purchases under the head of the household, who was usually a man. But it seems that more men than women actually visited the store, because Rex tended to note when someone other than the person charged picked up an order, and his daybooks show that women made only 10 to 12 percent of all purchases.[94] There is no way of knowing, of course, how many women accompanied their husbands to the store to select goods that Rex then charged to the husband's account, but apparently few women came alone.

Cultural norms in some regions, particularly the American South, prevented women from shopping, so this low percentage of female buyers is not unusual, and indeed the Rex figures are high compared to some regions. Elizabeth Perkins found that 10 to 14 percent of shoppers in rural Kentucky were female; Daniel Thorp notes that fewer than 4 percent of account holders at the Lowrance, North Carolina, store were women, and they were all widows. Allan Kulikoff found that Chesapeake men were also the family shoppers; they took responsibility for shopping as part of the overall duty of plantation management. Stephanie McCurry estimates that females made up only 2 to 4 percent of customers in South Carolina low-country stores. She explains that wives stayed home to tend to domestic duties while husbands shopped on their periodic trips to town; consequently, store visits were linked to "male privileges," such as voting and militia drilling. In the Hudson Valley, too, men tended to travel distances to trade while women used local networks of exchange.[95]

This was not the case in urban places, at least not in the northern cities of Philadelphia, New York, and Boston, where women were highly visible as customers as well as shopkeepers and tavern operators. Patricia Cleary points out that in Philadelphia shopping was a social activity for females such as Elizabeth Drinker. Cleary sketches a peculiarly female "sphere of trade" in which city women patronized women retailers, women retailers preferred to sell dry goods over such masculine goods as hardware, and stores were information centers that served the same purpose for women that coffee shops did for men.[96] Though Cleary may overstate the case for an urban female commercial sphere, it seems likely that city women were more visible actors in the economy than their rural counterparts. During the American Revolution, for example, urban women were linked specifically with shopping and consumption as they boycotted British imports and led protests against shopkeepers and merchants who withheld scarce commodities or violated nonimportation agreements.[97]

As in the South, community norms (and never-ending household and farm chores) may have kept most Schaefferstown women from leaving home and trading in person at the Rex store as frequently as men did. Descriptions of women's roles in the Pennsylvania German culture are antiquated and sorely in need of updating, but existing sources consistently describe the culture as highly patriarchal, with women's and men's areas of responsibility clearly delineated. Pennsylvania German women worked in the home and on the farm, including helping with field work when needed. They contributed substantially to the family economy on many levels, but they were expected to limit themselves to domestic concerns (children, home, and religious affairs) while men handled business matters and made decisions about dispersing the family income.[98] Rex's method of recordkeeping reflects these prescribed roles. When a family sold butter at the store, even though that product was made by the wife, the husband received credit in his name. If a married woman worked for Rex, he credited her husband's store account; for example, on November 11, 1797, Rex gave Andrew Foorman 2s. 6d. credit for "1 day's work done by his wife."[99] In the case of a female-headed household, Rex would give a woman store credit; Widow Houser's daughters worked for Rex after he retired from the store, and he credited the widow "by 2½ days' work by her girls 3/7."[100]

Jeanne Boydston's work on women's labor in the early republic reminds us that although women were largely invisible in the public sphere, they contributed to the household and regional economies in significant ways, including dairying, making lace, baking, and raising fruit and vegetables.[101] Rex's books provide brief glimpses of such activities among Schaefferstown women and hint at community networks of exchange beyond the store. For example, some of the town's women worked as seamstresses. Widow Christina Stiegel sewed for Rex in May 1791 in exchange for 4s. 6d. in store credit. Although this is apparently the only time she sewed for Rex, she probably worked regularly as a seamstress, for she owned three flat irons and a tailor's "goose." We know that in August 1799 Widow Shreiner made John Hanspike a shirt, because he borrowed cash from Rex to pay the bill. Catherine Gass sewed three shirts in July 1802 for Rudolph Kelker, who used his store credit to pay her. The women of the family were also in charge of spinning the yarn for the family's supply of homespun. On at least one occasion the widows Duppler, Wilson, and Houser each sold tow linen to Rex.[102] Unlike some cultures, Pennsylvania Germans expected the females of the community to work on the farm and in the fields as needed. Some women earned store credit (and after Rex left the store, cash) by working for Rex digging potatoes, pulling and breaking flax, and making hay.[103]

While females appear less frequently than males among Rex's customers, their economic contributions as producers and consumers are clearly discernible. Schaefferstown women churned butter and made other goods in lesser amounts to sell to the storekeeper to earn extra money for their households. They worked as seamstresses, spinsters, and occasional farmhands. Sometimes they performed these chores as part of the family economy, but other times they worked for others or sold their products for cash or store credit. And women were consumers, no matter who made the actual purchase of fancy combs, beads, and other items that flew from Rex's shelves into Schaefferstown homes.

It is impossible from existing sources to tell how Schaefferstown's German female population felt about the predominantly male environment of the general store, but at least one non-German woman yearned for a feminine touch at the store counter. In August 1798 Rudolph Kelker, a supervisor at Cornwall Furnace, wrote to Rex to order fabric and notions for Ann Long, whose husband was a furnace manager. After spelling out the particulars of the order, Kelker added that Mrs. Long "wishes *Mrs.* Rex to pick the thread suitable to the fine muslin" (emphasis added).[104] Though Samuel Rex was probably as knowledgeable as any other country storekeeper, some females preferred the particular skills and knowledge of another woman.

Schaefferstown Producers at the Store

Taking in locally produced goods for store credit was a common practice in Schaefferstown and other areas of the country, but historians disagree about what this practice meant to customers and storekeepers. Christopher Clark suggests that storekeepers accepted commodities because it was the only way they could hope to be paid, or because commodities were the only currency available. But Daniel Thorp finds that North Carolina storekeepers relied on local suppliers for produce and manufactured items. Johanna Miller Lewis's research also shows that North Carolina artisans supplied storekeepers with goods they needed for resale and personal use.[105] Rex's business activities provide insight into commodity payments in the Mid-Atlantic region. Rather than take goods as a last resort, Rex accepted only items he could use for himself or resell profitably. Indeed, he solicited some items because he needed them in his business; this practice worked to the customers' advantage as well, and Rex's market for these items drove production.

Sometimes, depending on his and his customers' needs, Rex took in only a small quantity of an item. In this case the exchange took place because a small producer brought in a few items to trade, or because Rex wanted a particular commodity for himself. Other local sales to the store were in bulk and were conducted on wholesale terms. Moreover, Rex and the local producers both had choices. He did not take every item that was offered; occasionally he took products on consignment rather than buy them outright. Nor did all craftsmen feel compelled to pay Rex in goods. Some reserved their products for other venues and paid for store purchases in cash. In short, when Rex accepted a good at the store, both buyer and seller got what they wanted: the producer earned cash or store credit, and Rex obtained a commodity to use or sell profitably.

Some writers call exchanges of commodities at the store, or settling one's account with goods, "barter."[106] But barter is an inaccurate and perhaps too simplistic a term for such transactions, given that they were negotiated at clearly understood prices. Even when Rex and a customer traded commodity for commodity, the goods carried a specific value: the cooper knew the value of the kegs he used to pay for a watch, which also carried a particular price tag. More important, seeing commodity payments as remnants of a local economy, or barter, underestimates the market involvement and sophistication of rural people and the role of the storekeeper who coordinated quite complicated exchanges for them. The term "commodity payments" or "commodity money," rather than "barter," more accurately describes what transpired when customers sold goods for store credit.

Customers from all ranks and occupations sold goods to Rex, but they did not all benefit equally. As table 2 shows, Rex spent three to four times more on farm products than on manufactured goods. Since craftsmen rarely had the land or means to raise farm products, farmers, who were already better off than craftsmen, stood to gain the most from selling goods at the Rex store. (Figures 10 and 11 show customers' commodity payments ranked by monetary value.)

Commodities I: Manufactures

Some exchanges of goods at the store were extensions of the other local exchanges that went on daily among community residents.[107] Weavers, hatters, saddlers, shoemakers, and women who knitted mitts (or mittens—Rex used both terms) brought their products to the store in small quantities when they

Table 2 Comparison of Credits for Country Produce and Manufactures

Customer Credits	Ledger 5, 1798–1806 (%)	Daybooks, 1791, 1798, 1806–1807 (%)
Farm Produce	15	42
Manufactured Goods	4	9

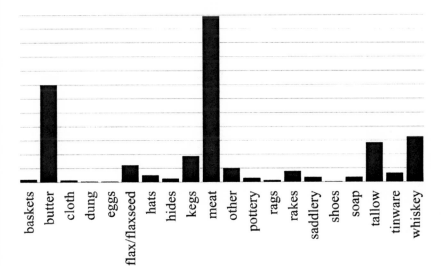

FIG. 10. Commodity Credits, Rex Daybooks, 1791, 1798, 1806–1807

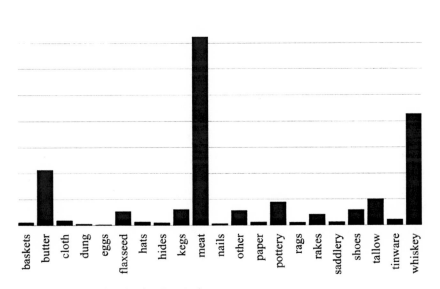

FIG. 11. Commodity Credits, Rex Ledger 5, 1798–1806

needed to buy goods or obtain cash or credit for other purposes. But, as noted above, Rex did not accept all commodities; if he was unsure of the market, he tested an item's sales potential before giving credit for it. In January 1795 he took Abraham and Philip Hoffer's ten hats "to sell on commission." In 1797 he took mitts from Mrs. (later Widow) Wilson on a trial basis and returned some to her unsold. Eventually, her skill or the market improved and Rex bought her mitts regularly.[108] Conversely, sometimes it was Rex who initiated the purchase of the commodity; he could buy household needs most conveniently, especially when he was short of cash, by using store credit. In this way he purchased shoes and boots for himself and his wife from local cordwainers; he paid the town doctor for medication; he bought a new coverlet, a good saddle, and a milk cow from other customers; and he put fresh meat on his table by buying it regularly from butcher Jacob Miller. Whenever possible, Rex paid for commodities with credit because the recipients would then use that credit to buy, at retail rates, store goods that he had purchased wholesale, so these deals were advantageous for him on several levels.[109]

Alternatively, some of Rex's purchases from local suppliers resembled those he made in Philadelphia. These sales were larger in scope, they provided him with replacement store inventory, and he acquired them on wholesale terms. Indeed, Rex (like other storekeepers in the area) was a ready market for local producers who depended on such sales for their livelihood. In this category were tobacco products, almanacs, earthenware, tinware, brushes, rakes, and barrels. Craftsmen who were producing at this level dealt with Rex on a more businesslike basis than producers who used commodities for occasional purchases, or who sold Rex the "coverlid" he needed. Some local manufacturers, including tinsmith Jacob Folmer, wrote detailed though crude invoices (see fig. 12). John Flower's pottery bills, by contrast, are expressed in the same business terms used by city merchants; the total price is discounted by "commission" of 3s. 9d. on the pound (fig. 13). However, Flower's invoices are written in Rex's neat scrivener's hand (there is evidence that Flower could not write), and this raises the intriguing question of how he and Rex arrived at terms of the sale. Nevertheless, Flower was satisfied enough with the arrangement to supply Rex with large loads of pots for years.[110]

Such transactions provided these large producers with more substantial earnings than did the smaller deals described above. Moreover, these producers were not selling their wares in order to obtain goods from Rex. Some, including Flower, took partial payment in store goods, but most wanted cash. Folmer, for example, made the rounds of many country stores to sell his tin, and he could pick and choose where he bought goods.[111] Tobacconist Christian Demuth and printers Albright and Lahn came out from Lancaster to sell snuff and almanacs to Rex, but since they lived in a city that abounded with all kinds of specialty shops, they had no need for credit at Rex's store and understandably preferred cash.[112] Still, they usually had to wait several months to receive the entire payment because it was Rex's habit to give the supplier a down payment at delivery and pay the balance when the supplier brought the next wagonload of goods. When Flower brought in his large load of pots in July 1800, Rex noted on the receipt that he still owed £4 for earthenware the potter had delivered in April.

Some area tradesmen found it convenient and mutually useful to sell goods to Rex for cash or store credit, but others preferred to sell in different markets.

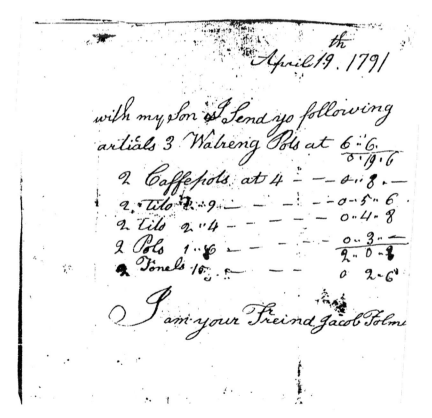

FIG. 12. Jacob Folmer Tinware Invoice, April 19, 1791. Jacob Folmer sold tin goods to a number of area businesses in addition to the Rex store. This invoice shows sales of coffeepots, pots, and funnels. Leon E. Lewis Collection, reproduced by permission of Orpha M. Lewis.

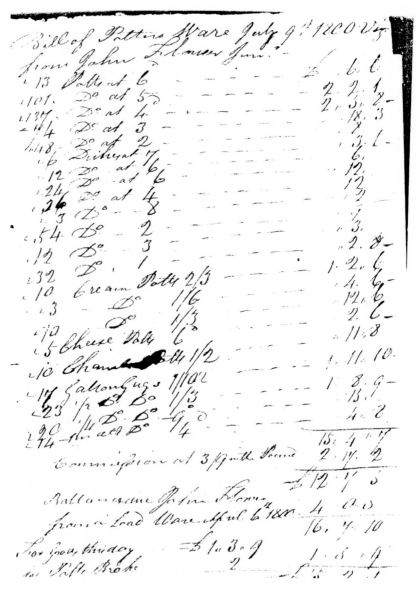

FIG. 13. John Flower Pottery Invoice, July 9, 1800. John Flower could not write, so Samuel Rex wrote the invoices for the pottery Flower delivered to the store. On behalf of Flower, Rex deducted a "commission" of £2 17s. 2d. (3s. 9d. "on the pound" from the total price); he also took off two shillings for pottery that arrived broken. Leon E. Lewis Collection, reproduced by permission of Orpha M. Lewis.

Philip Brecht bought materials and tools from Rex, but he paid his bills with cash or butter, never with locks or smith work. Brecht probably sold locks directly from his East Main Street shop, and, according to family lore, also delivered them in bulk to Steinman's store in Lancaster.[113]

In a few cases Rex had long-term arrangements with tradesmen that went beyond ordinary purchases and sales of goods. These cooperative agreements demonstrate the interconnected nature of Rex's local network and show the different relationships between the storekeeper and tradesmen of varying economic status. For a few years Rex had a regular agreement with nail smith John Sweitzer. Every few weeks Sweitzer picked up a bundle of iron rods at the store; he worked the iron into different types of nails for Rex, and Rex paid him in store credit.[114] Sweitzer, who was a tenant in the smallest house in Schaefferstown, spent his credit on food and supplies, including meat, since he did not have the means to raise his own livestock.[115] His store purchases exceeded his earnings for nail making, however, so he also worked mowing and reaping to pay Rex. Apparently, Sweitzer had trouble paying other bills as well; at one point he had to surrender his nail smith tools to a creditor, and Rex bought them back.[116] Though this gesture aided Sweitzer, it also helped Rex. When he bailed out Sweitzer, Rex kept him at work making nails so he could pay off his mounting store debt. Rex's arrangement with Sweitzer also shows the storekeeper's agility in moving goods through the local economy. Ironmaster George Ege used iron rods to pay his bills at the store.[117] As we will see in the next chapter, iron itself was not a moneymaker, but nails were, and so Rex put the iron out to Sweitzer to be made into nails that he could sell profitably.

Tanner John Kline (Klein) also had a regular and exclusive arrangement with the storekeeper. Simply put, any time Rex took in a cowhide from a customer he turned it over to Kline at cost. When he credited a customer for a hide, the next entry in his daybook was invariably a debit to Kline for the hide at the same price. Some entries include the cryptic notation "1s. in the hide," but the extra shilling is reflected in the price Rex allowed the seller and the price he charged Kline. Rex always marked up other local commodities that he resold, so his failure to do so with hides is puzzling. It seems, though, that this was a standard practice, because Samuel's brother Abraham used the same arrangement at his Mount Pleasant store, a few miles from Schaefferstown.

Several explanations come to mind. Tanners earned a commission when they custom-tanned hides. Perhaps Rex did not physically handle the hides but merely recorded the transaction as a bookkeeping service so that both parties had an impartial record of the exchange. If this was the case, the only benefit to the storekeeper was community goodwill. It may be that Rex received a reciprocal favor to compensate him for the hides. In January 1800 Rex credited Kline 11s. 6d. for "glew," but if Kline was regularly supplying Rex with glue or leather in exchange for hides, these transactions do not appear in the books.[118] Most likely, the price of hides was established by custom, and hides functioned as commodity money with a fixed value. Raw hides were not much use to anyone in the community except the tanner, who could set the price. When a customer sold a hide at the store or used it to pay a store bill, Rex had little choice but to turn it over to Kline, since he was the only tanner in town. But by brokering the hides Rex kept the local economy moving, and even though he did not make money on the transactions, booking deals for hides brought farmers and the tanner into the store, where they might buy other goods that did make Rex a profit.

The goods and cash that craftsmen and tradesmen earned at the store varied. Shoemaker James Maddoch brought shoe heels into the store a few dozen at a time, but these small deliveries never earned him much income. In 1800 his credit for heels totaled £1 11s., which he used to buy assorted goods, including a silk handkerchief. Other craftsmen did better from their sales. In December 1800, May 1801, and October 1801, John Flower delivered earthenware worth more than £37 4s. to Rex. He took £23 in cash, 130 pounds of red lead, and some household goods. In 1800 Jonathan Shoeneman sold Rex 120 rakes and twenty-two wooden shovels worth £10 14s. He bought goods with part of his credit and took the £5 19s. 10d. balance in cash.[119]

Peter Moore parlayed the cash he earned from selling goods and working for Rex into a new career. From November 1799 to July 1800 Moore earned £18 in store credit for butter kegs and hauling iron. He took about £4 in cash and used the remaining credit to purchase store goods that included thirty-four quarts of molasses and nine pounds of sugar. According to a local historian, Moore kept a hotel in a "log weather-boarded, yellow-painted building, on the corner of the Square." He is not listed as owning a tavern in the 1798 direct tax rolls, but his large purchases of molasses and sugar hint that by 1800 he was making beer in bulk. On April 15, 1803, he bought a pound of yellow ochre, two pounds of yellow paint, and three pounds of white lead from Rex, presumably to paint his hotel the vivid color recalled by local residents.[120]

Commodities II: "Poark" and Other Farm Products

Because Rex brokered country produce to regional ironmasters and to merchants in Philadelphia, his market for meat, especially "poark," was particularly strong. He bought smoked meat in small amounts throughout the year, but he made the greatest purchases from November through January, when the cold weather kept fresh meat from spoiling. This was the time of year when farmers slaughtered their hogs, and it was the season when the ironmasters laid in their annual supply of pork to feed their workers.

Pork was a favorite among Pennsylvania Germans, who were well known for swine production and for their ability to use all of the pig "but the oink."[121] A nineteenth-century observer noted, "Whenever you see hog-sties built in front of dwelling-houses, you may rely upon it, you are in the state of Pennsylvania."[122] The German's familiarity with swine culture was occasionally the subject of even more deprecating humor. Traveler Augustus Foster claimed that a German member of the Pennsylvania House of Representatives argued that he should serve on a committee to monitor damage by hogs in the city of Lancaster, because, as he put it, "I have been porn mid Pigs, pred mid pigs, and all my Life long lived mid pigs and I ought sure to know their Ways petter than any other person."[123] Despite biting jokes about their fondness for the meat, Germans knew that pork was economical and versatile. It was good fresh or smoked, and almost all parts of the animal were useful. Even the pig's head, feet, and stomach sac went on dinner tables, its intestines made casings for sausages, and its skin provided leather.

Although pork production was nothing new to Pennsylvania farmers, those in Schaefferstown enjoyed an exceptional opportunity to profit from raising hogs. When Rex put out the call, farmers from miles around responded by bringing in anything from a side of meat to a small herd weighing well over half a ton. Rex bought whole animals and cuts of meat; he paid the same price per pound for meat as he did for live hogs, because he could sell parts of the animals for additional profit, even after he paid someone to do the butchering.[124]

In sixteen years in business, Rex took in nearly eighty thousand pounds of meat, mostly pork, from about 150 different customers. Of this number, eight were craftsmen, two were widows who lived in the village, and 140 were farmers. Rex's top supplier was Henry Mock, who sold Rex 4,501 pounds of pork over five years for total receipts of more than £91, followed by Jacob Umbenhend, who sold 4,028 pounds of pork over four years and earned just less than

£80, and George Waggoner, who sold 3,695 pounds of meat over three years for a total of £74. Like Mock and Umbenhend (whose estates are discussed in Chapter 1), Waggoner also had a sizable farm of some three hundred acres; clearly all three men had the land and means to raise extra animals for sale. Of the few craftsmen who sold pork to the store, cooper and hotel keeper Peter Moore topped the list. Unlike most craftsmen, Moore owned farmland—some thirty acres, where he could raise livestock—and he sold six hogs (weighing a total 1,182 pounds) to Rex in three years.[125] His meat sales earned him a gross profit of £23, or just less than £8 a year. Most craftsmen sold considerably less than Moore, and few sold meat to Rex more than once.

Some Schaefferstown farmers found the Rex store a convenient outlet for their distilled products. The tax return of 1783 for Heidelberg Township shows seventeen residents operating stills; four of these residents reported having two stills on their property. In 1798 there were reported to be six stillhouses in the township, while Henry Schaeffer operated a double-pot still in his farmhouse basement.[126] Rex bought apple and rye whiskey (and, less frequently, peach and cherry liquor) from these local distillers by the barrel. His daybooks show a modest amount of whiskey coming through the store, but his receipt book tells a more complete story. From November 1791 until January 1802, Rex purchased 5,169 gallons of whiskey (an average of 470 gallons a year), worth more than £990, in quantities ranging from four and a half to six hundred gallons at a time. It is not apparent why he recorded these purchases in his receipt book rather than the daybook, or why he entered other whiskey purchases in the daybook but not in the receipt book, but it seems reasonable to conclude that when Rex visited farmers personally he carried the pocket-sized receipt book with him and left the larger daybook behind on the store counter. He may have entered the whiskey he intended to sell in Philadelphia in his receipt book and the whiskey to be resold locally in the daybook. Perhaps by omitting the whiskey from the daybook (which was open to public inspection), Rex was attempting to conceal certain transactions.[127] Whatever his reasoning, whiskey was profitable. In 1795 Rex paid 45d. for a gallon of whiskey and sold it in Philadelphia for 70d., giving him a profit of 55 percent before paying for transportation. Although Rex did not sell drinks by the glass, he sold whiskey by the pint and quart. At 10d. a pint or 1s. 6d. a quart, this is the equivalent of 72d. to 80d. for a gallon, making his local sales even more lucrative than his city sales.

Once Rex took a slightly different approach to brokering whiskey. In 1802 he hired local farmers Henry Buffameyer and Henry Schaeffer to distill "for the halfs" several wagonloads of apples (whether the apples were from Rex's property or the result of another deal is not stated). When the whiskey was ready, rather than take his share from Buffameyer, Rex sold it back to him.[128] This deal is unique in Rex's books, but it shows how he seized whatever opportunities came his way, including a bumper crop of apples, to make a profit.

Schaefferstown farmers did not rely on storekeepers alone to provide a market for goods. They usually sold their grain to millers or itinerant grain merchants, not to Rex, but occasionally Rex entered the profitable grain and flour trade as a broker. In March 1801 he bought sixty bushels of wheat for £22 10s. from George Strickler, who delivered the grain directly to Jacob Thomas's mill, west of Schaefferstown. Thomas ground the wheat into thirteen barrels of flour, and Rex paid a local man £5 12s. 6d. to haul the flour to Philadelphia. Two months later the Philadelphia firm of Dubs & Earl paid Rex £53 13s. 6d. for the flour, for a profit of £25 6s.[129] While his other business duties or competition may have prevented Rex from brokering grain and flour regularly, when he retired from the store he began to grow grain himself and tap into the profitable network already in place among Schaefferstown farmers.

Although food grains passed through the store infrequently, Rex often handled flaxseed, and these deals emphasize his role as a broker for local exchanges as well as the region's close connection to the city market. Flaxseed was in demand in Philadelphia for export to Ireland, but Rex had a regular customer closer to home.[130] Michael Grabill, of Elizabeth Township, owned an oil mill where he pressed flaxseed into linseed oil, an essential ingredient in paint. Grabill's relationship with Rex did not end with purchasing the seed. Grabill sometimes sent his oil to Philadelphia with Rex or had Rex pick up a payment for oil there.[131] Local farmers probably preferred to sell to Rex rather than directly to Grabill, even though he lived in the region, because Rex was centrally located and offered immediate payment in the form of store credit.

The Grabill transactions are significant because they reveal Rex's vulnerability to market fluctuations and the flexible relationship that existed between him and his customers. Usually reselling flaxseed was profitable, but sometimes Rex misjudged the price he paid and had to sell seed to Grabill at cost. Because Grabill also traded in Philadelphia, he knew the market prices and was apparently willing to pay Rex something—but not too much—in fees. Throughout August 1797, for example, Rex bought flaxseed at 10s. a bushel, but when he sold it to Grabill on August 26, the price apparently had fallen, and he handed over eighty-three bushels at the price he had paid, 10s. each. Whether Grabill informed him of the market slump or Rex learned of it by other means is not apparent, and if they exchanged angry words as they struck the deal, Rex did not record them. It could be, since the two men wanted to do business in the future, that they agreed to split the difference so neither would take a big loss. However, the next day Rex reduced the price he paid for flaxseed to 7s. 6d. so he could mark it up for a profit when he sold it to Grabill.[132]

Pork, whiskey, and grain were the most expensive commodities that Rex's customers sold to him, but butter was the most frequently traded. Joan Jensen describes women in Chester, Montgomery, Bucks, and Delaware counties, who regularly sold their own butter in the metropolis, as living in a "butter belt" around Philadelphia.[133] However, women who lived a distance from the butter belt could not always take their butter directly to the city, and so they turned to the country store. A total of 139 customers sold butter to the Rex store in 1791, 1798, and 1806–7. As previously noted, Rex almost always credited a male head of the household for products brought into the store. Only eight of the 139 customers who received credit for butter in this period were women, and seven of the eight were widows.

Customers of all occupations and ranks sold butter to Rex. But, as with pork, farmers, who had the means to raise more cows, sold butter more often than tradesmen. Of the forty-five people listed in Rex's ledger 5 (1798–1806) who sold butter, only six were craftsmen, and of the 116 people who sold butter to the store in 1791, 1798, and 1806–7 (as listed in Rex's daybooks for those years), only four were craftsmen.

Using butter for extra income was so commonplace that Rex did it too. After he retired from the store, he used the butter that his wife made to buy goods at his brother's store.[134] Rex's probate inventory shows that at the time of his death he still owned four cows, along with milk pans and a butter churn. With a herd of four cows, Mary Rex or a hired girl could have made about 140 pounds of butter annually. The Rexes had no children, but they did have an apprentice clerk. In addition, nieces and nephews and other relatives stayed with them from time to time. If their household averaged four people, figuring a yearly consumption of fifteen pounds of butter per person, they would still have had about eighty pounds left over to sell.[135]

Rex's customers brought in from one to one hundred pounds of butter at a time. When a customer presented butter to Rex, he weighed it and credited the customer's account accordingly; then he scraped it into a firkin or keg that probably already contained butter brought in by a previous customer. Storekeepers typically mixed butter with little regard for quality, as there was no way to distinguish one dairymaid's product from another when packing it for resale. Rex would have simply added one customer's two pounds of butter to another's five pounds and so on until the container was filled. Then he would have sealed the barrel, branded his name on the lid, and held it in the cool cellar until his next trip to the city.[136] Because Rex and other storekeepers kept butter for months before selling it and exporters might then send it on a long sea voyage before it reached consumers, maintaining freshness was important.[137] Salt, brine, sugar, and saltpeter were said to preserve butter for one to three years. Elinor Oakes, in her study of the dairy trade, found that properly treated butter was one of the least perishable of all export foods; only ships' bread lasted longer.[138]

Rex sold some of this local butter from the store, but he sold most of it in Philadelphia. Because he held butter so long before taking it to the city, as with flaxseed, determining the price to pay so he could sell at a profit was tricky. He varied the price he paid for some produce according to quality, and he also shifted price when he heard from his city contacts that the Philadelphia market price had changed. Despite the problems of pricing, as table 3 shows, butter was a regular source of profit. When Rex resold butter locally, he added a markup of 1d. per pound, and when he took it to Philadelphia he received from 2d. to 4d. a pound over the price he had most recently paid. Jensen cites women who earned as much as 1s. 6d. and 1s. 10½d. for a pound of butter in Philadelphia in 1798 and 1799, but in May 1799 Rex sold his butter in the city for only 13d., and in November 1799 he sold it for 14d. a pound.[139] The difference may be that Rex sold his butter to agents who paid less because they added an additional markup when they resold it. What Rex may have lost in price per pound, however, he made up in volume over Jensen's women, who sold only thirty or forty pounds of butter at a time. Rex's butter shipments ranged from as little as 159 pounds to as much as 5,034 pounds.

What could butter buy at the Rex store? Farmer John Moyer, who lived on a large farm in Millbach, found it worth his while to carry butter five miles to sell it in Schaefferstown. In 1806–7 Moyer brought in from four to twenty-eight pounds of butter at a time, for a total of 127 pounds, which earned him £6 in store credit, or enough to buy 120 pounds of sugar or 45 pounds of coffee. The purchases that farmers John Royer and Jacob Hoffman made during a typical store visit in May 1807 provide a concrete example of the buying power of butter. Royer used his credit to buy silk gloves, coffee, and other goods worth 13s.

Table 3   Rex's Profit on Butter Sales

Date	Price per lb. Rex paid	Price per lb. Rex charged at the store	Price per lb. in Philadelphia	Profit to Rex
1791	6d.	7 to 8d.	8d.	1–2d.
November 1794	11d.	12d.		1d.
April 1795	12d.		16d.	4d.
November 1796	9d.		11d.	2d.
November 1797	9d.	10d.	13½d.	1–4½ d.
January 1798	12d.	13d.		1d.
May 1799	12d.		13d.	1d.
June 1800	11d.		13d.	2d.
November 1800	12d.	13d.	13½–14d.	1–2½d.
May 1801	13d.		14d.	1d.
July 1801	12d.		13½–14d.	1½–2d.
September 1802	8d. to 9d.		9d.	0–1d.
August 1803	10d.		11d.	1d.
May 1804	12d.		18d.	6d.

4d., while Hoffman bought coffee, sugar, wine, wine glasses, muslin, rice, and sewing notions totaling £1 13s.[140]

Pork and whiskey sales to the store were even more lucrative than butter sales. In December 1799 farmer Adam Mock sold Rex 326 pounds of pork worth £6 15s. 10d. Over the next three months Mock used his store credit to buy a variety of goods, and in April he took the remaining £3 12s. 4d. Rex owed him in cash. In January 1801 Jacob Garret sold Rex 261 gallons of whiskey for £45 13s. 6d. Rex applied some £22 to Garret's store bills from the preceding year and paid Garret the remainder in cash. (Whiskey sales may have helped compensate for Garret's lack of good farmland, since his 146-acre property was "clay and gravel.")[141]

There was still another commodity that Rex's customers brought to the store for credit—their worn-out clothing and linens. Rex paid from 2d. (1795) to 3d. (1806) a pound for rags, and then stockpiled them until a papermaker or his representative called. In one daybook entry Rex noted that one of these papermakers, James Chalfint, was "at Mr. Weiss," suggesting that the papermaker came into an area and boarded at a local home while he made his rounds.[142] Sometimes the papermaker would simply pay Rex in cash for the rags, in amounts that ranged from 28s. 6d. a hundredweight in 1795 to 37s. 6d. a hundredweight in 1806. At other times Rex took writing paper and wrapping paper as part of the payment.

Selling produce, manufactures, and the occasional sack of old rags helped Schaefferstown families buy a wide variety of goods for themselves and their homes, and in some cases enabled them to earn cash as well. Butter sales were less profitable than pork and whiskey sales, and generally butter did not yield cash payments, but its sales helped a large number of people at all economic levels buy store goods. Jensen suggests that selling several hundred pounds of butter a year would enable Mid-Atlantic residents to buy "most of the commodities the family needed for the household."[143] While Rex's customers' lesser sales of butter probably did not purchase all the supplies that a farm family needed annually, these sales still put staples in the larder and enhanced their lives with such pleasant items as wine glasses and silk gloves.

Bridging the Gap: Rex's Place in the Community

In addition to the economic services detailed above, the bilingual Rex provided his German-speaking customers with still another service: he served as a culture broker by bridging the terrain between them and the English-speaking majority. In eighteenth-century America, storekeepers, as well as clergymen and teachers, frequently served in this capacity for German-speaking immigrants.[144] Indeed, storekeepers were culture brokers for rural people, linking city to countryside, even when there was no language barrier. Lu Ann De Cunzo explains that Delaware storekeepers "mediate[d] between the movement of goods, services, information, and ideas between cultural groups." Storekeepers occupied a "contradictory point at the boundary between local exchange and long-distance trade," and yet they adroitly managed to operate in, and serve as middlemen for, both arenas.[145] Gregory Nobles argues that Northampton, Massachusetts, merchants were "economic and cultural innovators, the central agents of social transformation in their communities."[146] Rex likewise supplied Schaefferstown people with merchandise, new fashions, and new ideas thanks to his regular contact with Philadelphia. Furthermore, both as a storekeeper and in retirement, Rex added another dimension to his role as a culture broker because he also wrote legal documents—in English—for his customers.

If Pennsylvania Germans in the new nation combined traditional culture with elements of the larger Anglo society, in Rex this combination was writ large. As a fellow Pennsylvania German, he both literally and figuratively spoke the language of Schaefferstown. In fact, his writing shows that he spoke English with a pronounced German inflection and that he occasionally preferred German words to English. When he took a "verbal" order, he recorded it as "werbel," a reflection of the Pennsylvania German speaker's tendency to switch v's and w's.[147] If he sold a wet horn (see fig. 14), he consistently entered it in his daybook as a *Kump*. When he wrote about the death of a great-nephew, he described the boy's illness as "choking rheum or what in German is called the *Stick Feiss*."[148] Although he may have spoken with an unfashionable accent, Rex was at ease in and knowledgeable about places where English was the language of choice. He periodically traveled to Harrisburg, the state capital, to file legal documents, and he interacted even more frequently with the business community of Philadelphia. A man with a foot in two camps, the ethnic German yet worldly Rex could thus assist rural customers with equal skill, whether they needed advice on legal matters, a will drawn up, or the latest goods from the city. While some Schaefferstown people may have known enough English to navigate the public sphere and conduct their own business deals in Philadelphia, many relied on Rex's legal expertise, writing skills, and business knowledge.

As a storekeeper, Rex had to maintain yet another dual identity by combining community and market postures. Over time as a friend, a neighbor, and in some cases a relative by marriage, Rex became a respected member of the community; he developed a close enough relationship with some of his customers

FIG. 14. *Kump*. Rex occasionally referred to an item in his inventory by its German name. Farmers would have used a *Kump*, or wet horn, to hold water to moisten tool blades before sharpening. Author's collection. Photo by author.

to serve as a godparent to their children.[149] But he was also a businessman who priced goods according to the Philadelphia market and who needed to operate his store profitably. And while deals at the store seem to have been made in a spirit of mutual respect and advantage (at least there is little surviving evidence of strife between the storekeeper and his customers), Rex had to look out for problems that could erode his profits. And he did encounter problems from time to time. It was the storekeeper's loss if butter was sour or lard turned rancid, so Rex was alert to customers who tried to sell inferior goods. When Christian Read brought in nineteen pounds of lard in January 1807, Rex's clerk did not notice that two pounds were spoiled. Rex caught the problem later and reduced Read's credit accordingly. Sometimes Rex and a customer disagreed over a transaction. In November 1803 he charged George Becker "by a present made to credit his daughter of 6 lb. of cotton which she says was paid, but never was." In May 1803 Rex rather petulantly credited David Kramer £2 16s. for "an allowance of coal baskets, which he says I had, but I know nothing of." In October 1804 Rex gave in to Casper Ellinger's claims and paid him £10 wages for goods that Ellinger said he had hauled to the city.[150]

Rex also kept his eye on his clerks and the family members who sometimes tended the store for him. When he returned from a trip he reviewed the books closely; this showed him what business had transpired in his absence and also gave him the opportunity to correct mistakes. The occasional errors or omissions in the daybooks were relatively easy to correct, but Rex had a dispute with apprentice Samuel Roop that was more serious. Roop came out from Germantown to learn the "art and mistery of a storekeeper" and was indentured to Rex for a nine-year term beginning December 1, 1795. Before this time was up, in March 1804, Rex was summoned to Philadelphia to answer the charge that he had reneged on some aspect of the indenture. The source of Roop's dissatisfaction is not stated in the summons, but it implies that Rex failed in some way to live up to his promise to train the young man and to provide food, clothing, and education. The outcome of the lawsuit is unknown.[151]

Rex's brother-in-law and erstwhile business partner Michael Valentine brought him even more headaches. Valentine was a poor (or unlucky) businessman who called on Rex time and again for loans; by the time Valentine died, he owed Rex a sizable debt.[152] And, as we will see in Chapter 3, even though Rex generally enjoyed good relations with the ironmasters and the clerks and managers at the furnaces, these friendships did not shield him from the vagaries of market prices or even the threat of a lawsuit over bad meat.

CHAPTER THREE

FEEDING THE FURNACES:
THE IRON COMMUNITY AND THE REX STORE

Hopewell Forge, 15th Oct. 1802

D[ea]r Sir,

I have not yet had an opportunity of speaking to you personally about a supply of Pork. I expect that you will lay in the usual Quantity to wit 4 or 5 Tons. Please write me the first opportunity that offers what you can make me certain of. I can advance you money on it now if you wish.

I rem[ain] respectfully yours etc.

Henry B. Grubb

[To] Sam. Rex Esq.

LIFE ON IRON PLANTATIONS, where ironmasters such as Henry B. Grubb supplied food and housing for workers in a rural industrial setting, was quite different from farm and village life in the rest of Pennsylvania.[1] While iron plantations resembled small towns and employed a number of people in different capacities, they could not produce all the provisions they needed. Ironmasters near Schaeferstown obtained provisions and supplies directly from local farmers and craftsmen, but, as Grubb's letter indicates, they also made large purchases, particularly of meat, from storekeeper Samuel Rex. In addition, ironmasters used the Rex store as a de facto company store, where workers could charge purchases to their accounts at the iron sites. This relationship worked to the good of all parties. Farmers and craftsmen benefited directly and indirectly from the increased trade, ironworkers and ironmasters enjoyed the wide range of services and goods that Rex could offer, and the storekeeper reaped the rich rewards of having customers whose business was so regular and substantial. In fact, between one-third and one-half of Rex's store income came from the iron-producing community.

The South-Central Pennsylvania Iron Community

By the time Rex arrived in Schaefferstown, the iron industry had been established in the region for more than half a century. Before William Penn even visited America, he wrote, among other frankly promotional enticements, that his new colony was "thought capable" of producing iron.[2] Though the earliest attempts to manufacture iron in Pennsylvania failed, Penn's intuition ultimately proved correct. Pennsylvania had all the components needed for an iron industry: rivers and streams, huge stands of forests, limestone (used as flux to separate impurities from ore), and, most important, rich iron deposits. By 1716 blacksmith Thomas Rutter had set up the first successful iron forge: a bloomery on the Manatawny Creek near present-day Boyertown. Other ironworks arose in Berks and Chester counties as well as in the "lower counties" that would become Delaware. As the population of Pennsylvania expanded westward, iron production followed. In 1737, when Peter Grubb established a bloomery at Cornwall, it marked the beginning of the area's iron industry and the discovery of what was for two hundred years North America's largest supply of iron ore.[3] Other entrepreneurial ironmasters were quick to build charcoal furnaces, iron forges, and slitting mills; by the 1760s Pennsylvania had taken the lead in North American iron production.[4]

Cornwall Furnace and mines were just five miles west of Schaefferstown; five miles to the south was Elizabeth Furnace, and within a day's ride were Mount Hope, Berkshire, and Colebrook furnaces, and Hopewell, Speedwell, and Charming forges. Schuylkill Forge lay thirty miles north of Schaefferstown, and Hopewell Furnace, forty miles to the east in Berks County.[5] Businesses in Schaefferstown reaped the benefit of trade with these sites as teamsters driving wagons loaded with ore and iron passed through the village and stopped for supplies. In 1767 tavern keepers Paul Gemberling and Alexander Schaeffer were involved in a dispute over the cost of repairing the road from Schaefferstown to Cornwall Furnace, which suggests townspeople were aware early on of the importance of the iron trade to the village.[6] A local historian writing in 1908 boasted, "Schaefferstown was a way station on the road, and here ore teams, with six horses to each team, stopped and rested for the night."[7] Sometimes there were unplanned stops, too. In 1804 innkeeper Michael Valentine sent a bill for 14s. 3d. to Hopewell Furnace for the provisions a driver and team used when they were stranded at Schaefferstown while returning to Hopewell from Cornwall in a snowstorm.[8]

While the teamsters brought substantial business to Schaefferstown with their individual purchases, Rex's relationship with the iron-producing community extended even further. Rex sold supplies to the ironmasters; he also acted as their company store, accepted goods from them in payment for their bills, and served as a middleman and banker. His did business with at least ten different furnaces and forges, but all of these were controlled by only three ironmasters: Henry Bates Grubb, Robert Coleman, and George Ege.

Although the Grubbs were the founding family in the regional iron industry, by the time Rex opened his store Robert Coleman had assumed the leading role. Coleman was an Englishman who had risen, by dint of hard work and marriage to an ironmaster's daughter, from an office clerk to become the richest ironmaster in the country. After working for his father-in-law, James Old, at Speedwell Forge and Reading Furnace (Chester County), Coleman struck out on his own. At first he leased a forge and furnace, but soon he began buying properties. Between 1780 and 1802 he gradually acquired most of the major furnaces and forges in the area around Schaefferstown. Coleman's first purchase (1780–84) was Elizabeth Furnace, the 10,124-acre iron plantation in Elizabeth Township, Lancaster County, just south of Schaefferstown, where he lived with his family. In 1791 he built Colebrook Furnace on a tract of 7,684 acres near Mount Gretna, and by 1795 he had acquired 80 percent interest in the Cornwall plantation and ore mine. By 1802 he owned (except for a one-sixth share in the mine) all of Cornwall's 9,669 acres, including the furnace itself, Speedwell Forge, and Upper and Lower Hopewell forges. He also owned Spring Forge in York and a portion of Marctic Forge in Lancaster County. Estimated to be worth more than £50,000 by the end of the eighteenth century, Coleman was as politically powerful as he was affluent.[9]

Though Coleman was the industry leader, Henry Bates Grubb, grandson of the original owner of Cornwall Furnace, was still a competitor in regional iron production. From 1795 to 1798 he, along with his brother, A. Burd Grubb, operated the two Hopewell Forges and Mount Hope Furnace, near Manheim. In 1798 Henry Bates Grubb bought out his brother's interest, and to finance the purchase sold half of his properties to rival ironmaster Robert Coleman. In 1802 Coleman and Grubb divided their holdings, with Grubb retaining Mount Hope Furnace and a one-sixth interest in the Cornwall ore mines and Coleman taking the two forges.[10]

George Ege, the third ironmaster who used the Rex store, owned the former Berkshire Furnace, a fifty-six-hundred-acre property near Robesonia, seven miles northeast of Schaefferstown. Under Ege's ownership, Berkshire became known as Reading Furnace.[11] Ege, nephew of the ill-fated ironmaster and glassmaker Henry Stiegel, also owned Charming Forge, a few miles north of Robesonia, and Schuylkill Forge, in Port Clinton, thirty-three miles northeast of Schaefferstown. In 1788 Ege bought from the Grubb family perpetual rights to remove enough ore from Cornwall mine to fuel one furnace. As a result of this agreement, which continued in force after Coleman took over Cornwall, Ege sent wagons to haul iron ore from Cornwall to Berkshire Furnace, some twenty miles away, a route that went through Schaefferstown.[12]

Coleman, Grubb, and Ege employed furnace managers who frequently interacted with Rex. Positioned between the laborers and the powerful ironmasters, they were part of what Anthony F. C. Wallace describes as "an amorphous and embryonic middle level, probably with little clear awareness of itself as a group."[13] Sometimes managers were employees, comparable to hired overseers on southern plantations, with which iron villages are often compared.[14] Like overseers, managers were men with unclear social status; they did not have the same social position as the ironmasters, but they were a cut above the laborers (some of them slaves but most free) whom they supervised. Some managers were hired workers, while others were ironmasters' sons who were learning the business (as did storekeepers' and merchants' sons) through hands-on experience. By 1801 Robert Coleman's older son, William, was in charge of Cornwall and a younger son, James, was running Speedwell Forge.[15] Peter Coleman, whose exact place in the family is not clear, managed Hopewell Forge. Reflecting business practices of the day, in which the lines between personal and business affairs were frequently unclear or nonexistent, when ironmasters and managers bought supplies for the furnaces and forges from Rex they sometimes transacted the deals in their own names, but other times they used the company account.[16] Some managers, cognizant of their nebulous standing, struggled to demonstrate their legitimate place in the class structure. When manager William Boyd asked Rex to send hog "guts . . . suitable for making sausage" along with Cornwall's meat shipment, he immediately regretted his word choice. Struggling to appear more cultured, Boyd closed his letter with an apology for the use of "so vulgar an expression."[17]

Coleman and Grubb were highly successful, but Ege ran into financial problems toward the end of his career. He was hit hard by the Panic of 1819; unable to pay his creditors, including Rex, he eventually went bankrupt. Even if they did not face such extreme economic crises, ironmasters were hampered by the lack of skilled workers, depleted ore mines, high transportation costs, poor roads, and sometimes their own inept management. Even prosperous ironmasters were chronically short of cash; they had difficulty securing capital for their operations and obtaining prompt payment for their products.[18] Like merchants and shopkeepers, ironmasters did most of their business on credit; when payments did not come in on time, they had to borrow to meet their obligations. They often sought major financial backing from wealthy merchants, but for their day-to-day operations they also looked to rural shopkeepers such as Rex for credit, loans, and the financial means to pay their workers.

Life on the Iron Plantations

Despite the volatility of the early American iron industry, ironmasters lived well, attaining the position of gentry in their respective neighborhoods. Writing in 1940, Lancaster County resident Herbert H. Beck noted that, until the 1880s, the leading families of the Lancaster-Lebanon iron-producing area were the Colemans and Grubbs. The awe that ordinary people felt for the wealthy and prestigious ironmasters even a century later comes through clearly in Beck's glowing description of them as "Lords of the Barony of the glorious Furnace Hills."[19]

In Rex's time the ironmasters were captains of industry, living in a high style that foreshadowed the wealth and prestige of nineteenth-century industrialists like Andrew Carnegie.[20] The mansions that Coleman, Grubb, and Ege occupied were far grander than any of the other homes in the region, and they clearly represented the ironmasters' high economic and social status. The Coleman family home at Elizabeth Furnace dazzled tax assessors in 1798; at 45 × 40 feet and with 468 lights in its twenty-two windows, it outstripped all other properties in surrounding Elizabeth Township, at a time when many neighboring dwellings had only a single window cut in their log façades. The assessors declared the Coleman mansion in "complete repair" and worth $2,000. Grubb's mansion at Hopewell Forge was only slightly less impressive; valued at $1,200, the two-story dwelling had eighteen windows. (Grubb built himself a new, larger, and more elaborately landscaped mansion on the grounds of Mount Hope Furnace when he took up residence there after 1800.)[21] In 1798 William Coleman had not yet moved into the mansion at Cornwall; instead, furnace superintendent Rudolph Kelker lived there. During Kelker's tenure the house was assessed at only $900, but it was considerably improved, including extensive landscaping, when the Coleman scion arrived.[22] Ege's twenty-four-room mansion at Charming Forge was particularly grand. The main section of the house, which Ege added in 1780 to an existing and far less elegant structure, was built in full Georgian style with a spacious entry hall and a spiraling stairway that ascended three stories.[23] The social and economic distance between the ironmaster and his workers is apparent in the location as well as the size of the Charming Forge mansion. It sits atop a small rise, literally looking down on the workers' houses, stables, gristmill, sawmill, and the forge itself.

Along with the forge or furnace, the ironmaster's mansion was the centerpiece of a small village. Ironmasters provided workers with company-owned housing, and they also ran a store where workers could purchase food, clothing, and other necessities on credit. The furnace clerk kept running accounts of workers' purchases and rent charges and balanced these debits against credits for work on the plantation. Thus, workers were at the mercy of their employers, who set their wages and also determined the prices they paid for rent and provisions. Such an arrangement caused unrest by the late nineteenth century in company towns such as Pullman, Illinois, where workers suffered severe hardships when owners reduced wages but continued to charge high rents and exorbitant prices at the company store.[24] However, historians who have studied Hopewell and Cornwall company stores have found prices comparable to other stores in the region and concluded that the stores functioned more as a convenience to workers than a profit center for ironmasters.[25] Moreover, at least some ironworkers had options. They did not have to buy everything at the company store, and at some sites they could draw cash from the company clerk.[26] Those working for Coleman, Grubb, and Ege could use Rex's store and charge purchases and cash advances against their wages.

Housing varied at different iron plantations. At Cornwall, Coleman offered workers houses that were valued between $120 and $635, with the better homes reserved for assistant managers, clerks, and other higher-status employees. The average house at Cornwall was assessed at $220, 80 percent of the average estimated value of a house in Schaefferstown ($268). Workers at Elizabeth and Mount Hope furnaces lived in much less impressive surroundings. Tax assessors valued the thirty houses at Elizabeth at less than $100 each. Mount Hope workers lived in small stone and log structures that were little more than huts; they ranged in size from 12 × 12 feet to 14 × 18 feet and were estimated to be worth between $30 and $80 each.[27] Some sites, including Charming Forge, provided dormitory-style accommodations and meals for single men.[28] Still other workers lived off the grounds and labored only part time for the iron company. Privileged employees such as clerks might occupy furnished rooms in the main house.[29]

Despite the mean houses that some ironworkers lived in, skilled ironworkers earned good money in the labor-scarce economy of the early republic. Johann Schoepf noted in 1783 that imported European iron was cheaper than American iron because American workers commanded such high wages.[30] While Rex was giving 3s. 9d. a day to customers who worked for him to pay their store bills, furnaces offered some of their employees nearly twice that amount. In 1799, for example, Mount Hope worker Neal McLafferty earned 6s. 5½d. a day for "coaling." Professional employees were salaried; Cornwall Furnace manager Rudolph Kelker earned £250 and clerk James Moore earned £75 annually.[31] Ironmasters needed a wide variety of workers to manage the business, dig and process iron ore, and feed and maintain the plantations; Mount Hope books show payments to workers for general labor, housekeeping, driving wagons, and running the plantation's gristmill.[32] At some furnaces skilled workers earned piece rates and perquisites such as free or subsidized housing, board, free garden plots, and firewood, but unskilled workers had fewer benefits.[33]

The relatively high wages and the large number of jobs attracted a heterogeneous workforce to the iron sites.[34] Ironworkers in Rex's region had surnames that indicate English, Scots-Irish, Irish, Welsh, and German ethnicity; a non-German name in Rex's daybooks is almost invariably a signal that the customer worked at an iron site. In addition, a number of ironworkers are specifically identified as African Americans. From the earliest days of the iron industry, Pennsylvania ironmasters used slaves and free blacks in iron production, and the ironmasters in the region around Schaefferstown were no exception.[35] In 1780 Curtis Grubb registered twenty-four slaves, including seven children and one "runaway," in compliance with the commonwealth's act for gradual abolition; that same year there were thirteen slaves at Cornwall Furnace.[36] The sixteen slaves owned by Samuel St. Clair and listed in the 1790 census almost certainly worked at Cornwall. Although the Dauphin County records are not broken down by township, St. Clair is listed between Cornwall Furnace managers Rudolph Kelker and Richard Sheldon, suggesting that he lived at or near the furnace and leased his slaves to the ironmasters.[37] By 1798 Robert Coleman still owned five slaves who worked under Kelker's supervision at Cornwall.[38] George Ege owned nine slaves in 1790 and seven in 1800; he is said to have freed some twenty-five slaves in 1810.[39] During the time he was a customer of the Rex store, Grubb's Mount Hope workforce included at least six African Americans.[40]

It is not clear from Rex's books what percentage, if any, of the African American ironworkers who shopped at his store were slaves. Whether slaves or free-men, however, African Americans' minority standing is highlighted literally and symbolically by Rex's practice of including their race as part of their names or as a notation in his daybook. Most of these customers were known only by one name (e.g., "Negro Ish") or by their skin color and occupation ("black hammerman at the forge"). Only one, Henry Clemons, used a surname, and in this case Rex almost always added the clarification "Mr. Grubb's black man." Though illustrative of blacks' low standing in the community, these entries also show that African Americans participated in the local economy despite lack of status. Elizabeth Perkins explains that Kentucky storekeepers' credit sales to slaves illustrate relationships of trust between whites and blacks. These trans-actions are important because they show slaves as consumers and as equal eco-nomic actors with free white customers.[41] The same is true of Rex's customers of color. One task that African Americans frequently performed was picking up store goods and delivering cash payments for their employers or owners. Grubb's clerk at Hopewell Forge sent Rex an order for dishes, spices, and cod "per Negro girl," and James Willson, manager at Berkshire (Reading) Furnace, trusted Negro Ish to deliver $100 cash to Rex.[42] African American customers also used the services of local craftsmen; in October 1799 Rex credited tailor James Huston with 10s. "for making a coat for Henry Clemons." African Amer-icans, like most other workers at the iron furnaces, seldom had the means to produce goods to sell at the store. They did, however, use their store accounts to pay third-party debts; in November 1799 Rex credited Clemons's account with "orders" (paper instruments requesting payment) from Negro Casteel totaling £2 10s.[43] Though Rex took pains to identify people of color specifi-cally by race, suggesting their inferior status as "others," they enjoyed the same services that Rex offered all his customers. If people of color were on the lower end of the social and economic scale in and around Schaefferstown, they were still participants in the network of relationships that made the economy work.[44]

Furnace workers, excepting slaves, could choose to stay at one site (in some cases families handed jobs down from one generation to the next) or they could use their skills to move on to a better job at another iron plantation. The Coleman family's ownership of many different sites permitted the managers to transfer workers from one furnace or forge to another as they needed more or less help, and the interconnected nature of the iron industry in general also led to cross-pollination among the sites. Carters hauled ore from mines to furnaces and brought pig iron from furnaces to forges. Because Ege had mining rights at Cornwall, Berkshire Furnace workers "raised ore" alongside Cornwall's miners.[45] Finally, some skilled workers, such as the potters who cast the hollow ironware in molds, were needed only part time, and they went from site to site as work was available.[46] The fluidity of iron furnace employment has caused problems for historians as they try to determine the number of people needed to operate an iron furnace. Frederic Miller was unable to learn the exact number of workmen at Cornwall, but he concluded that "at no time was the number employed very large." Joseph Walker, on the other hand, after a careful study of Hopewell Furnace books, found some 186 different men employed there from 1805 to 1807, although not all of them worked full time. Of these only a few workers actually made the iron, while a large number of supporting laborers did other tasks at the plantation.[47]

Of necessity, iron plantations were located in the countryside near the ore banks, streams (for water power), and forests (while in blast, furnaces burned an acre of wood, in the form of charcoal, a day).[48] Because ironworks were located in such out-of-the-way places, writers addressing popular and scholarly audiences alike emphasize their self-sufficiency. While noting that furnaces bought goods such as sugar and salt from outsiders, Miller declares Cornwall "economically . . . almost self-sufficient." Sharon Hernes Silverman describes Cornwall as "a small, self-contained village—nearly feudal in its hierarchy of ironmaster and his workers." Arthur Bining acknowledges that by the end of the eighteenth century, some plantations were in a fairly populous district, but he believes that early on workers did not often leave the plantations.[49] Walker, however, more accurately points out that iron plantations, like early America's farms, could never really remain aloof from the outside world or be totally self-sustaining.[50] Ironworkers mingled as they moved from one site to another to work. Teamsters drove wagons between mines, furnaces, and forges and stopped at stores on the way. Farmers and artisans worked part time for furnaces and sold their produce and manufactured goods to the ironmasters. In short, the ironmasters, managers, and laborers at the ironworks were in frequent contact with outsiders, including storekeepers who supplied them with goods and services they could not find on the plantation.

Ironworkers at the Store

Rex's relationship with the iron-producing community probably began with his time clerking for Kreider, for he enjoyed a steady business with ironmasters and workers from the day he opened his own store. His first customer on that day, December 22, 1790, was ironworker Thomas Atchinson, who hauled ore between Cornwall and Berkshire furnaces. This initial sale was a harbinger of even better things to come; in Rex's daybooks for 1791, 23 percent of sales (by count) were to ironworkers and ironmasters, and 80 percent of his credits (by value) came from the iron-making community. By 1798 Rex's trade with area farmers and tradesmen had increased markedly; as a result, the percentage of business from the iron furnace declined relative to the local trade. Still, even as his trade with the other groups grew, Rex continued to conduct a substantial amount of business with the iron-producing community. In his daybooks for 1798, 8 percent of transactions (by count) were with ironworkers, and these accounted for nearly 31 percent of his credits by value. By Rex's last year in business, 1806–7, 11 percent of daybook transactions (by count) were with ironworkers, and they accounted for 31.7 percent of the total value of credits. Analysis of Rex's ledger 5, 1798–1806, shows an even greater percentage of income coming from the iron producers. Forty-seven percent of total credits in ledger 5 came from the iron-producing community in the form of bar iron, book credit, cash, and orders (see table 4).

Rex's sales to the iron-producing community fell into two categories: individual sales to ironworkers and bulk sales to the ironmasters. Ironworkers often bought large quantities of goods at one time because they came to the store less frequently than customers who lived nearby. Their relatively high wages and the ability to charge purchases against future earnings may also have encouraged them to buy more. In addition, Rex offered a better assortment of goods than

Table 4 Percentage of Rex's Business Coming from Iron-Producing Community

	Rex's Transactions with Iron Community (as % of Rex's total transactions)	Value of Rex's Transactions with Iron Community (as % of Rex's total business)
Ledger 5 1798–1806	n/a	47.1
Daybooks 1791	23	80.3
Daybooks 1798	8	30.9
Daybooks 1806–1807	11	31.7

the company stores and could cater to the upscale needs of someone like iron-worker Richard Pendegrass. In June 1799 Pendegrass ran up a bill of more than £9 for seven different types of cloth and other goods; two months later he was back to buy silver knee buckles and other merchandise totaling £4.[51]

Ironworkers frequently arrived at the Rex store in groups as they drove con-voys of ore wagons through town. On October 7, 1799, for example, five iron-workers stopped in the store; besides various purchases of tobacco, pipes, and coffee, each man also purchased more than two yards of velvet or other cloth.[52] In July 1800 Paddy Haggerty and William Burnett shopped together; inspired by either Rex's selection or admiration of each other's purchase, each man bought, among other items, a cravat.[53]

Occasionally, women were among the groups of workers who came to the store. Peggy McGinley stopped at the Rex store with her brother and two other men from the furnace in December 1800. Taking advantage of the opportu-nity, McGinley brought a shopping list of things to pick up for friends and co-workers and instructed Rex to whom each order should be charged.[54] A few furnace women, of varying ranks, sold goods to Rex. Ann Long (wife of a man-ager) sold lard at the store. Her purchases included calico, silk, and indigo.[55] Black Nantz (at "Colemans") and Catherine Crass of Hopewell Forge sold soap to Rex. Nantz earned 13s. credit but did not buy anything immediately, while Crass used her credit to purchase calico, striped cloth, ginger, sweeping brushes, and a milk strainer.[56]

Rex's bulk sales to the plantations varied; ironmasters at times bought "kunk" shells (probably used to summon workers), tools, housewares, and provisions such as molasses and salt mackerel. The volume of these sales, and the furnace records themselves, show that Rex did not supply all the needs of the iron-masters but that he was one of several storekeepers who sold them goods.[57] Having accounts at more than one store allowed iron furnace drivers to pur-chase supplies at whichever place happened to be on their route that day. Over-land transportation was expensive; having teams bring back goods while on other business was a good way to economize. In fact, returning with an empty wagon was so undesirable and costly that the Mount Hope clerk docked carters 15s. if they "disappointed a team."[58]

Henry Grubb in particular relied on Rex to supply a large proportion of his plantation's needs, even though other stores were closer to Mount Hope. Grubb bought food staples in large quantities on a monthly basis, and among other items he routinely stocked up on what seemed to be his personal favorites—

green tea and "segars."[59] There are several possible reasons, both economic and personal, why Grubb chose to patronize Rex rather than a store nearer his furnace. Grubb, who was financially strapped when he took over his brother's share of the family business, may not have had the extensive network of contacts that Ege and Coleman enjoyed, and so he shopped where he could establish credit. It is also likely, however, that Grubb preferred to do business in Schaefferstown because he wanted to avoid Manheim storekeeper Samuel Peter Heintzelman. Grubb was Heintzelman's kinsman, but the relationship was unwelcome and unacknowledged, as Heintzelman's mother was Grubb's illegitimate half-sister, born to his father and a housekeeper less than a year after Grubb's mother died.[60]

In addition to the regular day-to-day business, ironmasters and managers sometimes placed special orders with Rex. Common sense dictated that he mark up prices if he was going to make a profit, but when he filled special orders for the influential Colemans and their higher-ranking employees, Rex sold the goods from Philadelphia at cost. Speedwell Forge manager David Eaton asked Rex to procure a saddle and bridle in the city, and Rex charged Eaton what he paid, £8 2s. 5d. He extended the same courtesy to Rudolph Kelker, who ordered a bridle worth £3 15s., and to William Coleman, who wanted a cheese from the city.[61] (These requests reveal the men's upscale taste; rather than order a saddle in Schaefferstown or buy locally made cheese, they preferred Philadelphia products.) Rex followed the same policy with certain goods he obtained for the ironmasters from local craftsmen.[62] By not marking up the price on special purchases, Rex performed a service for the furnaces in a spirit of community cooperation, just as he lent goods for funerals, and he also tacitly acknowledged the ironmasters' rank and power. By declining to profit on special orders, Rex earned the continued lucrative patronage of the ironmasters. The ironmasters likewise benefited from Rex's willingness to serve as their personal link to the Philadelphia shops, where he might select for them better food and equipment than what was available locally.

These special favors were personal and occasional. When he provided goods in bulk, Rex did not hesitate to charge the ironmasters for his services. He invariably charged an 11 percent markup, for example, when he sold them the mine and coal baskets that he purchased from David Kramer.[63] These sturdy baskets were essential equipment for the furnace operation; workers used them to carry ore to the stacks and to haul leaves and other fuel when they made charcoal.[64] At one point manager Matthew Irwin wrote to Rex on a rather desperate note: "I hope you have procured me some coal baskets. I have entirely depended upon you and expect you will write me a few lines to send for them, which will be very agreeable as I am just in a [illegible] wanting."[65]

Rex also brokered grain purchases between area farmers and ironmasters and workers.[66] In 1791 he sold forty bushels of corn and seventy bushels of rye to Alexander Montgomery and Thomas Atkinson, who used their credit in Berkshire Furnace books to make the purchase.[67] In April 1806 Rex paid £18 5s. cash to Jacob Peylor for seventy-five bushels of rye "on account of Hopewell Forge."[68]

Grain sales were insignificant, however, compared to Rex's steady sales of meat to the ironmasters. In September 1801 clerk William Stuart wrote to Rex from Mount Hope Furnace, "The season is fast approaching in which we procure bacon for the use of this place. . . . We are in expectation of you procuring a quantity for us, for which Mr. Irwin will undoubtedly pay the best current price."[69]

Rex sold both live animals and dressed meat to the ironmasters. Buying live hogs had advantages for the ironmasters; winter was a slack time because the furnace was out of blast, and workers could be put to work preparing the meat. When the furnace employees did the butchering, they could determine how to get the most economical cuts out of the animal, salt some for "corned pork," and custom-smoke hams and bacon. Butchering also enabled the ironmasters to sell surplus lard and tallow back to Rex. And since they purchased the lard barrels from Rex, who bought them from local coopers, these transactions stimulated the local economy on several levels.[70]

Occasionally individual ironworkers purchased hogs directly from Rex, but more often ironmasters bought the pork and resold it to their workers either whole or by the piece. In February 1798 the Mount Hope Furnace clerk debited ironworkers' accounts at the rate of 5½d. a pound for whole hogs and 6d. a pound for cuts of meat.[71] Sometimes furnace managers contracted individually with their workers for meat purchases. Rex noted in October 1796 that Rudolph Kelker still owed £45 4s. 2d. for bacon, "which he is to pay me for his hands when they have settled with him."[72]

While clerks at times stressed their employers' willingness to pay the "best prices," occasionally they (and their employers) disagreed with Rex on matters of pricing. In the winter of 1795, before agreeing to buy pork, Boyd discussed terms with Rex and informed him that "the price of pork in this part of the country is fixed at 4½d. I believe it is the standard of all the iron works. As the pork is plenty this season [I] have no doubt but you can raise an ample stock at that price." Rex agreed to furnish the meat but continued to haggle over how much he would be paid. On December 12 Boyd again wrote to Rex, this time invoking a higher authority: "Concerning the price Mr. Kelker desires me to inform you that 4½d. is the most he can give. . . . Mr. Coleman was here yesterday, says he gives no more and it will not suit for us to raise it."[73]

Unfortunately, because of a gap in Rex's daybooks, the price that he paid for pork that year is unknown, but the letters quoted above reveal tensions in negotiations between Rex and the ironmasters, as each party sought to maximize profits. On a lighter note, a letter from John Fletcher, the manager at Elizabeth Furnace, who like Rex seems to have supported the Federalist Party, hints playfully that politics also had a hand in pricing. After arranging to pick up a load of pork, Fletcher commented, "Was it not to stall the Democrats in your place pork could be purchased lower[;] however we must work them a little."[74]

Rex's anxiety about pricing was justified. In 1799, after purchasing a quantity of pork at 5d. a pound, Rex found himself overstocked in a buyers' market, and he had to sell the meat at cost. The following two years proved more rewarding. Rex again took in large amounts of pork—more than twelve thousand pounds in 1800 and twenty-five thousand pounds in 1801—and sold it at a profit of one-quarter to one-half pence per pound. Relying on volume rather than a high markup apparently produced an acceptable profit; in 1801, with the quarter-pence markup, Rex made more than £57 on his sales of 54,739 pounds of meat. These pork sales were good for area farmers as well as for Rex. His call for pork in 1801 reached beyond Schaefferstown and its outlying farms; Peter Spengler, who lived near Myerstown, drove his three hogs (weighing a total of 604 pounds) to Rex's store and earned nearly £13.[75] Pork purchases sometimes put a strain on Rex's money supply. In December 1800 he paid out so much cash for hogs that he had to borrow £37 10s. from Philip Erpff.[76] No wonder that when Grubb placed his order in 1801 he offered to advance Rex some money if he needed it to buy the meat.

Rex never again achieved the record sales of the winter of 1800–1801. The following winter, 1802–3, after he purchased a quantity of pork, the market price in Philadelphia fell as the American economy contracted in response to a temporary lull in the war between France and England. City merchants, pinched because of the decline in export trade, reduced the price from 5d. to 3d. The effect of the correction rippled out into the countryside, and ironmasters lowered the price that they would pay for meat.[77] Rex stood firm. He sold two pigs at cost to local customers and salted the rest of the pork so he could store it for a later sale. During the winter of 1803–4 Rex must have expected the market to rally, because he bought more pork, but the hoped-for recovery did not mate-rialize. Rex sold some meat locally at the price he had paid but held onto the rest; he bought twenty-eight barrels from Peter Moore and paid George Desinger 6s. 3d. to pack the pork into the barrels.[78]

Over the next few months Rex shipped barrel after barrel of salt pork to Philadelphia. In February he sent twelve barrels of pork, along with other pro-duce, and instructed his agents in the city, Dubs & Earl, to sell the butter, lard, and tallow but to store the meat. In April he sent one barrel, and in May he sent eight more barrels of pork "to be stored." By June 4, when he sent another fifty-three barrels of meat to the city, the market was improving, and Rex finally instructed the agents to sell.[79] As long as he could afford to have his assets tied up, it paid Rex to be patient and wait for prices to recover.

Apart from pricing issues, Rex and the ironmasters were sometimes at odds over the amount of meat they would buy from him. A loose ledger page dated December 1803 (perhaps from a lost "pork notebook") shows that Rex agreed in advance to buy meat and occasionally paid a deposit even before the farmer brought his animals into the store to be weighed. An entry for December 3 reads, "Bought of John Cockley 2 hogs to be delivered at Shaeffers Town . . . bought of Jacob Peylor 2 hogs at 30/ hundredweight; paid him on account $4." When prices fell or when the ironmasters refused to take as much as Rex antic-ipated, he was left with too much meat on hand. What is more, farmers living close by supplied the ironworks directly, threatening to undercut his prices and making it even more difficult for him to judge how much pork the furnaces would need from him. Now and then managers bailed Rex out, as when John Fletcher wrote that one wagonload of meat was really all they needed but that he would take more as a favor. "We have got a large quantity since I seen you from the country, more than I expected. . . . I will take the two loads but no more."[80] William Coleman was less helpful when he wrote to Rex in some frustration in December 1801. His letter shows that buying pork was as prob-lematic for ironmasters as it was for the storekeeper: "You mentioned to Mr. Moore yesterday that you expected I would take five thousand weight more, but must inform you I cannot take more than the first quantity mentioned. I have promised to take a great deal of pork from our neighbours which has not come in yet. I scarcely know what to do about it, as we have at present as much as we will have in for the ensuing season."[81] Furthermore, both ironmasters and storekeeper also had to worry about the quality of the meat. In December 1797 William Boyd wrote from Cornwall:

A person of the name of Hawk has deposited some hogs with you which was suspected to have been bitten by a mad dog. I must request that if you received the pork, you will by no means send it among ours, as the mere suspicion of such a thing is of such a horrid nature as to give the most alarming uneasiness. . . . We were nearly imposed upon last year by the same means and Mr. Coleman was determined to prosecute the person at the utmost, and nothing but the most abject concessions prevented him experiencing the rigors of the laws. I hope if you have before heard the circumstances you would not take his pork.[82]

Ironmasters were understandably concerned about their workers' health, and Rex was risking a lawsuit—or worse—if he deliberately or unwittingly sold them bad meat.

Schaefferstown tailors and seamstresses also benefited from Rex's steady trade with ironworkers who bought cloth at the store and then paid to have it made into clothing. Even Robert Coleman, who could have afforded to shop anywhere, used the services of Schaefferstown tailor James Huston, who bought cloth, buttons, silk twist, and thread for Coleman's new coat at the Rex store.[83]

Paying craftsmen with store credit was just one of the store's financial services that ironworkers used. Borrowing cash was another; in fact, Rex's loans to the ironmasters and managers were sometimes rather large. In 1800 and 1801 Grubb borrowed a total of $705, and in April 1806 Peter Coleman borrowed $250 from Rex "to pay Jacob Thomas." Although Rex allowed borrowers up to a year to repay loans without interest, the ironmasters at times needed only temporary cash. In March 1801 Grubb wrote to Rex, "I have to trouble you for the loan of 150 dollars for a couple of weeks, at which time it shall be returned."[84] Like special purchases, interest-free loans helped Rex stay on good terms with these important customers. Money lending also worked both ways; though Rex never approached the ironmasters for cash, in May 1800 he borrowed £37 10s. from John Fletcher.[85]

More important than occasional loans of cash or brokering payments to craftsmen was the ironmasters' ongoing arrangement to use their credit at the Rex store to pay their employees. These transactions worked in several ways. An ironmaster, manager, or clerk might issue a written note or "order" to instruct Rex to pay a worker a certain amount of cash, allow him book credit, or provide her with a specific item. In December 1801, for example, James Moore

wrote to Rex from Cornwall, "Please let Hugh Gallagher have cloth and trim-
mings for one sailor jacket on account of this place."[86] And in December 1805
the Cornwall clerk sent John McKinney to pick up molasses and glass for the
furnace and appended a postscript to the note: "Also let McKinney have two
pounds coffee and a gallon of molasses on account."[87]

Other transactions were more complicated. In May 1791 three ironworkers
arrived at the Rex store to spend four orders in amounts ranging from 6s. 6d.
to 20s. William Boyd had issued two of the orders and Rudolph Kelker had
issued the other two, but all were drawn on Cornwall Furnace.[88] Sometimes
Rex received the word personally from an ironmaster or manager. In January
1791 Richard Sheldon gave Rex a "worbel" order to deliver goods to Peter Paul
"to amount of 3.10.2." In June 1791 William Campbell of Berkshire Furnace
likewise told Rex to supply goods worth £2 to £4 to three furnace workers
and to pay £2 in cash to a fourth man.[89] Sometimes the order was insufficient
for an ironworker's needs; "Negro" Cuff Jones spent £1 17s. 3d. "above his order"
in April 1801.[90]

Taking a customer's word that he or she was permitted to charge goods on
another's account involved a certain amount of trust on Rex's part; at least once
a transaction turned out to be fraudulent. On May 16, 1799, Mrs. James Dicks
came to the store, ostensibly to pick up goods for Robert Coleman and Isabella
Johnston. Dicks selected nearly £3 worth of store goods and charged them to
Johnston, and she charged more than £4 in merchandise to Coleman's account.
Somewhat later her deception came to light. Rex adjusted his accounts and
noted in the margin of the daybook, "These goods were got by James Dicks's
wife and it appeared afterwards they were for herself."[91]

Rex enjoyed less status within the iron-producing community than in
Schaefferstown, and he was on different terms with different people at the iron
plantations. Rex and the ironmasters provided useful services to one another,
but the ironmasters had the upper hand in their dealings and did not mingle
socially with the storekeeper. The social distance between the two groups is
evident in the old-fashioned deference that Rex displayed toward the ironmasters and their higher-ranking employees by according them courtesy titles. Rex
was on more comfortable terms with the furnace managers and clerks, who
seem to have been his social and intellectual equals. Long after Rex left the
store, James Willson of Reading Furnace valued Rex's expertise enough to
write and ask his advice on whether to accept a position as cashier of Reading Farmers Bank.[92]

Some of Rex's associations at the furnaces developed into friendships. During the holidays Fletcher occasionally rode into Schaefferstown with some of the other "Forge Boys" to share an oyster feast with Rex at Valentine's tavern.[93] In 1799 when Fletcher agreed to take more pork than he really needed, it was a gesture based on kindness and sympathy, as Fletcher advised Rex, "Take care of yourself in purchasing."[94]

There were other links between the iron community and Schaefferstown; at least one family from the furnaces attended church in the town. Fletcher and his wife, Margaret, were members of the German Lutheran congregation, where they had their daughter baptized, and chose to be buried in the Schaefferstown cemetery.[95]

Cornwall Furnace supervisor Rudolph Kelker had a particularly close—and perhaps unique—relationship with Rex. Kelker was a frequent visitor to Schaefferstown not only to buy goods but because his illegitimate son lived and went to school there, apparently under Rex's supervision. Rex saw to the boy's material needs and kept a running tab for the father. At various times from 1791 to 1801, Rex charged Kelker for such expenses as school supplies, a leather-covered trunk, and cash paid to the tailor for making the boy's clothes. When Kelker fell ill (a few years before his untimely death in 1801 at the age of thirty-three), he named Rex one of his executors, and he trusted Rex to invest his son's inheritance and provide for the boy's maintenance until he reached maturity.[96]

Iron as Commodity Money

Ironmasters paid their bills at the store with a combination of commodities, cash, and paper instruments, including credit in the company books, orders for iron, and orders for cash drawn on Philadelphia merchants. Aside from lard and tallow left after butchering and the iron rods that Ege used to pay Rex, most commodity payments were iron bars that weighed about forty pounds each. (Bar iron was used so regularly as payment for goods that in some regions it was called "merchant iron.")[97] Although the furnaces produced cast-iron objects and Rex sold cast ware in his store, the ironmasters never paid Rex with castings. Rex carted iron pots, skillets, and kettles from Philadelphia rather than buy locally, perhaps because he and his customers preferred the less expensive English products he could buy in the city.

Rex resold the ironmasters' lard and tallow in Philadelphia and Harrisburg. He may have made the initial contacts for these sales personally when he went to the capital to file legal documents at the courthouse, but when it came time to deliver the goods he paid a carter to haul them. In April 1801, for example, he paid Jacob Mumma to deliver two bags of tallow weighing 170 pounds to Benjamin Kurtz in Harrisburg. Unlike most of his transactions, Rex received an immediate cash payment for the tallow; Kurtz sent £8 10s. along with Mumma on the return trip.[98] When he sold tallow and lard, Rex usually made a profit of 2d. a pound, but the price he paid depended on the product's quality. On November 12, 1804, for example, he gave David Eaton 11d. a pound for 222 pounds of tallow, but on the same day he allowed Peter Coleman only 10d. per pound for his 230 pounds of tallow.[99]

While Rex could sell tallow and lard at a profit, bar iron was a different story. Iron, like cowhides, had a fixed value on the local market, so Rex could use it as commodity money (that is, spend it like cash) for local transactions, but he could not usually mark it up in price. That is, with few exceptions, when Rex sold iron to a customer he turned it over at cost, essentially running it through his books as he did hides. Some transactions even appear in accounts as linked pairs; a daybook entry for April 26, 1799, for example, debited Nicholas Hawk £18 15s. for half a ton of iron and credited Cornwall Furnace the same amount for the same weight of iron.[100]

Perhaps because of the high price of iron, Rex sometimes set a deadline for the customer to pay so that he would not have the debt on his books for too long. In January 1799 Rex debited Philip Baker for half a ton of iron (at the cost he credited the furnaces) to be paid "the first of May next."[101] In May 1802 he credited the Elizabeth Furnace account by one ton of bar iron (at £37.10s.) and immediately debited Andrew Boyer for the iron at the same price. He requested that Boyer pay half the price "first October next and the other half first April next." Boyer was a bit late with his first installment (he paid it in November), but he apparently made satisfactory arrangements for the second payment because in May 1803 he bought iron from Rex again. This time he purchased an order on Elizabeth Furnace for a ton and a half of iron (again at Rex's cost) and again agreed to pay it in two installments over the next year.[102]

Understanding some of Rex's iron deals is problematic, because he did not enter the value of every transaction for iron in his books. Furthermore, while iron prices stayed remarkably stable between 1798 and 1807 (a ton usually sold for £37 10s.), some iron commanded more. In a rare profitable deal, in February 1802 Rex credited £11 5s. to the Speedwell account for five hundred pounds of iron "delivered George Stroam" and debited Stroam for £11 10s., for a 5s.

markup.[103] At this price the iron cost the equivalent of £45 a ton, an all-time high price in Rex's books. Possibly this iron was superior to the run-of-the-mill product that he usually dealt in and thus brought a higher price and allowed him to add a markup. In a similar transaction that shows iron selling at a higher price than usual, in October 1798 Rex sold half a ton of bar iron to Philip Brecht for £20. At the same time he credited Henry Grubb for the iron, but because he failed to write in the amount of the credit, it is impossible to tell whether Rex made a profit.[104]

Rex and his customers also circulated orders for iron; like iron bars, papers representing iron acted as currency. Usually the order was drawn on the ironmaster's own business, but sometimes it was drawn on another iron site. That is, one ironmaster would use the order to pay a debt to another ironmaster, who would use it to pay Rex. Rex typically moved the order further through the network by selling it to a smith. In March 1803 Rex received an order drawn on Peter Coleman and credited to the Elizabeth Furnace account, and sold it (at cost) to blacksmith Peter Lydig.[105]

In rare circumstances deals for iron orders could be profitable. Rex once purchased an order at a discount rate, probably because the seller needed immediate cash. In March 1799 Jacob Stoner offered Rex an order drawn on Ege for one ton of iron. Though the market price of iron was £37 10s., Rex paid Stoner only £25; he gave him £15 in cash at once and promised "the remainder to be paid in groceries."[106] In this case Rex's zeal for profit, or perhaps just his pragmatism, superseded the community norms that set the price of iron. One can imagine Rex saying, in effect, take it or leave it—I am short of cash, and this is all I will pay—to Stoner (much as the ironmasters told Rex when it came to pricing pork). Stoner was desperate enough for cash to accept the low offer.

Rex sold some iron as far away as Philadelphia and Chestnut Hill. Paul Paskoff writes that transporting iron long distances overland was extremely difficult: "What was a gentle slope for farming could be a formidable obstacle to wagoners and the iron producers who hired them."[107] Daniel Thorp, however, has found that North Carolina storekeepers moved shipments of goods hundreds of miles between the backcountry and Charles Town, "without herculean effort or crippling costs."[108] Indeed, a ton of iron weighed no more than a ton of any other commodity, and beginning in 1791 Rex sent iron to Philadelphia merchants as readily as he did farm produce.[109]

The market for iron in the city was more competitive than that in the country because of short supply and high consumer demand, so Rex's iron brought a higher price in the city.[110] Grocer Thomas Miller paid for the iron Rex sent him in 1791 at the rate of £28 7s. 6d. a ton; this probably gave Rex a modest profit, as he was crediting commodity payments of iron at £26 10s. and £28 that year.[111] In September 1792 Philadelphia merchant Henry Darroch wrote that he had resold Rex's shipment of bar iron at the "highest price which was £35."[112] In June 1801 William Lane indicated that he, too, was willing to pay top dollar for iron. Lane wrote from Philadelphia that he had just received Rex's shipment and would pay £42 5s. a ton, "which we believe is higher than any of the iron sellers give. Should take it as a particular favor to send immediately the iron you may have for this market and you may rely upon it we shall always allow you as high a price as you could possibly get."[113] Rex's profit on iron and other goods that he sold in Philadelphia was eroded by transportation costs; he paid carters 3s. 9d. per hundredweight (112 pounds) or the equivalent of £5 for each ton of goods.[114] Because delivering goods was so costly, Rex was as loath to "disappoint" a team as the ironmasters were. Whenever he sent carters to Philadelphia, he offset the expense by having them bring back full loads of goods that he could resell profitably from his store.

Rex's deliveries of iron to Chestnut Hill were far less frequent than local sales or sales in Philadelphia. In August 1799 and February 1800 he shipped a total of three tons of iron to his brothers John and Enoch, who were now operating the family store; each time he charged them his price, £37 6s. a ton.[115] If the brothers reimbursed him for the carters' wages or repaid him in another commodity, Rex did not record the transactions; instead it seems these deals were made in a community spirit of exchanging favors. There is evidence that such courtesies extended even to in-laws. In May 1800 Rex sent a ton and a half of bar iron, along with fifty-six pounds of butter, to John Weiss in Germantown. He charged Weiss the price he had allowed the furnaces for the iron, and also sold him the butter at cost.[116] Rex's sister Mary married a George Weiss, so it is likely that John Weiss was a relative by marriage; otherwise the deal is puzzling.

Like his handling of the cowhides that he resold to the tanner at no profit, Rex's bar iron trade seems counterintuitive. Forgoing a profit on sales to family members is understandable, but why not mark up sales of iron to his other customers in Schaefferstown? The answer may be that ironmasters formed cartels and agreed to fix the price of iron, and as a result the market price of iron was stable, at least for transactions that occurred close to the furnaces.[117] In addition, Schaefferstown smiths were attuned to the market price of iron because it was essential to their production. Though Rex offered convenient terms, the smiths were not willing to pay him more than the going rate at the furnaces. Just as city merchants adjusted prices for pork and flaxseed, ironmasters controlled the price of iron in the countryside. In dealing with fluctuating prices, Rex's best course was to wait until the price rose, as he did with pork. In dealing with fixed prices, such as those for hides and iron, the best method was to sell at once. The apparent lack of profit on iron was offset by the benefit of converting it into a more profitable form, or using it like money to keep the economy moving, thus building networks that led to more lucrative deals. Rex did not make money on iron rods, but he did make a profit on the nails that Sweitzer made from the rods. He could sell iron at face value locally or go to the trouble and expense of hauling it to Philadelphia, where prices were higher. Even when he did not make a profit on iron or paid dearly to transport it, keeping it and other commodities flowing through the economy as interchangeable parts of the whole was as key to Rex's success as it was to the prosperity of Philadelphia merchants. Like city merchants, Rex knew that sometimes it was necessary to sacrifice a profit on a few transactions in order to keep his business moving and make money on subsequent exchanges.[118]

Resembling the exchanges farmers and craftsmen made at the store, the deals iron community members made with Rex were useful to all parties, though not without some tensions. Rex enjoyed profits from his steady trade with the iron community, and ironmasters found in Rex a reliable source of food and other essentials for the plantations, as well as a way to pay their workers' wages. The workers benefited, too; for them, the store was a place where they could hear the news, pay a debt, obtain cash or fancy yard goods, or simply buy a lantern, bottle of rum, and warm mittens to see them home at the end of a long wagon trip.

Keeping the Books Regular

Like all storekeepers, Rex sold goods on credit.[119] He kept track of customers' indebtedness and payments to the store with a single-entry bookkeeping system. He kept a paper-bound daybook (see fig. 15) where he entered each sale of merchandise at the time it took place as a debit and each payment of cash or a commodity as a credit. Periodically he posted the transactions to the customers' accounts in a large, leather-bound ledger, where entries were arranged alphabetically.[120] While the daybooks provide a fascinating glimpse of daily activity in the store, the ledgers present a more accurate picture of how customers satisfied their accounts, because when a customer made the final payment to close his account, Rex posted the transaction in the ledger only, bypassing the daybook. Rex's ledgers reveal that his customers were hardly cash poor; in fact, when it came to paying their store accounts, cash was their preferred medium.

In Rex's 1791, 1798, and 1806–7 daybooks, customers' commodity payments (craft goods and produce) accounted for about 47 percent of credits. Iron made up 25.6 percent, cash accounted for 16 percent, and labor made up just over 6 percent of the credits that customers accrued on a daily basis. This pattern of transactions shows that customers seldom carried cash with them to pay for

FIG. 15. Samuel Rex Daybook 24 (September 12 to December 5, 1803). These typical pages show Rex's single-entry system. He recorded debits ("Dr") for customers' purchases and credits ("Cr") for their payments of cash, sale/payment of goods, or labor. He recorded store transactions in the daybook as they occurred and periodically transferred customers' accounts to a ledger, where he used a double-entry system. The entries in German show that Rex was away and that someone else was tending the store. Photo by author. Used by permission of Historic Schaefferstown, Inc.

everyday purchases. Instead they ran up bills for months, even years, at a time, offsetting their debits periodically by selling goods to the store, when they had them to spare and Rex was willing to buy them, or, less frequently, by working for Rex. Occasionally they might pay cash on account, but cash payments in the daybook are far less common than commodity payments.

Eventually, however, a customer had to pay his bill or face the wrath (and legal action) of the storekeeper, and these arrangements are reflected in the ledger entries. Rex's ledger 5 (1798–1806) shows that customers used a variety of methods to pay down their accounts, but cash accounted for the largest percentage of credits he received—just over 30 percent of the total. Paper instruments accounted for nearly 20 percent of the total payments in the ledger, while produce and craft goods accounted for 14.4 percent and 4.3 percent of the credits, respectively. Labor was not a significant method of paying; only 4.5 percent of the total ledger credits came in this form. See table 5 for a complete breakdown of credits from the ledger and daybooks.

Studies by other historians of country stores provide comparisons to the Rex analysis. At the Lowrance store in North Carolina, the greatest percentage of store credits (82 percent) was cash, while the smallest amount (7 percent) was labor. The remaining credits (11 percent) were for local products. Unlike Rex, the Lowrance storekeeper seldom received paper instruments. A different pattern occurred at the Williams store in Deerfield, Massachusetts, where the storekeeper received the most credit in the form of second-party notes and orders (30 percent); other credits were cash (24 percent), real estate (16 percent), and commodity payments, mostly of livestock and wheat (15 percent). Here, too,

Table 5 Customer Credits from Selected Rex Daybooks and Ledger 5

Customer Credits	Ledger 5, 1798–1806 (%)	1791 Daybooks (%)	1798 Daybooks (%)	1806–1807 Daybooks (%)	Total 1791, 1798, 1806–1807 Daybooks (%)
Assumption	1.8	0	0	0	0
Book Credit	4.5	0	0	0	0
Cash	30.1	14.0	16.3	16.2	16.0
Country Produce	14.4	8.9	40.1	43.1	39.0
Craft Goods	4.3	2.9	14.1	6.3	8.0
Iron	11.5	45.5	19.2	25.3	25.6
Labor	4.5	0.4	2.0	9.1	6.3
Paper Instrument	19.6	28.4	8.3	0	5.0
Second-Party Cash	9.2	0	0	0	0

labor was the smallest percentage of the total (14 percent). From the Hasbrouck store in the Hudson River Valley in 1799, still another model emerges. The largest percentage of credits came in the form of commodities, including agricultural goods (24.1 percent), barrel staves and oak wood (21.5 percent), and textiles and clothing (5.3 percent). Cash payments made up 18.2 percent of the total, and service to the storekeeper amounted to only 1 percent. There were no paper instruments.[121]

It is not surprising that Rex and Williams had a considerably larger number of paper instruments and assumptions than the North Carolina storekeeper did. Not only was Rex operating in a slightly later period and closer to a metropolis where circulation of paper was common, but he was also dealing extensively with ironmasters who paid their workers by assuming their debts or issuing orders. The residents of the long-established village of Deerfield likewise were probably more accustomed to circulating notes than were people living in the North Carolina backcountry; in addition, Williams did considerable business with the military, and they may have paid him with notes. In all four places customers sold farm and manufactured products to the store, and in New York customers favored commodity payments over cash. Customers in all regions used some cash to pay off store accounts, although the percentage of these payments varied from place to place. All of this indicates that early Americans had economic resources besides the local store and emphasizes that stores were only one component in networks of exchange.

But what could a customer do if he or she could not pay the store bill? If Rex's bookkeeping methods were traditional and his pace of collection leisurely because of community norms, he was methodical and zealous in pursuing unpaid accounts, so that he could pay his own bills and keep his business operating profitably. To this end, although he never struck a year-end balance or tallied the value of his inventory, he attended closely to his books. If he judged that an account had gone too long without payment, he took measures to make sure he would be paid.

Rex handled each case on an individual basis. Sometimes he charged no interest at all on a loan or overdue account, but more often he added 6 percent—a rather standard amount at the time. A few times he noted (to avoid future disputes, perhaps) that he added interest with the customer's consent. He was inclined to be lenient for longer periods if a customer was making partial payments, but he sometimes demanded payment in less than a year. In the case of ironworkers Peter Swoap (in 1791) and Barney McBride (in 1803), who must have seemed suspicious, Rex waited only nine months to send the unpaid accounts for collection.[122]

Rex's most benign way to secure repayment was to have the customer sign the daybook to acknowledge that a balance was outstanding. This constituted a book debt but included no provisions for repayment. If a customer lived some distance away, Rex might send a pointed reminder; in 1801 he wrote to John Barr of Shippensburg, Cumberland County, to remind him that his bill of £8 18s., now five years overdue, had accrued interest of £2. 16s. 4d.[123] Barr's response is unknown, but a letter from another customer suggests the difficulty that some people had in paying their store bills. Will McClafferty, who had moved to Allegheny County, wrote to Rex in November 1801 that he would "make every exertion possible" to repay the money he owed. "I have got 200 acres of land . . . in hopes of making well out on it. A man's wages are from 3/ to 3/9 per day. Money is scarce. But rest assured D[ea]r Sir I shall not neglect you."[124]

In other cases the customer could sign a note or bond using the printed forms that Rex kept on hand as part of his inventory. Bonds had more force than notes because they carried a penalty. For a £50 debt a creditor might sign a £100 bond, promising to pay the higher amount if the debt was not repaid by the deadline. Rex's outstanding notes and bonds were payable anywhere from one month to one year hence, and they ranged in value from as little as £4 to as much as £140.[125] Once he had signed the note or bond, a customer could immediately borrow more cash or charge more goods. This policy enabled customers to obtain cash and supplies even in hard times, but the service came at an increasingly high cost if they could not meet payment deadlines.

Customers who let their accounts go too long would face Rex's most draconian collection method—a lawsuit filed against them with a local justice of the peace. Rex did not hesitate to initiate suits against customers of all occupations and ranks. Where Rex sent the bill for collection depended on where the customer lived, as each justice had jurisdiction over a particular bailiwick. In 1807 Rex sent three overdue accounts to a justice in Myerstown. The justice settled two of the three cases in Rex's favor but returned one because the person was no longer living in the county.[126] Rex sometimes added interest and legal fees to the accounts he "put into suit," but often he was willing to settle for the principal amount outstanding. Some of the amounts that Rex sued for were quite small; the consequences for his customers were nevertheless dire. Those who could not pay might have their goods seized and sold or be hauled off to jail. In March 1798, when Rex sued Peter McDonagan, Justice

Henry Schaeffer directed the local constable to "levy the Goods and Chattels of the said Defendant, and according to Law, make Sale thereof, sufficient to pay the said Debt and Costs, together with the Costs of serving this Execution. . . . But for Want of Goods sufficient, take, in Execution, the Body of the said Peter McDonagan and convey him to jail for the said County, there to be detained, until the Debt and Costs aforesaid are paid or satisfied, or he be otherwise, from thence, legally discharged."[127]

Even ironmasters were not immune to lawsuits for nonpayment. Though Rex deferred to these powerful businessmen in most matters, when George Ege could not pay his account at the store, Rex sued. Ege's trouble began in 1803 with his purchase of five dozen coal baskets worth £7 10s. Four years later Ege charged 4,407 pounds of pork at £91, and in 1811 he took on an employee's £10 debt. After Rex filed his lawsuit, he received "two notes of hand" from James Old, a prominent ironmaster and Ege's relative by marriage. Either the notes did not cover all debts or they just kept rolling over and accumulating interest because by 1820, some thirteen years after Rex left storekeeping, the bill was still outstanding and the resulting seventeen years' worth of interest had swelled the original £109 8s. debt to a whopping £205 15s.[128]

A Market Economy Embedded in Community Life

Negotiations among Rex and the ironmasters, farmers, and craftsmen took place in the context of both local arrangements and a maturing market economy. In this close community, word spread rapidly when a farmer sold sick hogs to the local storekeeper; the agricultural cycle dictated payment schedules; short-term loans were made free of interest; and community norms forced Rex to treat hides and iron as commodity money and move them through his books at cost. In such an environment, Rex had to guard his reputation carefully. If he were known as a man who sold tainted meat or marked up a product too steeply, he risked losing his place in the crucial networks on which his business depended. In addition, an ironmaster's lawsuit over bad pork would mean not only a financial loss but an attack on his honor—even his masculinity—that Rex wanted to avoid.[129] It is hardly surprising that some aspects of Rex's relationships with his customers, even when they were representatives of the iron industry, were more characteristic of a personal, local economy than an impersonal market-driven system. A letter from Cornwall Furnace manager Peter

Leib demonstrates the degree to which these transactions were based on shared values of knowledge, understanding, and trust. Leib had come to the store while Rex was absent. He was reluctant to ask Rex's brother (who was clerking) for credit because he did not know him, but he was confident that Rex would honor his request: "You have a pair of rose blankets in your house would suit me very well, and [I] want them badly, but had not money enough to pay for and did not like to ask your brother for trust, but told him to lay them by for me. . . . I will either give you Cr[edit] or pay you some time in the spring."[130] Rex agreed to give Leib credit, and he sent the blankets to Cornwall on the teamsters' return trip, relying (as it turned out, in vain) on Leib to pay when he promised.[131]

On the other hand, at the same time that they were involved in these face-to-face exchanges, Rex and his customers were part of a market-driven system in which local prices were based on Philadelphia rates, farmers raised extra hogs to sell at the store, and an ironmaster could use legal threats to protect his business interests. In fact, as we have seen, many of Rex's customers, whether from Schaefferstown or the iron community, did business with him when it was to their advantage to do so, but also used networks other than Rex's to meet their needs. The same combination of community and market orientation characterized business conditions in the city. In the next chapter we follow Rex and his teamsters to Philadelphia, where they rubbed shoulders with sea captains, mechanics, clerks, and prosperous merchants on the busy streets of the largest city in the nation.

CHAPTER FOUR

"ORDERS THANKFULLY RECEIVED, AND CAREFULLY EXECUTED":
REX AND THE PHILADELPHIA MERCHANTS

SAMUEL REX WAS BUSIER THAN USUAL on Thursday, November 14, 1799. His first customer, Henry Weiss, needed powder and lead; Jacob Buffamoyer stopped by later for thread and twist. As the day went on, Rex weighed tea, coffee, sugar, pepper, and tobacco, poured quarts of molasses and wine, and cut lengths of linen, rattinett, and serge. Some people came in just to pay on their store accounts, but a group of ironworkers came to shop. Among them was Paddy Forrey, who wanted a quart of whiskey and two pairs of knives and forks. Toward the end of the day Nicholas Hawk picked up a half-ton of bar iron, Widow Weaver came in for two quarts of salt, and Mrs. Donnelly bought a pair of shoes. In all, Rex waited on twenty-two customers. With business this brisk, it was a good thing that he was about to leave for a shopping trip in Philadelphia.[1] Besides laying in new stock, Rex had another reason to go to the city: he had goods to sell there. He had been collecting butter from his customers for months and had forty-seven kegs and one tub of butter stacked in the cellar.

While scholars have long noted the importance of the agricultural hinterlands to Philadelphia's economy, they have been vague about how country goods made their way to the city. This gap in the literature is puzzling, because Philadelphia, from its earliest days, served as a market outlet for rural production; William Penn had precisely this goal in mind when he situated the city between two navigable rivers.[2] Yet in 1959, when Arthur H. Cole described Philadelphia merchants assembling their export cargo, he noted, "Unhappily we know precious little about the process. Apparently, the staves and the salt fish, the flour and the pit iron walked themselves to the ports."[3] In the 1970s both Diane Lindstrom and David Dauer lamented that historians still had not studied adequately the crucial urban center–hinterlands commercial link. Moreover, despite recent interest in consumption as a subject of historical analysis, scholars have not addressed the physical movement of goods between urban ports and the countryside. As Richard Bushman observes, we understand far more about wholesale international trade than about American retail sales.[4]

Rex's store records provide concrete information on how rural-urban trade functioned in early America and specifically reveal the ties between such different places as Schaefferstown and Philadelphia. Following one of his shopping trips, Rex's customers could experience vicariously the exciting consumer world of Philadelphia shops and beyond, by seeing, touching, and perhaps even buying some of Rex's newest offerings. For some locals, the link to the city was even more tangible; these men worked for Rex driving wagons to and from Philadelphia on his regular shopping excursions. The interest in rural-urban trade was reciprocal. Just as country people enjoyed imported goods brought from the city, urban merchants welcomed deliveries from the country and cultivated relationships with storekeepers who could deliver farm products in bulk and buy large orders of goods each time they came to the city.

Philadelphia and Its Business Community

For his November 1799 trip Rex hired farmers Nicholas Swanger and Casper Ellinger, who often worked for him, to drive wagonloads of produce to the city and haul goods home again. Rex did not record the type of wagons the men used, but Pennsylvania farmers commonly drove heavy Conestoga wagons with teams of four to six horses. Traveler Johann Schoepf noted that "people from a distance, especially Germans come into Philadelphia in great covered wagons" on market days.[5] Such wagons could carry up to three thousand pounds of cargo, and they were as familiar a sight in the eighteenth and nineteenth centuries as tractor trailers would become two hundred years later. Horses pulling fully laden wagons had to stop frequently to rest, and the average distance they could travel in a day was between twenty and thirty miles.[6]

On long trips some wagoners carried provisions for themselves and their teams and slept in their wagons, while others stayed at taverns along the way. Schoepf noticed German farmers going to market, sleeping in their wagons, and living on bread and cheese they carried with them. Theophile Cazenove observed farmers sleeping on the floor of an inn while on their way to

Philadelphia; they lay with their feet to the fire, and for cushions they used the bags of oats they had brought to feed their horses.[7] One possible route for Rex and his carters was the newly completed Lancaster Turnpike, which offered a number of places that they could stay for the night—no fewer than sixty-one taverns in a sixty-six-mile stretch of road.[8] However, early maps (see fig. 1) show that there were other routes to the city that might have been more convenient for Rex. If he wanted to stop and visit his family or do business in Chestnut Hill, he could have headed northeast to Womelsdorf, then east to Reading and on to Germantown Road, entering Philadelphia from the north.

Rex's carters—especially on their first visit to the city—would surely have been struck by the great contrast between Philadelphia and Schaefferstown. Both places were established on commercial rather than manufacturing or religious principles, and both were centers of commercial exchange, but there the similarity ended. Whereas Schaefferstown was a rural town of fewer than one hundred log and stone houses, a deserted market house, and a handful of taverns and general stores, Philadelphia was a cosmopolitan center, and so large that it was divided into a dozen wards. The city's population of sixty thousand included about five hundred merchants and hundreds of shopkeepers.[9] The market house on High (also called Market) Street extended from First to Third Street; on market days, Wednesdays and Saturdays, people flocked into the city and the streets "swarm[ed] with buyers and sellers."[10]

Founded late in the seventeenth century, Philadelphia was America's premier seaport by 1776. Like other northern cities, it languished in the early 1780s, a victim of the depressed economy that followed Britain's closing of West Indian ports to American trade and the declining European demand for American products. To compound its problems, after the war Philadelphia saw an influx of ex-soldiers and former slaves swell the already high number of unemployed. Commenting on the desperate straits of city laborers, British consul Phineas Bond observed in 1788, "Scarcely an artificer of any sort can at this time meet a decent support."[11] By 1790, however, the city's economy had begun to recover, and in the final decade of the eighteenth century Philadelphia reached its zenith as the wealthiest city in America, the country's busiest port, and the nation's banking center.

The city was a political as well as an economic hub. Until 1799 it was the state capital; from 1790 to 1800 it was also the national capital, and until 1797 home to President George Washington, who occupied a grand residence on High Street. Philadelphia was also a cultural and social center, with the finest taverns in the country, as well as libraries, a hospital and university, and two theaters.[12] If Rex and his carters had time for entertainment, they could have enjoyed John Bill Ricketts's "Pantheon Circus and Amphitheatre," Charles Willson Peale's natural history museum, and the occasional traveling exhibit of oddities such as lions and elephants.[13]

Despite these attractive features and the restored economy, Philadelphia, like other large cities, had its share of problems, including poverty and disease. Not all residents could afford to attend the theater, dine at a tavern, or buy a museum ticket. Many Philadelphians lived hand to mouth in squalid housing. Overcrowding and poor sanitation bred deadly epidemics that threatened residents of all ranks. Disease was a chronic problem in the late eighteenth century, especially between 1793 and 1798, when yellow fever swept through the city annually and those who had the means fled to the countryside. (Germantown was a popular retreat.) During the worst of these epidemics, some merchants relocated their stores temporarily to Lancaster, and country storekeepers had to choose alternative sources of provisions.[14]

Still another difference between Philadelphia and small towns was the diversity and density of its population. Although first settled by English Quakers, Philadelphia soon became a city of immigrants, home to a variety of ethnic and religious groups and a sizable free black population. Germans, many of whom had sold themselves as "redemptioners" to pay for their trip, made up the greatest number of new arrivals before the Revolution.[15] In the 1790s, French refugees from the Continent and Saint Dominique poured into the city.[16]

Philadelphia streets formed a neat grid pattern that stretched for several miles between its two rivers, but most of its residents chose to congregate in the streets closest to the Delaware River, where population density reached as high as 1,411 people in a few city blocks.[17] Some scholars have argued that ethnic and racial groups mingled rather than settle in the enclaves and ghettos that would characterize Philadelphia in later years.[18] Mary Schweitzer cautions, however, that the heterogeneity of the city may be overemphasized since many Philadelphians preferred to live close to others of the same occupational, social, or ethnic backgrounds.[19] Germans, for example, tended to live in the northern part of the city and in the Northern Liberties, a suburb north of the city proper. Moreau de St. Mery, a French émigré who resided for a time in Philadelphia, was of the opinion that "above Third Street in Northern Liberties . . . there are only Germans."[20]

One might expect that the northern part of the city and the Northern Liberties would have been Rex's destination on his trips since he was of German descent and was shopping for a largely German clientele, but this was not the case. When Rex went to Philadelphia, he headed for the heart of the city: the streets nearest the Delaware River.[21] Although commercial and private residences commingled in the city, here there was a high concentration of businesses because of proximity to the wharves and the public market house. On High Street alone, 248 out of a total 373 residents listed in the 1801 city directory were storekeepers, merchants, or artisans who operated shops.[22] (See Appendix D for a list of all the merchants that Rex patronized.)

As Rex and his carters walked through Philadelphia on these buying trips, they would have noticed that, unlike the widely spaced one- and two-story houses in Schaefferstown, city buildings nestled closely to each other; many were quite narrow but rose to three or four stories. Philadelphia houses were mostly built of brick, as insurance companies deemed wooden structures fire hazards. In fact, until 1781, when a rival company opened for business, the city's only fire insurance company refused to insure frame structures.[23] Even so, not everyone chose brick. Rex frequently dealt with Martin Dubs, who had his business in a 22 × 40-foot frame building, and he also did business with auctioneer John Connelly, whose "accompting house" was a 10 × 15-foot wooden structure.[24]

Other stores where Rex shopped ran the gamut from modest to expensive, though what was modest in Philadelphia would have been quite pricey back in Schaefferstown. They ranged in value from William Guyer's eighteen-foot-square brick building, assessed at $1,000, to ironmonger Richard Wistar's four-story building at Third and High streets, a 30 × 30-foot brick pile valued at $7,500. A few businessmen whom Rex patronized lived and worked in what were probably quite opulent surroundings. Merchant Robert Harwood's residence at 30 South Front Street was assessed at $12,000; the building may have served business purposes, too, as it was owned by his firm, Waddington & Harwood.

Rex would also have observed that many city houses had businesses on the first floor, with living quarters on the upper stories—a city version of country innkeepers' living arrangements in the rooms above their taverns.[25] The "celebrated and beautiful" Ann Baker Carson, for example, had a china shop on the first floor of a 16 × 26-foot city house, and she shared the second-floor living space with nine other people.[26] Tax assessors in 1798 duly noted that the two chambers over Robert Henderson's city store were "always occupied by the tenant of the adjoining dwelling house." Even the wealthiest merchants lived above, or adjacent to, their places of business. Stephen Girard resided at 23 North Water Street; he had his private counting room on the first floor and a public counting room in the building next door.[27] There was little distinction between private and commercial buildings, and some storekeepers and merchants worked in private residences altered for business use.[28] In March 1785 Isaac Snowden offered to rent a brick house next door to his own home, noting that the rental "with ease would make a large store."[29] Rex regularly patronized Davis & Co., Wiltburger & Smith, and Samuel Eldredge, all of whom had businesses in converted residences on High Street.

If Rex and his wagoners were uncertain whether a place that looked like a house was really a store, they would have looked for a signboard. Moreau de St. Mery noted that city artists created "beautiful signboards with backgrounds of different colors," trimmed in gold and silver, and he vowed to obtain one of these when he opened his own bookstore.[30] Such signs served as handy ways for businessmen to identify their establishments. Country storekeeper John Huber asked city merchant Adam Zantzinger to send the goods he ordered to the sign of the Camel on Second Street. Samuel Wetherill & Sons had their store "at [the sign of] Galen's Head." Benjamin Poultney sold hardware at the sign of the Crown and Anvil, across from "the sign of the Conestogoe Waggon." William Coats's store was "at the sign of the Sugar-Loaf."[31]

Even if exterior arrangements differed, when Rex entered a city store he would have felt at home, for many accoutrements resembled those of his own shop. A late eighteenth-century broadside for William Coats's shop (fig. 16) shows a shelf-lined storeroom filled with bottles, barrels, and boxes, along with the necessary tools of the trade, including a scales, measures, and a funnel. Some city stores were paneled with cedar, an aromatic wood that would have helped to repel destructive insects, but it seems unlikely that country storekeepers would have had the means to panel their shops in this manner.[32]

Through the probate inventory of middling Philadelphia merchant Philip Boehm, taken room by room, we may step beyond the public areas of one city store.[33] Boehm had his shop and office on the first floor of a three-story building, and he lived above on the second and third floors. His office contained his clock, desk, and bookcase; the six Windsor arm chairs and several tables would have permitted him to hold private business consultations there. The adjacent sales room included weighing and measuring equipment, as well as a brace and bit and a box of sand for blotting wet ink. Boehm's sales space was stocked with wine, domestic and imported rum, tea and teakettles, pepper, oil, and rice. He

WILLIAM COATS,

Takes this method of acquainting the P U B L I C in general, and his F R I E N D S in particular, that he has for S A L E, at his S T O R E, at the fign of the Sugar-Loaf, contiguous to the Public Wharf, in Front-Street, and near Pool's Bridge, Wholesale and Retail;

WEST-INDIA and PHILADELPHIA RUM, Jamaica fpirits, brandy, geneva, annifeed, cordials; Madeira, Lifbon, and Teneriff WINES ; lamp oil; loaf, lump and mufcovado S U G A R S;molaffes ; green, fouchong, and bohea T E A; chocolate, rice, oatmeal, ftarch, indigo, pepper, ginger, allfpice, cloves, mace, cinnamon, and nutmegs; cotton ; 3d, 4d, 8d, 10d, 12d and 20d, nails ; powder and fhot, foap and candles, brimftone, allum, falt-petre, copperas, raifins, currants, madder, red-wood, fine an d coarfe falt, W E S T O N's S N U F F, muftard, Florence Oil, &c. &c. &c.

Sea ftores, fhallop-mens bills, &c. put up with care, and all orders from Town or Country thankfully received, and carefully executed.

P H I L A D E L P H I A, Printed by J O H N D U N L A P, at the *Neweft Printing-Office*, in *Market-ftreet*.

FIG. 16. William Coats Broadside, 1772. Coats's advertisement shows the necessary tools for operating a store in the country or city and also highlights the connection between rural storekeepers and the urban merchants who supplied them. Reproduced by permission of The Library Company of Philadelphia.

kept a truck for a hogshead, a spade, shovel, bucket, watering pot, and empty barrels in a storage room that may have been accessible to the selling space and therefore vulnerable to theft, since he did not use it for his valuables. A more secure storage area contained extra stock: some 3,400 gallons of rum, 1,600 gallons of wine, and 1,924 gallons of "oyl."[34] Like Rex and Valentine, Boehm used his cellar for storage; there were another 390 gallons of Philadelphia rum and a hogshead packed with teakettles stowed there.

In eighteenth-century terminology, Philadelphia businessmen included "merchants," wholesalers who bought and sold in foreign markets; "grocers," who sold imported food items at retail; and "shopkeepers," who purchased stock from the merchants and sold at retail a general selection of goods. As time went on, however, the distinctions between the groups became less clear. After the American Revolution, British firms extended credit to anyone who wished to import a cargo on his own and, much to the consternation of established wholesalers, petty shopkeepers, even those from the countryside, began styling themselves as "merchants."[35]

Indeed, Rex may have been tempted to enter overseas trade himself in 1795, though the details of his plans are sketchy. A letter from Philadelphian John Martin to Rex refers to a potential agreement with one Captain Quinn. Martin had spoken with Quinn, but regrettably he had not succeeded, and he suggested that Rex "proceed in the manner we proposed as there is no likelyhood of his [Quinn's] leaving the city at present."[36] Although he never imported his own goods, Rex did transport cargoes from city to countryside, and he came to think of himself as a "merchant." Some city firms who dealt with Rex addressed correspondence to "Samuel Rex, Esq., Merchant," a title that may also have served to flatter the country storekeeper and solicit his continued patronage.

City merchants, like their rural counterparts, operated as individual proprietorships and in partnerships. In both places good help was essential, and city storekeepers and merchants, like Rex, took on young males as apprentices or paid clerks. These men often used a clerkship as a stepping-stone to owning their own shops or entering into partnership with former employers.[37] Rex quite frequently patronized shopkeepers and merchants whom he had met while they were working as clerks in other establishments. He had known Samuel Eldredge, who would become one of his regular business associates, when Eldredge was still clerking for William Wister. The rise of city clerks to business proprietors was not unlike Rex's own career path, which also began with a clerkship.

As in the countryside, city women who needed to earn their own living found shopkeeping a respectable option. Although parents did not apprentice girls to merchants to learn the trade, widows often took over a family business, and occasionally daughters succeeded their mothers in millinery or dressmaking shops.[38] Ann Baker Carson "determined to enter into the sale of china and queens-ware" to support herself after her husband deserted her in 1807.[39] Rex patronized three widowed shopkeepers, including Barbara Beates, who took over the family tobacco shop when her husband, Conrad, died. In fact, despite the presence of a male relative who worked in the shop, Barbara was the proprietor; Rex's receipts were signed by William Beates (perhaps a son learning the business by working as a clerk?) "for Barbara Beates."[40]

Still other aspects of city merchants' operations were similar to rural practices. Philadelphia was the busiest commercial center in America, but its businesses still functioned on a personal level. Merchants and would-be merchants conducted deals with people they knew well or whose good reputation they could confirm with a trusted third party. Informal face-to-face discussions at city coffeehouses allowed businessmen to meet one another and keep abreast of important matters. The personal touch extended to the salesrooms and warehouses; merchants and shopkeepers at all income levels lived above their stores and, along with clerks and apprentices, waited on customers and prepared receipts for their purchases. Some merchants even took to the road to do business with customers, reversing Rex's periodic journeys to the seaport. Eldredge traveled into the countryside regularly to visit customers, solicit their future business, and fill special orders. In August 1799 he called on Rex in Schaefferstown and collected the £53 that Rex owed him.[41] And in December 1801 Eldredge wrote to Rex from Lebanon, "I shall be in Womelsdorf this evening ... perhaps you may have commands for Philada. If so they shall merit my best attention." While these excursions helped strengthen Eldredge's relationship with his rural customers, they were time consuming. He apologized that his schedule did not permit him to travel to Schaefferstown on that particular trip, because he had "been long from home and must return as soon as business permits."[42]

In this traditional milieu, personal endorsements from merchants carried considerable weight for a young man entering the world of commerce. When John Dull, Eldredge's former clerk, "commenced himself in the crockery line" with Benjamin Shoemaker, he wrote to former clients, including Rex, to announce the news. To demonstrate that Dull left him on good terms, Eldredge wrote a recommendation on the back of the letter. "By opening an account with the firm of Shoemaker & Dull you will oblige me and I trust thereby form a valuable connection as I am convinced they are determined to do business on the most amiable terms."[43] Personal contacts were also important when businessmen hired a clerk or took on an apprentice. When seventeen-year-old Londoner Richard Vaux sought a clerkship in Philadelphia, his father wrote to city merchant Edward Pennington asking for help in placing the young man in a good firm.[44] At the same time, negative evaluations of a person's trustworthiness or credit rating raised suspicions about these individuals and damaged their reputations. Although Philadelphia was large and diverse, word spread as swiftly in the city when a resident was not to be trusted as it did in Schaefferstown when sick dogs bit hogs. In reference to a question about a business associate's credit, Philadelphia grocer Thomas Miller advised Rex, "I have not Time at present to call on Mr. Sickle in regard to his Note, but from what I know of his punctuality, you had [illegible] better have nothing to do with his Note."[45]

Rex tapped into this urban network of relations as well as his family network when he began to trade in Philadelphia. He would already have known the merchants and clerks who had traveled out from Philadelphia to deal at his father's store, and when he set up his own business, his brothers and father offered advice and assistance. Samuel's father even accompanied him on early buying trips. On October 2, 1791, John Rex, Samuel's older brother, wrote to him that a younger brother (Enoch) could not be spared to come to Schaefferstown to tend Samuel's store while Samuel bought supplies. Enoch was needed at home because "Father intends to go up there [Philadelphia] with you."[46] Building on these ties, Rex, his family in Chestnut Hill, and some Philadelphia businessmen formed a triangular arrangement in which Rex shipped country goods to his family and his family paid him by depositing cash or credit at one of the city stores. In June 1792 Rex's brother informed him, "Father will pay... for the Iron you sent him in Philadelphia at any of the Merchants. Please send a few lines what the Iron comes to and which Merchants he shall pay the Money to."[47]

By the time his father died in 1793, Rex had built up enough goodwill among city merchants that he no longer needed his experienced hand selecting merchandise, but when John and Enoch took over the store, they also worked cooperatively with Samuel. In addition to buying iron from him, they advised him about where he might sell goods profitably. In February 1794 John wrote to Samuel that Germantown innkeepers Abraham Heydrich and John Hart would each buy a load of apple liquor at 6d. per gallon or "as much as any other man" would pay. "If you think you can deliver 2 loads down for that price you can bring some with you when you come down. Please to write concerning the liquor as soon as possible."[48] Visits between Chestnut Hill and Schaefferstown worked both ways. Samuel's brothers John and Abraham came to Schaefferstown often enough to meet their future wives there. (John married Margaret Valentine, Mary and Michael's sister, and Abraham married Elizabeth Schaeffer, granddaughter of the town's founder.) Long-distance personal relations, as well as business ones, were all part of the interwoven network that connected city to countryside in early America.

Having good contacts was just one aspect of shopping in the city; a storekeeper also had to make the right decisions about buying goods. Rex compiled a list of everything he bought to stock the store initially, and this "Invoice of Sundry Goods Sent Samuel Rex from Sundry Persons in Philadelphia, December 11, 1790," shows that he spent a total of £456 5s. 2d. to set up his business. (Besides the expected store goods, there were some one-time purchases, including a "compleat" money scales and a larger set of scales and weights.)[49] Rex's list shows that he purchased goods from twenty-five merchants, thus establishing the pattern he would follow for the next decade and a half. That is, he patronized a variety of establishments to get the product mix that he judged would satisfy—and tempt—his customers. Rex's first purchases are broken down by product category in figure 17.

Rex's invoice presents a one-time snapshot of the goods that were necessary to start up a country store, and his subsequent invoices and receipts show his buying patterns for keeping the store stocked thereafter. Using the surviving records from the November 1799 trip with Swanger and Ellinger, we can recreate a typical journey to Philadelphia and follow Rex about the city as he sold his country produce and assembled a load to take back home.[50]

Rex and his men left Schaefferstown on Friday, November 15.[51] Assuming that his wagons traveled the estimated thirty miles a day, the trip took at least two days, so they probably arrived sometime on Monday. One of their first stops would have been Dubs & Earl's store at 247 High Street to unload the wagons. Over the next few days, while Rex took care of his other business, the merchants inspected and weighed the barrels of butter the men had hauled from the countryside.

On Tuesday, November 19, Rex began buying inventory to take back to Schaefferstown. He visited Benedict Dorsey & Son's store at 3 and 5 South Third Street, between Market (High) Street and the Harp and Crown Tavern,

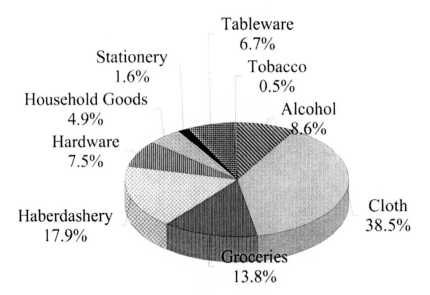

Tableware
6.7%

Stationery
1.6%

Tobacco
0.5%

Household Goods
4.9%

Alcohol
8.6%

Hardware
7.5%

Cloth
38.5%

Haberdashery
17.9%

Groceries
13.8%

FIG. 17. Samuel Rex's Purchases in Philadelphia, 1790. Rex spent £456 5s. 2d. for inventory and furnishings to set up his store in December 1790. This chart shows how he allocated that money.

and bought two barrels of coffee beans and a twenty-pound keg of indigo. Then it was on to Barbara Beates's shop at 209 High Street for £42 worth of tobacco and cigars.

The following day Rex sought out Godfrey Baker at 59 Sassafrass Street and selected more than twelve dozen books and two boxes of window glass. Baker totaled up the bill (£26 18s. 10d.) and gave Rex a 2 percent discount if he paid within three months. Another stop was Baker & Conegy's "elegant" brick store at 28 Chestnut Street, where Rex paid just over £19 in cash for children's hose, handkerchiefs, green cloth, and other dry goods. Rex bought still more dry goods—bed barget, linsey, and woolen gloves—and paid cash at Nottnagle & Montmollen & Co., 22 South Front Street.[52]

On Thursday, November 21, Rex spent much of his day on High Street. At William Chancellor & Company, he chose, among other items, six dozen Barlow and butcher knives, hair ribbons, and sewing silk; clerk Zachery Evans received his payment of £8 12s. At John Davis & Company, Rex selected "mixt" cloth, calico, velvet, and shawls and paid just over £42 in cash for his purchases. Moving along to Widow Elizabeth Cottringer's china shop a few doors up the street, Rex selected a large assortment of glassware (mugs, decanters, flasks, and milk jugs), along with enameled cups and saucers (in blue and white), nests of bowls, plates, teapots, and chamber pots. Like many other merchants the storekeeper visited, Cottringer deducted 5 percent from his bill of some £23, but, perhaps because of the difficulty of packing the fragile china, she charged him 3s. 9d. for the shipping crate. The final stop was Bickam & Reese, where Rex spent another £11 7s. 6d. Figure 18 shows Rex's receipt book and the entries for these payments.

On Friday Rex bought five hundred gun flints from Thomas Hockley and spent more than £17 at the shop of merchants Hugh and John Jackson; he paid cash at both places. Nearing the end of his stay in the city, Rex stopped back at both the Beates and Dorsey shops and paid for his earlier purchases; at the same time he may have had the goods he bought loaded on one of the wagons.

On Saturday, November 23, Rex went back to High Street once more to finish up his business. At Dubs & Earl's store he learned that his shipment of 3,520 pounds of butter would yield £219 17s. 4d. Martin Dubs paid Rex in cash and marked his receipt book. Before leaving Philadelphia, Rex also visited merchants Wistar & Cooke and ironmongers Wistar & Konigmaker to pay the money he owed them.[53] Rex's only other piece of business was to meet with Samuel Eldredge and pay him £241 19s. 6d. for "an acceptance of William Lane."[54]

By Tuesday, November 26, Rex was back behind his store counter in Schaefferstown, and so was at least one of the carters, Ellinger, whose presence is demonstrated by his purchases of store goods that day. Swanger may have stayed on in Philadelphia to load the remaining goods; it seems that he did not return until three days later. That is, when Rex entered Ellinger's November 26 store purchases in the daybook, he noted a payment of 15s. made to Ellinger in Philadelphia, but he did not record the 7s. 6d. he paid to Swanger in the city until November 29, when Swanger came into the store and bought tar and oil.

The Go-Betweens: Hiring the Carters

Ellinger and Swanger were part of a large contingent of carters plying the roads between the city and countryside. Eighteenth- and early nineteenth-century accounts confirm that hired teamsters and farmers carried enormous quantities of goods at regular intervals from south-central Pennsylvania to Philadelphia. In 1743 Lewis Evans described the "High-Dutchers" (Germans) from Tulpehocken

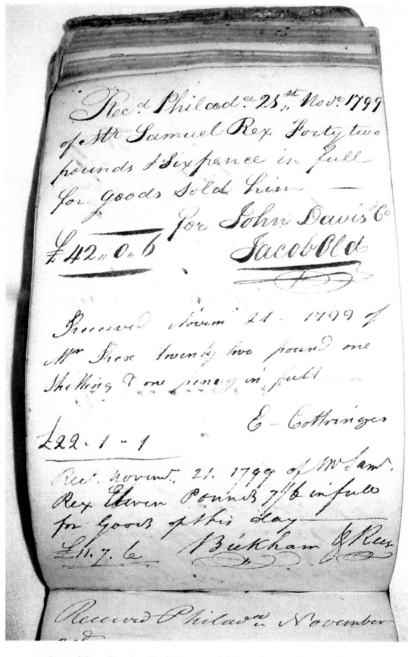

FIG. 18. Samuel Rex Receipt Book. Rex used this pocket-sized receipt book to record payments he received locally and in Philadelphia. This page shows payments from John Davis & Co., Elizabeth Cottringer, and Bickham & Reese during his November 1799 trip. Photo by author. Used by permission of Historic Schaefferstown, Inc.

driving their flour seventy or eighty miles to Philadelphia each spring and fall.[55] In 1776 another observer claimed that "between 8 and 9000 waggons, each drawn by four horses," conveyed farm products to market in Philadelphia.[56] Benjamin Rush, more conservative in his estimates, said that each September and October it was common to see between a hundred and 150 farm wagons carrying produce to Philadelphia on the Lancaster and Reading roads.[57] Cazenove described seeing fourteen Lancaster farmers at an inn in Downing's Town, Pennsylvania; each was driving a "big 4-horse wagon, with 12 barrels of flour, to Philadelphia."[58]

Carters also attracted negative attention from travelers. The consensus was that taverns catering to wagoners were low class and crude, though not so low as drovers' taverns. Wagoners' taverns, where as many as thirty teams might be pulled up for the night at one time, were reputed to be sites of hard drinking and frequent brawling. In fact, Schoepf ventured that Pennsylvania German farmers who drove goods to market were likely to drink all their profits in taverns before they made it back home.[59]

Some farmers did take their own grain to market, but farmers who wanted to avoid the trouble sold it to local stores.[60] Given Rex's habit of buying farm produce and hiring farmers to drive his goods to the city, it may well be that the farmers who drove goods to market were working for storekeepers—ironically, perhaps, transporting for wages some of the very goods they had raised and sold at the store. Daniel Thorp sketches a similar picture of goods moving to market in the Carolinas. There, pack animals and wagons traveled between the North Carolina interior and Pine Tree (later Camden), South Carolina, a five-hundred-mile round trip that took three to four weeks. Even before the Revolution, a regular freight company, along with independent carters, served this route.[61]

Historian Elva Tooker found that commercial freight lines also operated in Pennsylvania by the early nineteenth century; these companies regularly drove goods between Philadelphia and the hinterlands. Wagoners working for a freight line set up offices in rural towns and solicited cargoes bound for the city. They followed a similar practice in Philadelphia, where they made temporary headquarters at a tavern or store so that urban merchants could meet with them and arrange to ship goods back to the countryside.[62] Rex did not have such a standing company at his disposal. Local historian Charles Zerbe claimed that by the early twentieth century freight lines to Philadelphia, Baltimore, and Pittsburgh were headquartered in Schaefferstown, but these firms came far too late to benefit Rex.[63]

Rex relied instead on local men who combined driving with other lines of work. His roster of drivers (Appendix E) included more than seventy men who varied in economic standing and occupation. More than half of them (forty-seven) drove only once for the storekeeper, while others drove for him from six to ten times. None seems to have been a full-time wagoner, and some combined hauling with farming or craft work. Wealthy farmers such as Peter Sheetz Jr. drove for Rex from time to time, and enterprising cooper and tavern keeper Peter Moore used driving as still another way to make money.[64] Farmers' sons, laborers, and tenants also worked for Rex, sometimes driving under the direction of their parent or employer.[65] Some men who drove to Philadelphia also worked for Rex on shorter runs, as in May 1803, when he hired three of his carters to haul logs and stone for his new barn.[66]

The connection between city and countryside was multifaceted, and people besides Rex regularly traveled, or arranged for trips, to Philadelphia. In October 1804 Rex lent John Bomberger $130 "to send to Philadelphia with John Neip."[67] Because of the frequent trade between Schaefferstown and Philadelphia, Rex could sometimes piggyback his business onto someone else's. On one of his trips to Philadelphia to sell linseed oil, Michael Grabill delivered the £50 Rex owed to Henry Darroch and brought back a load of goods for Rex.[68] Rex extended the same service to Grabill; on November 31, 1794, he received £75 in Philadelphia for the oil miller.[69] It was mutually convenient for local people to work with Rex on these errands, but the deals they made resembled business transactions more than community exchanges, and they billed him at the going rate for carriage. Rex paid tanner John Klein (Kline) £4 15s. to haul twelve barrels of flour to Philadelphia, and he paid miller Jacob Thomas 15s. for bringing three hundred pounds of goods back from the city.[70] Drivers of ore wagons offered still another means of delivering goods, especially in Rex's early years of storekeeping, when he was still building up community relations with local farmers. In 1791 Rex hired Alexander Montgomery, a store customer and regular driver for Berkshire Furnace, to haul produce to Philadelphia.[71]

Some men who brought goods out from Philadelphia were strangers to Rex; they may have been city drivers hired by the merchant who sent the shipment, or they could have been farmers from other locales who agreed to carry a load to Schaefferstown on their way home. Wistar & Cooke sent red baize and butcher knives to Rex and noted on the reverse of the invoice that the bundle of goods was arriving "per H. Kring."[72] Henry Darroch promised to write to Rex when his remittance arrived, "per Stager."[73]

Farmers and craftsmen who were Rex's regular customers took their carters' wages in store credit or cash, so driving wagons was one more way for them to earn extra income and buy store goods. These deals enabled Rex to pay at least part of the transportation expense with his most cost-effective method, store goods. The drivers, however, probably wanted at least some of the wages for spending money while they were in the city, because Rex often gave them cash in Philadelphia. Having friends and neighbors haul goods had an added benefit. Rex knew them personally and knew that they could be trusted to not drink to excess in taverns and to deliver his merchandise and cash payments safely. He had no such assurances when outsiders hauled his goods, and he also had no choice but to pay them entirely in cash. When strangers Adam Nare and William Bullein brought goods out from Philadelphia in December 1803 and March 1805, Rex paid them each more than £6 in cash and had them sign his receipt book as proof of the transaction—something that he did not require of his regular carters.[74]

Although the carters earned good wages, they ran risks and incurred expenses. If a wagon broke or a horse went lame, the carter took the loss, since Rex paid by distance covered as well as the weight of the load. In August 1799, when John Weaver's wagon broke down fifteen miles into a trip, Henry Weiss had to pick up Weaver's load and finish the delivery. Rex's response was to prorate the fee; he credited Weaver only 19s. and gave Weiss the remainder, £3 16s.[75] Carters were also responsible for the maintenance of their wagons and teams, and they paid for supplies such as pitch and oil, oats for their team, and their own food and lodging along the way. If they took the turnpike, carters also had to pay the toll.[76] Still, there was room for haggling, and some carters seem to have negotiated better wages than others. (The rates ranged from 3s. 6d. to 5s. 6d. for carrying a hundredweight of goods.) Rex once sent two men to Philadelphia within two days of each other, and paid them at different rates. On October 1, 1804, he credited Casper Ellinger 3s. 9d. per hundredweight, but on October 3 he paid Joseph Kratzer 4s. per hundredweight.[77]

Wagoners not only bargained for the best rates, they also had the final say about the weight of the load they would carry. In September 1802 Martin Dubs sent two barrels of coffee to Rex with Henry Weiss and told Rex that he would have sent along a barrel of salt, but Weiss would not take it. Weiss probably did not want to overload his team, but he might have refused out of spite because he had been forced to load his own wagon at Dubs's warehouse. To add to Rex's vexation, Dubs tried to charge Rex a porter's fee, even though Weiss did the loading.[78]

Moreover, it is unclear just how many laborers were available. Rex's need for carters was probably greater than the carters' need for work, for they could haul iron for the furnaces if they did not like Rex's terms.[79] Thus, unless they were in debt to Rex or out of work, carters may have had more leverage than he did in bargaining. Rex was not powerless, though. While much about his relationship with the carters reflects a spirit of mutuality, when Weaver's wagon failed, Rex carefully figured how much he had earned and paid him just that, disregarding the rest of Weaver's anticipated wage and his repair costs. On the whole, however, Rex and the wagoners tended to seek relations of trust and respect on each side. He relied on them to deliver his shipments promptly and safely, and they trusted that he would compensate them in whole or in part when they returned.

Selling Produce, Buying Goods, Building Networks: Market and Community in the City

The networks of relations that connected urban merchants and rural storekeepers resulted in mutually advantageous exchanges of goods that met the needs of businessmen, producers, and consumers in both regions. Rex delivered to the city the country produce that he had taken in from his customers over the past few months, and he used the proceeds to help pay for imports to start the cycle anew. If Rex was happy when he reached Philadelphia at the end of two or three days in the saddle or bouncing in a wagon seat, his city agents were equally glad to see him arrive with wagonloads of produce they could resell to city shopkeepers or outbound sea captains. In fact, the anticipation with which city merchants greeted fresh country produce is evident in a letter to Rex from Henry Darroch. Writing in 1792, Darroch told Rex that he "would be glad how soon you send the keg [of] butter as I am in want for family use."[80]

The high value that many city merchants placed on trade with rural storekeepers also shows in the advertisements they circulated. William Coats's broadside (fig. 16) specifically welcomed orders from "Town or Country," which would be "thankfully received, and carefully executed." Abbot & Simpson announced that country storekeepers, among others, "may have their orders executed with the greatest punctuality and on the most reasonable terms." Daniel

Drinker likewise noted that country storekeepers would have their orders "carefully put up, on very reasonable terms."[81] In 1797 Adam Zantzinger shipped hundreds of pounds' worth of merchandise out to distant backcountry storekeepers, including John Huber in Lower Saucon Township ("on Bethlehem Road, 49 miles from Philadelphia") and Shannon and Brysson in Newville, Cumberland County ("take right hand at Mount Rock 3 miles & 131 miles from Philadelphia near Carlisle").[82] For city merchants, having dependable customers who periodically bought sizable orders and paid for them promptly made good business sense. Those dealing in provisions welcomed doubly a customer like Rex, who could also send a steady supply of farm products their way.

City businessmen angled for their rural customers' continued trade by emphasizing friendly service and good prices. Grocer David Bevan advertised that he had once been employed by "millers, farmers, &c in selling of flour" and therefore "waggoners from the country [who] are frequently at a loss" because they didn't know city merchants should feel at ease placing their trust in him.[83] Eldredge once sent Rex his bill for dry goods, declaring, "Hope they will prove to satisfaction as they are charged at the most reduced prices and well selected. You say you will be down in two weeks, I must wait patiently till you come and then will give you the best bargains."[84] Godfrey Baker sent a wagon to Schaefferstown loaded with £20 worth of goods and stressed his reasonable terms. "By the bearer we send you all the articles you want and at the old prices. The coffee mills have got higher in the prices. John Friend charged his but a week ago for no. 4 [size] 5/9."[85]

The rural-urban trade was so important that city merchants paid to improve the highways leading into the city. For years the deplorable condition of some roads impeded rural residents from trading in Philadelphia. North of the city, great stores that served as exchange centers, such as the one operated by Rex's father, were necessary because the abominable condition of Germantown Road (a dirt road that was impassable in poor weather) prevented farmers from continuing even ten more miles into the city to sell their produce.[86] In 1792 merchants from Philadelphia and Lancaster joined forces and lobbied for a new turnpike to connect those two cities; five businessmen from each place formed a commission to oversee construction. When completed, the highway was the best road in the nation—a physical link between city and countryside and a material acknowledgment of how crucial that heavily traveled road was to inland commerce and the national economy.[87]

Philadelphia was clearly the city of choice for Rex when it came to buying goods to please his customers, and he rarely bought from merchants elsewhere. In October 1793, when yellow fever broke out in Philadelphia, Rex went to Wilmington, Delaware, for supplies.[88] Wilmington must have been a poor substitute for Philadelphia in Rex's view, however; even though the fever returned to Philadelphia for the next five years, subsequent epidemics did not keep Rex away. His only other out-of-state purchase came on December 20, 1803, when he credited Benjamin Newman £1 15s.10d. for hauling fourteen bushels of salt from Baltimore.[89] Apart from these isolated instances and the goods he bought from Lancaster firms and local craftsmen, Rex relied on Philadelphia businesses for his inventory, and he traveled there at least fifty times over his sixteen years in business. He typically planned trips to the city in May and November when the shipments of the latest goods were arriving and the selection was at its peak, but occasionally the schedule varied. His contacts in Philadelphia apprised him of the best time to come. On April 30, 1800, Eldredge wrote to Rex, "There are several vessels arrived with Indian goods and one from Liverpool with English. The rest may be expected in about 2 weeks and they will probably be discharged in about ten days after arrival. I think if you are here about the first of June you will get a good assortment of goods."[90] Likewise, on September 24, 1801, merchant John Cooke sent a letter to inform Rex that the fall vessels had arrived with a "complete assortment of goods suitable to the present and approaching season."[91] Rex also went for shorter periods throughout the year on other business. Including travel time, he usually spent about ten days out of the store on a major buying trip; between personal visits he sent carters to Philadelphia to deliver goods and do errands for him.

Over the course of his career Rex patronized more than 250 Philadelphia businesses, including auction houses; he also sometimes bought goods on the wharves.[92] At the same time, he maintained a regular relationship with one or two city merchants who served as his regular agents. These men were Rex's closest link to the market; when he could not come to Philadelphia to do business for himself, they acted on his behalf.[93] Rex dealt with several agents in the early years of his business, but after 1796 he relied on Martin Dubs or the firm of Dubs & Earl.[94] Rex used his agents exclusively to buy, or broker sales of, country produce as well as to furnish him with some—but not all—of the goods he bought in the city. In addition to having an agent who dealt in provisions or wet goods (rum, molasses, coffee, and other imported liquor and groceries), from 1797 on Rex used Samuel Eldredge, who specialized in dry goods. Eldredge supplied a large portion of Rex's textile needs and occasionally took commodity payments of bar iron, but since he did not deal in wet goods, Eldredge never bought or brokered Rex's farm produce.[95]

Rex's purchases in Philadelphia, like his sales in the store, increased dramatically as his business expanded, although surviving documents probably do not show the full extent of his dealings in the city. Typically between 30 and 40 percent of his annual expenditures went, in equal amounts, to a dry goods firm and a wet goods dealer. In 1791 Rex spent more than £782 at thirty-six stores; 19 percent of this amount (£147) went to Darroch and 18 percent (£144) to Thomas Bartow, who traded in dry goods. In 1798 he spent £3,365 at one hundred merchants and shopkeepers, and he made his largest purchases from Eldredge (16 percent of the total, or £550) and Dubs & Earl (14 percent, or £457). By his final year, 1806–7, Rex was winding down his business, but he still spent more than £1,621 at thirty-three businesses, with 21 percent (£342) going to Dubs and another 20 percent (£324) going to dry goods merchants Wistar & Cooke. If, as Doerflinger notes, dry goods merchants in the revolutionary era relied on a core group of customers who each spent between £75 and £250 annually, Rex, who purchased between £144 and £550 worth of dry goods each year from 1790 to 1807, was a valued customer indeed.[96]

Urban demand for country produce seemed insatiable, but Rex (and the farmers who supplied him) rose to the challenge. In 1791 he sold only £67 worth of produce in Philadelphia, but by 1799 he had increased his sales to more than £484. By 1803, his best year for produce sales, Rex sold more than £508 worth of farm goods to city merchants. Put in more concrete terms, over the course of sixteen years in business Rex sold more than thirty-one thousand pounds of butter in Philadelphia, an average of nearly one ton per year. As much as these sales netted Rex, they were not sufficient to pay for all his purchases, and, like his own customers, Rex paid cash for the balance of his bills. Table 6 shows Rex's known produce sales to his city agents.

Rex's transactions with the agents who received his country produce took several forms. Sometimes they simply accepted commodities as partial payment for merchandise that Rex bought from them. In May 1801 Dubs & Earl noted that they had received from Rex £250 18s. 2d. worth of produce and £132 8s. 10d. in cash as payment in full for his grocery purchases.[97] Alternatively, Dubs & Earl did not buy Rex's produce themselves but took it into their warehouse and then shopped around for a buyer, in effect acting as a commission agent for these domestic products in the same way some firms did for goods imported from Europe or the West Indies.[98] When Dubs & Earl served in this capacity,

Table 6 Rex's Produce Sales to Philadelphia Agents

Date	Purchaser	Product	Price	Annual Total
1791	Thomas Miller	837 lbs. butter 307 lbs. tallow 34 lbs. beeswax 515 lbs. pork 920 lbs. iron	£67 6s.	£67 6s.
May 16, 1792	Henry Darroch	31 lbs. beeswax	£3 2s.	
June 30, 1792	Henry Darroch	159 lbs. butter	£6 4s. 3d.	
September 5, 1792	Henry Darroch	2,232 lbs. iron	£34 17s. 4d.	
October 13, 1792	Henry Darroch	1,442 lbs. butter	£47 4s. 6d.	£91 8s. 1d.
May 15, 1793	Henry Darroch	954 lbs. butter 29 lbs. tallow 53 lbs. beeswax	£49 4s. 2d.	£49 4s. 2d.
April 25, 1795	Dubs & Marquedant	1,112 lbs. butter	£76 2d.	
June 4, 1795	Dubs & Marquedant	whiskey, butter, lard	£119 1s. 6d.	
August 29, 1795	William Clark	butter	£110 4s. 11d.	
November 6, 1795	John Martin	apple whiskey	£56 10s.	£361 16s. 7d.
May 4, 1796	Martin Dubs	butter, beeswax, lard, tallow, rye whiskey	£158 10s. 10d.	
November 2, 1796	Martin Dubs	1,999 lbs. butter	£94 19s. 11d.	£253 10s. 9d.
November 23, 1797	Martin Dubs	1,054 lbs. butter	£59 5s. 9d.	£59 5s. 9d.
March 17, 1798	Dubs & Earl	butter, beeswax, lard	£50 6s. 3d.	£50 6s. 3d
May 29, 1799	Dubs & Earl	483 lbs. lard 703 lbs. butter 291½ gals. whiskey	£127 2s. 11d.	
November 23, 1799	Dubs & Earl	3,480 lbs. butter	£219 17s. 7d.	£347 6d.
June 5, 1800	Dubs & Earl	lard and butter	£117 8s. 11d.	
June 28, 1800	Dubs & Earl	1,082 lbs. butter 73 lbs. beeswax	£87 10s. 4d.	

Date	Purchaser	Product	Price	Annual Total
December 4, 1800	Dubs & Earl	butter	£42 6s. 8d.	£247 5s. 11d.
May 21, 1801	Dubs & Earl	2,742 lbs. butter 272½ gals. whiskey 107 lbs. beeswax 49 lbs. lard	£250 18s. 2d.	
June 1801	Wm. Lane	5,584 lbs. iron	£123 14s.[1]	£374 12s. 2d.
May 22, 1802	Martin Dubs	sundry produce	£237 17s. 6d.	
July 29, 1802	Martin Dubs	3,458 lbs. butter	£129 13s. 5d.	
November 25, 1802	Martin Dubs	5,034 lbs. butter	£188 15s. 9d.	£556. 6s. 8d.
May 20, 1803	Martin Dubs	sundries	£293 12s. 7d.	
November 1803	Martin Dubs	4,688 lbs. butter	£214 17s. 6d.	£508 10s. 1d.
May 2, 1804		2,775 lbs. butter 518 gals. whiskey	£216 18s. 9d. £116 2s.	£333 9d.
Totals		Butter: >31,499 lbs. Beeswax: >298 lbs. Tallow: >336 lbs. Lard: >532 lbs. Pork: >515 lbs. Iron: 8,736 lbs. Whiskey: >1,082 gals.	£3,299 13s. 8d.	£3,299 13s. 8d.

1. Lane gave the total price in dollars and cents ($280.86) but quoted the price per ton as £42 5s.

Rex still maintained a measure of control. In 1803 and 1804, when pork prices fell and Rex could not sell fresh meat profitably, he preserved it in barrels and shipped it to Dubs & Earl to store until the market improved. Also, Rex could stipulate a minimum price he needed for his goods; in October 1802 Dubs & Earl wrote to Rex that they had received his four casks of apple whiskey, "which we will endeavour to sell at the price limit enclosed."[99]

Rex's agents also advised him about current prices, the availability of merchandise, and the latest business and social news. In mid-May 1800 Eldredge wrote that there had been a few arrivals from Europe, but they were "not sufficient to make the assortment good."[100] In September 1802 Martin Dubs wrote with prices but ended on a somber note: "Country rum is now worth 70 cents, rice six dollars, butter very dull at 10 cents a pound. The fever we cannot say is very bad though the accounts of the board of health since Monday last are more alarming than any time previous through to this season, from eight to ten new cases have been reported in twenty-four hours and from 6 to 7 deaths. We are all in very good health and no fever in our neighborhood as yet."[101]

In addition, agents sought out special orders, provided warehousing, and shipped goods to Rex. In July 1798 Dubs & Earl sent a load of merchandise to Schaefferstown that included tobacco they obtained for Rex from Conrad Beates and explained that were still holding salt because there was not enough space in the wagon.[102] In July 1799 Eldredge wrote that he was sending Rex the thickset, ferret, and velvet binding he wanted, but he could not find any flannel, though he had tried "at all the stores in Market Street."[103] The agents helped Rex find the best buys and cooperated with each other in delivering goods. In March 1801 Dubs & Earl informed Rex that they had sent a small hogshead of sugar instead of the three barrels he ordered ("we thought it cheaper & hope you will think so also") and explained that the shipment also included goods that Eldredge had forwarded to their shop for Rex.[104]

For his part, Rex benefited from having reliable Philadelphia contacts to sell his produce, send him accurate information, and advise him about prospective business partners. It was advantageous to have Eldredge or Dubs search the city stores and wharves for his particular needs when he could not do it himself, and safely store his purchases until he picked them up. And rather than peddle his own farm produce in the city, Rex found it expedient to give the products to an agent who would take the entire delivery and who had the business knowledge to sell it at the best price. When Abraham Rex took over the store, he sent each of his adult sons to Philadelphia for a time to be his agent; in the absence of a reliable family member, Samuel Rex used the next best thing: trusted business associates.

Some historians theorize that businessmen in early America preferred to deal with members of their own ethnic or religious groups rather than outsiders, but these factors had little influence on Rex.[105] He was motivated more by pragmatism and sound fiscal practices than by loyalty to friends, ethnic ties, or long-standing business partners. Knowing the Pennsylvania German language and culture was a plus for him in Schaefferstown, but this knowledge was irrelevant in the city. There were Germans among his contacts, to be sure; a few businessmen even signed their bills in German script. But other businessmen Rex patronized, including his agents, varied in religion and national origin. It was the common language of business rather than German language or cultural concerns that linked Rex to his city trading partners. In addition, using a variety of stores and shops, besides his agents, gave Rex what Doerflinger describes as flexibility and leverage in the city market.[106] As an astute and aspiring "merchant," Rex learned much by doing his own shopping, visiting the stores and auctions to view the selection, meeting his urban counterparts, and assessing the business scene personally. Moreover, although his agents were knowledgeable about their merchandise and the city market, Rex knew best what would appeal to his customers.

Even more than in the countryside, doing business in the city meant combining traditional personal relationships with impersonal financial practices. By trading with a wide variety of partners, Rex found what he needed at a good price, but this pattern brought him into contact with more businessmen, some of whom he barely knew, than if he had limited himself to a small, closely connected network. Although city merchants formed ongoing relationships with some clients, they were attuned even more than Rex to the dictates of the market. This difference is apparent in the financial terms stipulated by city merchants. Back in his country store, Rex allowed most customers at least twelve months to pay bills, but city businessmen preferred a shorter cycle. Merchants encouraged prompt cash payments by quoting prices that included interest and then discounting the bill by 2 to 5 percent for early payment (see Richard Wistar invoice, fig. 19).[107] Early in his career, when he was short of ready cash, Rex often bought on credit. As the years went by, however, it seems that he was more likely to pay cash, either the same day or a few days later when he picked up the shipment, so he could avoid a penalty and also shop at establishments such as auction houses, where he could get better prices but could not buy on credit.[108]

City merchants were also quicker than Rex to dun clients who did not pay on time. Merchants needed to be paid promptly so they could meet their own obligations, yet at the same time they were sensitive to their customers' plights. During Rex's first year in business, one city merchant pushed him for prompt payment. On April 13, 1791, Thomas Miller sent a reminder to Rex that he still owed money for his purchases the previous year: "I should thank you for the remainder of balance as soon as you can, as I am very much in want of cash at present; the balance is £59. 15. 9., a considerable part thereof above 4 months standing (instead of two months which is the usual credit on groceries)."[109] Rex bought the groceries on December 11, 1790, so Miller waited only two days past the four-month deadline to call in the debt. Although he badly needed the money, Miller was cordial and sympathetic. He recognized that Rex had to buy

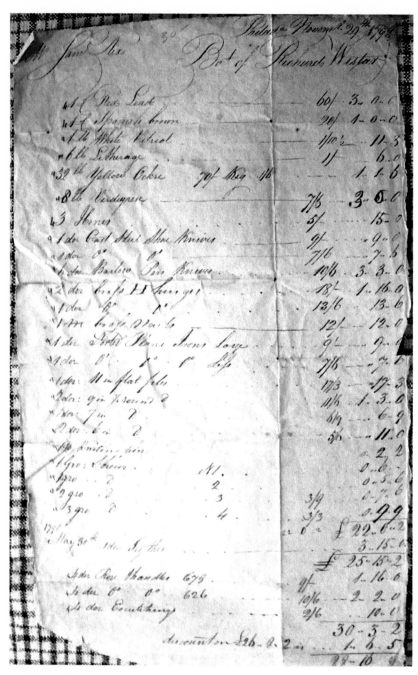

FIG. 19. Richard Wistar Invoice, Philadelphia, November 29, 1798. This invoice for hardware and tools shows that Wistar discounted a portion of Rex's bill. Photo by author. Used by permission of Historic Schaefferstown, Inc.

stock to keep his business running. To be sure, if Rex went bankrupt, Miller might never be paid, but Miller must have considered Rex a good risk, because he continued to trust him. At the same time that Miller sent Rex his bill, he shipped the additional merchandise, worth £11 6s. 6d., that Rex had ordered.

In some cases Rex enjoyed some of the close personal associations with city contacts that international wholesalers had been cultivating for generations. Clerk William Schlatter, writing to Rex on behalf of Eldredge about an order for goods, added a friendly postscript concerning Rex's family: "N.B. All the people at Ches[t]nut Hill are well."[110] When Eldredge wrote to Rex of his anticipated arrival in Womelsdorf, he invited Rex to come "pass the evening with me . . . should be happy to see you."[111] Even if a warm friendship did not result from such meetings, they were the equivalent of city merchants' coffee-house gatherings and would have helped Rex stay abreast of market developments and enabled Eldredge to gauge the needs of his country client. Quaker merchant Benedict Dorsey Jr. also had a closer-than-usual relationship with Rex, perhaps because of a tie through marriage to Schaefferstown. In 1795, when Dorsey sent Rex a bill for whale oil and gunpowder, he added the personal note that "Peggy would have been glad to have heard how her mother was and sends her love to her and you all."[112] Though details of Dorsey's precise link to the town are unknown, his letter, like Schlatter's, is one more indication of the network of business and personal ties that connected the disparate locales.

The absence of personal contact, or anonymity in business relations, was correspondingly detrimental. At times boxes of window glass arrived with "much broke," shipments came only partially filled, or fees were unjustly assessed for wagon loading. These disagreements were usually settled amicably, but Rex kept a careful eye on the goods and bills that he received, and he did not hesitate to point out errors. In December 1797 Richard Wistar sent Rex a replacement keg of oil and an apology. "I am sorry for the mistake of the other as I had no more of that kind and had to purchase it, but still I hope there will be no [illegible] attending it." Though the apology was sincere enough, Rex may have been piqued anew by the way the letter was addressed—to "Samuel Rex, Jonestown," an error that surely did not flatter him and displayed a decided lack of personal knowledge and attention.[113]

Although there were profound differences in their physical locations and variations in their handling of customers' accounts, Rex and the city merchants shared some common ground. As Miller's letter reveals, traders, whether international or domestic, country storekeepers, city agents, or export merchants, lived difficult—even "nerve racking"—lives.[114] Both Rex and his city contacts could be caught short of cash; they had to keep a sharp eye on their profits, maintain accurate books, and pursue delinquent customers. They were at the mercy of the vagaries of the economy and possibly unreliable business partners; they risked lawsuits and damage to their reputations if business deals went bad; and they were all subject to demands of creditors. City and country dealers alike had to be shrewd judges of customers and of goods; they had to be familiar with the different currencies that crossed their counters; and all needed reliable contacts in different locations. In transporting valuable cargoes long distances through dangerous passages, Rex also mirrored city traders. He used farm wagons, not seagoing vessels, and he imported and exported goods to and from the countryside, not from a foreign port, but he relied on the carters in the same way merchants relied on their captains, and he used his agents as merchants did supercargoes and delegates in distant cities. Moreover, dealings between Rex and his urban contacts were mutually beneficial. Just as Rex needed his city contacts, they needed him. They counted on Rex to buy quantities of goods regularly and pay for them promptly, and bring quality produce. In fact, when city businessmen assessed one another's creditworthiness, having good business contacts in the countryside was a crucial positive factor.[115]

Though Rex was only one of many country storekeepers doing business in Philadelphia, his sales and purchases there were significant. He did not wield the same authority in Philadelphia that he did in Schaefferstown or make associations with men of similar interests as close as those with the men at the iron furnaces, but the level of business he brought to the city and his good standing earned him a favorable reputation and the city merchants' respect.

Schaefferstown, the iron plantations, and Philadelphia were separated by geography as well as by significant economic and cultural differences. Nevertheless, Rex bridged the gap for residents of the three locales. He and his contacts inland and in the seaport formed a network that connected urban and rural consumers and producers and moved goods, currency, credit, and information from place to place. At the Rex store, Schaefferstown residents found Bohea tea and the proper vessels in which to serve it. Farmers and tradesmen bought the tools and raw materials they needed, along with imported textiles to dress themselves and their homes in style. After shopping at the Rex store, rural innkeepers could offer their patrons punch in enameled bowls and West Indian rum in double flint tumblers. Through deals brokered at the store, pork raised by Schaefferstown farmers fed ironworkers and city residents through the winter;

country iron supplied city forges; Schaefferstown whiskey fueled debates in Philadelphia taverns; and butter churned by Schaefferstown women arrived in city dining rooms and made its way (in country-made barrels) onto vessels bound for Europe.

But keeping a country store and managing a complicated network of relations was trying, and the effort was enough to exhaust even the most energetic and entrepreneurial man. After sixteen years of riding between the city and countryside in all weather, hauling hogsheads of whiskey and tubs of butter, and inspecting herds of swine, Rex was ready for a change. The next chapter follows Rex as he relinquishes his business to a new generation of storekeepers and begins life as a gentleman farmer in Schaefferstown.

CHAPTER FIVE

························

A LIFE OF "COMPARATIVE EASE"

IN MAY 1807 SAMUEL AND ABRAHAM REX took an inventory of Samuel's store. The resulting list, completed on June 1, was ten pages long, and the grand total of the goods came to £677 19s. 7½d.[1] The enumeration marked the end of an era for Samuel Rex and the beginning of a new one for his younger brother. Earlier in the month Abraham had left the tavern-store he had rented for the previous five years at Mount Pleasant, Pennsylvania, to take over at Schaefferstown. He sent two wagonloads of household goods ahead to Schaefferstown, then packed the rest of his goods and settled his wife and their two young children in the rooms above the store.[2] He made his first sale—a silk handkerchief to Squire Joseph Long—on May 20; by June 1 the brothers had signed a formal agreement and the transfer was final.

A local historian described Samuel Rex as living in "comparative ease" after he left the store, but Rex did not retire to a life of leisure.[3] He stayed involved in business, political, legal, banking, and religious affairs, and he seized new opportunities in the same entrepreneurial spirit with which he had run the store, but the focus and geographic scope of his interests changed.

From Storekeeper to Gentleman Farmer

Sometime before he sold the store, Samuel Rex and his wife, Mary, moved across the street into the former Gemberling-Boyer tavern and made it their private home. Because it was located prominently on the town square, the building was a convenient spot from which to observe the goings-on at the busy intersection, and living here enabled Rex to stay actively involved in village commerce even after giving up the store. For a few months after the sale was final, he still sold (whether at the store or from his home is not clear) sundry merchandise he had kept from the store inventory. By the fall of 1807 he had disposed of the last of the store goods, and thereafter he concentrated on investments, marketing farm crops, and conducting financial and legal services. Continuing to meld his commercial activities and personal transactions, Rex kept track of these ventures in the same books he had used as a storekeeper. Only the diminished number of transactions and their altered focus indicate the change.

Rex's commercial endeavors after selling the store offer a contrast to the New England model, in which country storekeepers used a "putting-out" system to supply component parts to customers who made hats and shoes in their homes. Over time, the putting-out system gave way to industrialized factories, the demise of individual artisan shops, and eventually a new class and social structure.[4] Less frequently emphasized than the rise of factories, in part because some historians have depicted industrialization as a teleological process, is the continuing importance of commercial agriculture in the early nation.[5] Rex's activities demonstrate the farming alternative; after leaving the store, rather than encourage manufacturing or the putting-out system (setting up nail smith John Sweitzer and others like him in small factories), he became a gentleman farmer. Rex hired wage laborers to work his fields, bought plantations that he rented to tenants, and supervised the growing of cash crops by improved agricultural methods.[6] At the same time, Rex pulled back from his former network of relations. He was still active in the local community, and he maintained close friendships with a few furnace managers. He even sold produce to the ironmasters on occasion, but he virtually severed his Philadelphia ties and concentrated solely on local transactions.

Rex built up his property holdings gradually. His earliest purchases were small pieces of land in and around Schaefferstown. Some were vacant town lots where he grew vegetables and fruit and pastured livestock; two of the parcels included houses that he rented out. Still others were "outlots," two-and-one-half-acre tracts on the edge of town used by town residents for gardens. In 1812 Rex began to buy farms. In partnership with Abraham, he acquired Henry Mock's 140-acre plantation, known as the Auburn Farm, near Schaefferstown.[7] In 1821 he bought George Hocker's 107-acre farm in Lebanon Township at a sheriff's sale.[8] At some point he purchased the "Koble Farm" in Berks County and the

"Swatara Farm." By the time he died, Rex owned a dozen town lots and out-lots and 350 acres of farmland.[9]

Rex's tenants paid their rent with a portion of their grain crops, and this provided Rex with his largest source of agricultural income. From 1812 to 1823 Rex's average share of the annual harvest from Auburn Farm was 190 bushels of grain. Toward the end of his life, when his health forced him to cut back on his activities, he took the rent in cash rather than crops.[10] As an "improving farmer," Rex was typical of many men of the era who sought new ways to in-crease farm yields.[11] He purchased dung by the wagonload from neighbors to fertilize his fields, dispatched carters to Philadelphia for plaster of paris (also used as a fertilizer), and encouraged his tenants to sow clover seed to nourish depleted soil.[12] Some agricultural improvers were theorists with little practical experience, but Rex enjoyed working the land himself. He jotted notes in his daybook about his crops and livestock, carefully listed the varieties of apples in his orchard, and recorded how many rows of each type of vegetable he sowed in his garden. He grazed cattle, horses, and sheep on his farms, had his hogs butchered in the fall, and recorded in his daybook the dates he hung the ham and bacon in his backyard smokehouse each March.

As he shifted his business interests, Rex continued to look both to traditional community networks and to distant markets and a money economy. He allowed his neighbors ample time to pay for the products and services he sold, but he also maintained a businesslike posture, as when, in August 1819, he credited "Jacob Garrett by five loads dung to be paid in pasture for his cows at the rate of one load for a month pasture." He used a monetary calculus to record the value of the deals he logged in his daybooks and transacted at least some sales at rates linked to the regional market. Peter Moore bought twenty-five bushels of rye from Rex in August 1811, "to be [paid at] the rising price." In July 1813, when Anthony Kapp bought fifty-eight bushels of barley, Rex specified "the price to be what barley may be about Christmas."[13]

Although he priced goods at market rates, in retirement Rex and his neigh-bors were part of a reciprocal economy in which they exchanged goods and services with the understanding that they would be returned in kind without interest.[14] Rex and Peter Sheetz Jr. often "loaned" each other cuts of veal after butchering a calf so that they could enjoy fresh meat more frequently. In Decem-ber 1814 Nicholas Swanger borrowed a pair of spectacles from Rex; in Novem-ber 1816 Joseph Shenk borrowed a thousand hinged shingles; and in June 1820 Jacob Snyder, Rex's tenant on the Mock Farm, borrowed three bushels of wheat.

In each case the borrower returned or replaced the item a few months later. While such exchanges exemplify a spirit of mutuality, Rex still kept careful records of the loans in his daybook.

But the local network did not operate independently from the outside world. When external forces affected the price of agricultural products, Rex charged interest on a commodity loan. As a result of unusual weather conditions (a killing frost every month in "the year without a summer," 1816) and the political and economic repercussions of the War of 1812, farm prices rose sharply from 1816 to 1817, only to drop precipitously during the Panic of 1819.[15] Thus, in May 1817, when Joseph Shenk approached Rex to "borrow" three bushels of buckwheat, Rex agreed but charged Shenk interest. He stipulated that Shenk return "four and a half bushels of the same," apparently as compensation for the price he could have obtained by selling the grain for cash in the strong market.[16]

By contrast, Rex's hiring of farm and household laborers underscores the pace of the rural economy and its dependence on agricultural cycles. Each year Rex engaged a young man to work during the peak farm season, from April to December. In 1813, for example, he "hired Peter Houser for 8 months from the first day of April at $5 per month." Periodically he took on day laborers to haul dung and do other farm chores. During busy times he assembled a crew of relatives and neighbors to help in his fields; in June 1814 he recorded the work done by a dozen "sundry persons in haymaking and harvest." Despite his businesslike records of the amount he owed the workers, Rex maintained the longer payment periods typical of country transactions; in fact, he was almost as slow to pay workers' wages as his customers had been to pay their store bills. On January 11, 1815, he credited "Henry Desinger by 10 days threshing" £2 5s. and paid him 15s. on account. It was not until more than two months later, on March 23, that Rex "paid him in full £1 10s."[17]

Though Rex scaled back his long-distance contacts, his sales of farm produce placed him at the center of the local economy, and the deals he made for this produce demonstrate how local networks outside the country store functioned. Local innkeepers bought meat, whiskey, cider, oats, and hay from Rex. Brewer Anthony Kapp bought grain to make the beer that he sold at Abraham Rex's store. Samuel also sold produce at Abraham's store, and he used farm produce to pay local debts.[18] In a particularly apt exchange, Rex used grain to pay local weavers for the tow and flax linen they sold him for his grain sacks.[19] Rex also was active in the regional flour trade. Sometimes he sold part of his wheat crop to a local miller; other times he had the grain milled into flour and sold the flour locally or regionally. Alternatively, local men bought wheat from Rex and arranged with him to send it directly to the mill for grinding into flour. Figure 20 lists the produce that Rex bought and sold after leaving the store.

Rex continued to make loans in varying amounts to community residents. Some were quite small; he gave Ludwig Howser 7s. 6d. to buy four shad, and he lent Joseph Long two dollars "for his wife to go to her Father's."[20] But he also made loans as large as $1,200; in fact, 10 percent of the 120 loans in his books in 1834 were for $800 or more.[21] On most loans Rex added 6 percent annual interest, but he did not charge interest to family and close friends. Rex never charged interest to his brother Abraham, who always repaid promptly

Sold	Bought
ashes	ashes
barley	barley (for sowing)
beef	calf skins
boiled oil	chestnut rails
buckwheat	clover seed
butter, lard, flour *	dung
cabbage	heifers and steers
calves	hogs
clover seed	lime
cider	a mare
cider oil	plaster
flaxseed	rye and rye straw
flour	sole leather
hams and bacon	veal
hay	wool
horse	
Indian corn	
oats	
pasture for a cow	
potatoes	
rye and rye straw	
timothy seed; timothy hay	
use of a horse	
veal	
vinegar	
wheat (red and white)	
whiskey, apple and rye	
wood	

FIG. 20. Farm Produce Sold and Purchased by Samuel Rex, 1807–1835. After retiring from storekeeping, Rex dealt in a number of agricultural products, including the grain that his tenants returned to him as part of their farm rent.

and who could be counted on to return the favor if Samuel needed cash. Nor did he charge any interest on the sizable loans he made to his brother-in-law, Michael Valentine. In Valentine's case, Rex may have concluded that adding interest was a pointless bookkeeping exercise, since Valentine was struggling financially and could not repay even the principal.

Fortunately for Rex's debtors, he charged simple, not compound, interest, but since the debts ran on for years, even simple interest mounted up and added to Rex's bottom line and his debtors' discomfort. Christian Garret's note of hand for £9 rose to £14 in eight and a half years, and Jacob Gass saw the amount of his debt to Rex more than double, from $266 to $602, in the twenty-one years he deferred paying it.[22]

Rex also continued his legal work; he prepared deeds, assessed household inventories, settled estates, and rode to the courthouse to "prove" wills. While much of the work was fairly straightforward, serving as the executor of an estate was a time-consuming job that could mean years of work untangling debts, selling real estate and personal property at auction, buying the tombstone, paying the widow's dower, and tracking down beneficiaries. Rex charged a fee for his work and gained status from managing complicated cases, but such work also opened him to public scrutiny, and at least once his handling of an estate was questioned.

The amount of money Rex had out on loan rose steadily. Though he never recorded annual balances while running the store, as he got older and considered his mortality, he tried to put his affairs in order, and he began periodically to calculate his worth. In January 1830 he figured the amount of notes and bonds due to him at £12,122 (more than $32,245). Four years later, in January 1834, he calculated that the amount outstanding had risen to $38,040 (by this point Rex had changed from using pounds to dollars as his money of account), and by January 1835 he had $39,237 in outstanding loans.[23] Determining just what these amounts meant to Rex's overall wealth is complicated by the fact that he owed debts to other community residents, but Rex owed far less money to others than they owed him. When he drew up his will, he left instructions that Abraham retain just £450 ($1,202) from the estate to repay his debts.[24]

The Rex House: Living in Country Style

Clients who called on Rex in his home to borrow cash, buy grain, or have a will prepared would have seen visible evidence of his increasing prosperity and status in his possessions and the design elements of his home. Appropriately enough, while his house was impressive, it also displayed material evidence of his membership in two very different communities, the rural Pennsylvania German village and the more sophisticated business environment exemplified by Philadelphia.

When Rex bought the old Gemberling-Boyer tavern in 1798, the exterior plaster between the visible half-timbers was painted in a red and black checkerboard pattern resembling bricks. (According to the federal direct tax assessors, "front part is frame fill'd with brick and the back part of stone.") Though this exterior treatment seems quite gaudy today, Rex's house was not the only one of its kind. Theophile Cazenove wrote that the "best" houses in Kutztown, Pennsylvania, had "boards on the outside and are painted like bricks."[25] Sometime after 1799 (the actual date when the Heidelberg Township assessors documented the house for the direct tax mandated in 1798), Rex covered the exterior with wide clapboards that produced a more refined and less overtly Germanic effect.[26]

By the time Rex bought the tavern, it had undergone some rather radical changes. A previous owner or owners had enlarged the building both upward (by adding three courses of logs to the top of the exterior wall) and rearward by removing a rear wall and extending the parlor and kitchen space into a stone lean-to addition. At the same time, the owner changed the floor plan to a central-hall model and installed corner fireplaces topped with elegant fielded panels in the front and rear parlors.[27] (The rear parlor is pictured in fig. 21.) Although all this was done before Rex bought the place, he surely noticed and approved of the interior's similarity to homes he had seen in Philadelphia. The house, especially the dual parlors with their formal accoutrements, was an appropriate backdrop for him as he entertained clients and guests, and it reflected his status as a gentleman and former "merchant." The effect upon entering these rooms would have been one of elegance and sophistication; the door leading into the front parlor had a doorknob in the center, allowing guests, had they been so inclined, to enter the room with a gesture resembling a courtly bow.[28]

At the same time, these elements also reflect Rex's country connections. The woodwork appears to be the product of a local builder who was not entirely familiar with the genre but who did his best to interpret it with exuberance, perhaps from a verbal description or rough sketch. The result, as described by Charles Bergengren, "concatenates every manner of wavy dentil, sawtooth, keystone, and more" in the cornices and chair rails.[29] In addition, the elegantly

FIG. 21. Rear Parlor, Gemberling-Rex House. By the time Rex bought the former Gemberling Tavern, a previous owner had greatly enlarged and remodeled it. Renovations included removing the entire back wall of the *Fachwerk* building and expanding it with a stone
lean-to addition, creating space for the rear parlor, shown here. Photo by author, 2000.

paneled corner fireplace in the front parlor—its position indicates English influence—boasts a very Germanic feature: hinged doors closing the firebox (fig.
22). In the slightly off-center passage, an elaborately carved open stairway also
speaks of the German roots of its carver; it boosts an unsupported banister with
a wavelike pattern and cutwork end pieces, of which no two are alike (fig. 23).
In short, the house's remarkable interior became a metaphor for its owner's social
persona. Both blended elements of folk ethnicity and urban sophistication.[30]

Although Rex had no use for the tavern's bar cage (fig. 24), he did not remove it when he made the tavern his home. He may have used the bar area,
which provided the only interior access to the cellar, for storage and opted to
keep the grill in place since it admitted light. The door to the bar cage remains
in the rear parlor, but at some point the portion of the bar that extended into
the front parlor was removed; whether this was accomplished by Rex or another
occupant of the house is unknown. (In the twentieth century, the surviving bar

FIG. 22. Fireplace, Front Parlor, Gemberling-Rex House. As remodeled, the Gemberling-Rex House had corner fireplaces, a placement that is typically associated with English design, but the hinged doors closing the fireplace in the front parlor are a very Germanic feature. In Rex's day this room contained a corner cupboard that held his silver and ceramics. Photo by author, 2007.

FIG. 23. Stairway, Gemberling-Rex House. This elaborately carved stairway with its free-hanging railing is a product of the pre-1799 remodeling. The stairway is in the center hall and faces the rear of the building. Photo by author, 2007.

FIG. 24. Bar Cage, Rear Parlor, Gemberling-Rex House. The paneled and grilled bar surround in the rear parlor is the only remainder of the eighteenth-century bar cage; there are "ghosts" on the wall in the front parlor showing that the bar extended into this space at one time. Photo by author, 2007.

space was given a new purpose; owners converted it into a powder room accessible by a doorway cut in the central hall.)

Some of the Rexes' furnishings further suggest that the couple aspired to gentility. They owned china teaware and a tea tray, their floors were carpeted, and pictures and maps hung on their walls. As befitted a man of his stature in the community, Rex had not one but two tall clocks. A corner cupboard in the front parlor displayed Rex's valuable ceramics and silver.[31] The china and silver seem to have held special significance for Rex, as well as an association with the woman of the household, who would have presided over tea rituals. In his first will Rex left his wife three tea trays and the "corner cupboard in the front parlour with all my silver plate, china, glass and every other thing in the same." When he made a new will after Mary's death, he left some of his silver to Abraham's wife as a "token of remembrance." Even if the house was the scene of some sophisticated entertainment, including teas, it must have been crowded by today's standards. Rex's probate inventory hints that he retained much of the furniture from the time the building was a tavern. The eight-room house contained six beds, five bureaus, a case of drawers, ten dining tables, six looking glasses, forty-three chairs, two settees, and two desks.

Wielding Power, Surviving Scandals

Most of the legal and financial transactions Rex conducted were smooth and trouble free, as well as profitable, but on a few occasions his ethics came into question. Rex had the use of the deceased's money while he was settling an estate, and he sometimes made loans of those funds. In October 1812 he lent his brother Abraham $145 "of my own money" and "of Jacob Umbenhend's estate, $135." The following year he advanced Abraham £37 10s. "of P. Wolfebarger's money" and John Reydel £97 10s. 6d. from Umbenhend's estate. In November 1814 he lent Michael Valentine £37 10s. cash and noted "S. Rex took this money of Peter Wolfebarger's estate."[32] Rex recorded in his daybook when he lent out estate monies and when he paid himself a fee, so he could produce documentation if the disbursements were questioned. Still, lending out money to people who paid no interest (Abraham) and those who could not afford to repay it (Valentine) seems like a curious, unproductive, and, possibly even unethical way to carry out one's fiduciary responsibilities.[33]

Rex may have avoided litigation, but a late nineteenth-century writer claimed to have detected a whiff of impropriety about his settlement of Philip Erpff's estate. P. C. Croll, a local Lutheran minister and antiquarian, claimed in 1895 that Erpff and his wife intended to leave a legacy of £50 to their godchildren and the balance to the Lutheran church, but an "outsider interfered with the husband and either by an alteration in the will or crookedness in the estate's settlement the church was deprived of the intended legacy." Though Croll did not name names, it was Rex who drew up Erpff's will, and he and Michael Valentine were the executors. The two men were also beneficiaries of a portion of the estate, so the implication is clear.[34]

The circumstances surrounding Rex's rise to prosperity in Schaefferstown may have contributed to such uncharitable thoughts as Croll's. Considering the nine-year age difference between Rex and his wife, observers may well have wondered whether Rex married Mary for her family's local connections. The same question might be asked, with even better cause, about Abraham Rex, who, through marriage to Henry Schaeffer's daughter, became part of the town's most prominent family. Furthermore, both Rex brothers prospered in Schaefferstown, while their in-laws slid into poverty. Samuel's star ascended as surely as Michael Valentine's fortunes waned. He lent Valentine money, and he helped him and his son set up in a store in Myerstown, but the Valentines turned out to be poor managers. Michael Valentine died owing far more than his estate was worth, and his son went to debtor's prison.[35] A similar situation occurred with Abraham's in-laws. By 1815 Henry Schaeffer Jr. (Abraham's youngest brother-in-law) was bankrupt, and Abraham, along with John Bomberger, another brother-in-law, assumed control of Henry's properties, including the old Schaeffer hotel and the right to collect the town's ground rents.[36] While it does not appear from extant papers that Abraham precipitated his brother-in-law's misfortunes any more than Samuel caused the Valentines' problems, the parallels are too striking to ignore.

As befitted a leading citizen of the town, Samuel Rex was active in local politics after leaving the store, and here, too, a faint hint of scandal attended him. Though he never stood for office, his political involvement is evident in a letter written to him by a member of the Coleman family in October 1823: "I am convinced if Rex would take a little pains in refuting the calumnies in circulation against Gregg he could get them all to vote right." A postscript suggests that Rex assisted voters in getting to the polls: "Tell Rex that old Lou Matthews will go to the election if he can get a conveyence."[37] Correspondence from Rex's nephew Samuel Bockius reveals further that Rex may have offered not only transportation to the polls but a monetary incentive to vote for a particular candidate or attend a political event. Bockius strenuously denied starting a rumor that Rex "hired horses and wagons to convey people thither [to a county meeting at Lebanon] and . . . paid them 75 cents per day to go up." But he conceded that he heard one attendee say that Rex "kept him free from expenses" and that hiring wagons had cost Rex about $30.[38] If Rex did not actually bribe people, he probably pushed the boundaries of appropriate community behavior by rewarding their attendance at caucuses.

Mirroring the actions of city merchants who founded the Lancaster Turnpike, Rex was an active member of the Berks-Dauphin Turnpike Road Company. He was an original stockholder, and he served on the board of directors from 1816 to 1820. As a board member, he participated in decisions on the design of the new "artificial road" connecting Reading and Hummelstown, inspected the road as work progressed, and handled the company finances. Rex gained only modestly from this service; the road directors voted to pay themselves $2.50 a day for running the road and attending meetings.[39] But it was probably Rex who arranged for the board meetings to be held at Michael Valentine's tavern in Myerstown (where Valentine moved after Abraham Rex took over the store). The business meetings would have helped Valentine's trade and also benefited Rex because Valentine was so deeply in debt to him. If his rank and wealth had their privileges, Rex used them, but he sometimes invited criticism in the process.

On a more positive note, Rex was active in the town's Lutheran church, where he served as treasurer from 1810 to 1815.[40] He also contributed generously to the congregation. When the church building needed repairs, and when a petition circulated to supply the parson with a gift of oats, Rex topped the lists with one of the largest pledges.[41] In his will he left $200 to be invested and the proceeds used to pay the minister and schoolmaster an annual stipend, but he directed that this gift remain in effect only while Parson William Beates served the church. He also bequeathed an acre of land to the town's two churches to increase the size of their common cemetery, which by now was getting full.

It is relatively easy to reconstruct Rex's economic, political, and philanthropic activities through his business papers, but details about his personal life are more elusive. In contrast to the occasional irritation with customers that comes through in his daybooks, a few entries show Rex's sense of humor. Inside the cover of the daybook that he kept while he ran the store in his father-in-law's tavern, Rex penned the words, "January 28, 1794. A good morning to your nightcap."[42] Was this to gently chide his wife or brother-in-law for sleeping too late? And in April 1797 he recorded two sales to a customer whom he identified as "Doctor Kill or Cure."[43]

A biographer in 1904 claimed that Rex's "pleasant manner made him many friends, and although he left no issue, in affection he was known as 'Uncle' by a great many residents."[44] This glowing tribute should be accepted cautiously, given the tendency of writers in this era to praise important men lavishly, but it is true that Rex was literally "Uncle Sam" to a number of nieces and nephews who frequently stayed with him as houseguests. Everyday happenings such as relatives' visits usually go unrecorded unless something out of the ordinary took place. We know about these visits because of several unusual occurrences that also provide insight into life in the village and the Rex household. In 1822 teenaged Polly Valentine (Michael's daughter) was staying with the Rexes. Rex depicts Polly as a girl of some spunk, who, "still being up" at ten o'clock, "surprised a thief who entered the granery" and tried to steal a bag of grain.[45] A more tragic incident took place in 1827, when three-year-old Isaac Valentine (Michael's grandson) contracted a sudden, fatal respiratory ailment while staying with the Rexes. Rex's account of the death reveals his grief:

> I had hardly got into the house until he [Isaac] inquired whether I had any mint stick for him. The next morning . . . he went with me to Brother Abraham's Store where I bought a suit of Winter Cloathes for him, which he carried to Mr. Garret's the Taylors himself and after noon took a large button up which he had found, to be put to his cloathes and asked whether they were not made. About 8 o'clock he showed great simptons of shortness of breath. I went to the doctor's, got some medicine. . . . About 3 o'clock on Sunday morning he jumped out of his bed, ran across the room twice in great agony . . . at 10 o'clock (in the evening) breathed his last and left us. . . . His death has left my Family in great distress.[46]

Polly and Isaac were just two of many young people the Rexes hosted in the former inn; a steady stream of teenagers, some relatives, stayed with the couple while attending one of Schaefferstown's schools. In 1812 Rex recorded a charge to John Bricker of £2 "for boarding his son when at school," but mostly Rex seems to have housed the youngsters gratis and sometimes even paid their tuition.[47] Other relatives worked for Rex. A few weeks after he was widowed, Rex hired his niece Eliza Valentine to work as his housekeeper.[48] Abraham's son, Samuel S. Rex, helped his uncle by writing his letters when Rex's hand became "much debilitated" in his old age.[49]

Toward the end of his life Rex made small and large monetary gifts to nieces and nephews, and his notations of the gifts in his daybook provide more insight into the role Rex played in his family. In August 1833 he gave $20 to Franklin, another of Abraham's sons, toward his expenses "of studying medicine," and two months later he contributed $10 toward Franklin's costs of traveling to New York for further medical training. Tragically, Franklin died in a train wreck while on his way home from medical school graduation, and so Rex made another present in March 1834—$10 to Abraham "towards the expense for re-moving the corpse of his son Franklin S. Rex from Jersey to Germantown." In March 1835 Rex gave nieces Eliza Valentine and Ann Rex "pin or spending money" of $7 and $25, respectively, "for going to Germantown or Philadel-phia" shopping.[50] Though many of his gifts were relatively small, Rex was ex-traordinarily generous to Margaret Valentine Mace and Polly Valentine Bucher, who may have been more like daughters than nieces.[51] During his lifetime he gave each of them furnished houses to live in, and he made the gifts perma-nent in his will. When Michael Valentine died, rather than take the roughly £1,726 that Valentine owed him from the estate, which would have left noth-ing for Valentine's heirs and creditors, Rex requested that the administrator pay all other debts first and give Rex power of attorney over the rest. He then divided the remaining funds among Valentine's heirs, who otherwise would have re-ceived no inheritance.[52]

In addition to Michael Valentine's money problems, there were other fam-ily embarrassments. Rex quibbled with his brother Enoch over the bills Enoch submitted for the care of their elderly mother. He found John Bockius, his sister Catherine's husband, so unsatisfactory that in his will Rex directed his executor to invest Catherine's bequest and pay her the interest personally so that Bockius could never "claim or control" his wife's inheritance.[53]

The picture that emerges from Rex's community and family involvement is, like that of his business life, complex. He was generous, but he enjoyed power. Sometimes he used his power unwisely, and often his generosity came with strings attached, as with the gift to the church that benefited a favorite min-ister, or his wish to distribute the residue of Valentine's estate personally. Given his propensity to manage, what did Rex expect in return? Probably he wanted affection, since he had no children of his own on whom to lavish attention; but he also wanted respect and more than a small measure of control. His relatives knew that he had the power of the purse and that they would benefit by staying on good terms with him. This is evident in letters that a less-favored nephew, Samuel Bockius, wrote to Rex; Bockius apologized contritely for past misunderstandings and disagreements—and then requested a loan for payment of debts. Although Bockius wrote twice in wheedling tones, Rex declined to help him.[54]

It is even more challenging to glean information about Rex's wife, who, like most women in this era, is largely invisible in surviving papers. Benjamin Rush observed that more Pennsylvania German women could read than could write, and this may have been true of Mary Rex.[55] She could apparently read—once Rex sent her a letter from Philadelphia—but she left no letters or other documents behind, and in 1806 she signed a property deed with her mark.[56]

We do know from Rex's correspondence that Mary occasionally helped him even before they were married by tending the store when he was out of town.[57] She may have also tended the store after they were married; as noted in Chapter 2, one customer specifically asked for Mary's help in choosing thread to match her cloth purchase. The only surviving letter from Rex to Mary (sent from Philadelphia, November 12, 1801) shows that he also relied on her to help with the business by receiving and inventorying goods and paying the carters: "With Swanger, Deal & Lesher, you will receive three loads of goods. I have agreed with Lesher for his load for the sum of £3.5.0. which you will please to pay him, and of Swanger & Funk's load you will take note of what packages and kasks each had loaden as they were loaded in a hurry and I do not just recollect what each has loaded. I expect to be home by Sunday evening."[58] The household furnishings in Rex's probate inventory reveal the range of Mary's kitchen chores (making sausage, drying apples, baking bread, churning butter) and her work in textiles (quilting and spinning).[59] She very probably also sewed the linen sacks Rex used for grain, as he did not record paying a seamstress to do it.

Mary occasionally traveled well beyond Schaefferstown. The records of St. Michael's Church in Germantown show that Mary and Samuel were sponsors at the baptisms of a nephew in September 1802 and a niece in August 1807.[60] Mary may have ridden to Germantown with Samuel in his carriage on these occasions, and in his sleigh when they went out in winter, but the couple also owned a sidesaddle that she would have used to ride horseback.[61] We catch another brief glimpse of Mary in the doorway of her home, greeting a caller.

In March 1822 Rex noted in his daybook that John Hostetter came to pay his $145 debt and left the money with Mary because Rex was away.[62]

When Mary died, leaving Rex a "mournful widower," he felt the loss keenly. The final vignette of Mary Rex comes in a letter from Rex to his sister. He explained that Mary's fatal illness began with a splinter in her left thumb—the result of picking up kindling wood for the morning fire. The wound became infected and caused "intolerable pain." They consulted Mary's nephew, Dr. Christian Bucher, who prescribed poultices, but the infection led to a "bowel complaint," and two weeks later Mary was dead. Rex remembered her in her old age for her diligence and her beauty: "On the morning of her death, she went down into the kitchen for to look after her affairs . . . [but fainted and had to be carried to bed]. . . . I have seen many persons die but I have never seen any person die so easy without a struggle and when dead she was the hand-somest corpse I have ever seen for her age."[63]

Rex survived his wife by three years, but his own health was failing. In 1833 he wrote that his hand was crippled and that he was "afflicted with weakness in my feet and legs. . . . I do not walk much except in Town."[64] On May 6, 1835, nine days before his death, Rex made his last daybook entry, a mundane note, written in a shaky hand, about trading one of his cows to a drover.[65]

Rex's estate accounts show that he had done quite well for himself in his several careers. He left behind a house valued at $1,333, household goods assessed at $641, and $550 in cash.[66] Besides his farms and town properties, his invest-ments included stock in the Berks-Dauphin Turnpike and two shares in a wid-ow's dower. His outstanding notes, bonds, and interest-bearing loans totaled $36,336.[67] Altogether the estate was valued at $52,297 (or about £19,587).[68] Though this figure is far less than the estates of the great Philadelphia merchants, who were worth between £15,000 and £35,000 in the late eighteenth century, Rex was as well to do as a modest city merchant. Stuart Blumin's analysis of the 1860 Philadelphia census shows that 27.4 percent of merchants and other upper-level property holders had real and personal property worth more than $20,000. Even in 1835, Rex's estate, minus book debts, was worth $15,961.[69]

By the end of his life Rex had climbed to a position of prominence in Schaef-ferstown. If he tended to enjoy his power overmuch, this fault did not hurt his overall standing. Even though he was not native to the close-knit village, wielded considerable economic and political clout, and had supported the unpopular Federalist Party, he had become a solid member of the community, one who shared agricultural and business interests, as well as a German heritage, with other residents. The debts that he and his neighbors and friends incurred with each other were bonds of obligation that further strengthened their ties. And while the townspeople could plainly see that Rex profited from his various commercial activities, they also knew that he was generous to his family, community, and church. In short, in retirement as in storekeeping, Rex enjoyed the confidence of most local residents, who trusted him with their financial, religious, and legal matters and were willing to pay the prices he charged for these services.

A Tale of Two Stores

Like his brother, Abraham Rex drew on the family network to launch himself in business. In 1801 he came to Schaefferstown and clerked in Samuel's store for a time. In 1802 Abraham went out on his own; he leased Jacob Hagy's tavern, barn, and eighteen acres of land in Mount Pleasant, Cocalico Township, Lancaster County.[70] Mount Pleasant no longer appears on maps, but it was near Schoeneck, a hamlet about ten miles from Schaefferstown, where Abraham and his wife had their oldest children baptized.[71]

Samuel assisted Abraham in starting his business in several ways; he sold him store inventory, helped him purchase start-up goods in Philadelphia, and drew up the rental agreement with Hagy.[72] If some of his business practices seem haphazard by modern standards, Rex's legal documents were formal and meticulously detailed, and because he was an experienced storekeeper, Samuel was probably especially particular about this document. Under the lease agreement, Abraham purchased all of Hagy's inventory except the country produce he had on hand. Hagy agreed to more generous payment terms than would have been possible in the city: "the whet goods or groceries at three months and the dry goods at nine months credit." The lease further stipulated that if they could not agree on a price for the merchandise, two "good judges . . . one to be chosen by each of them" would arbitrate. Hagy was responsible for renovations to the building, including enlarging the shop, providing boards for shelves and a counter, and replacing the fence around the house and barn. He also agreed to leave behind his scales and weights, a ten-plate stove, the large table and benches in the tavern room, sufficient dung for the garden, and a half-acre of potatoes. In a clause that shows the Rex brothers' business acumen most clearly, the lease further stipulated that Hagy could not open a store or a tavern within five miles.

For his part, Abraham agreed to pay £45 annual rent and half the cost for the carpenters to install the shelves; he would also haul the wood for the fence, give security for the rent and store goods, and leave the premises in good order. Even such a comprehensive lease did not provide for every contingency. Abraham's ledger shows that he paid an additional £1 a year to rent the tavern clock that Hagy left behind.[73]

Having arranged for his store building, Abraham tapped into the network of customers and suppliers that Samuel already had in place. Some of the same customers who had shopped at Samuel's store now came to Abraham's, and the brothers bought goods from the same local and itinerant craftsmen. Like Samuel, Abraham brokered deals for supplies for the ironmasters. He bought pork from Mount Pleasant farmers and sold it to the Colemans for Elizabeth Furnace and to James Willson at Reading Furnace.[74] Ironworkers also shopped at Abraham's store as they traveled through the region, but Abraham did not have a regular arrangement with ironmasters for paying their workers. Abraham also benefited from Samuel's Philadelphia network; he bought goods from and sold produce to the same city firms Samuel had used.[75] The brothers also provided support for each other. When one of them ran out of an item, he bought it from the other, as when Abraham debited Samuel for three dozen crooked combs and five hundred cigars and credited him with twenty-five pounds of coffee.[76]

Abraham's operation in Mount Pleasant was different from Samuel's in only one major respect: Abraham was the proprietor of both a tavern and a store, while Samuel Rex and Michael Valentine ran the store and tavern in Schaefferstown separately. Apparently Abraham enjoyed both occupations, because when he came to Schaefferstown he took over both the store and tavern within the former Schaeffer hotel. He ran both businesses until 1815, when he turned the entire operation over to his brother-in-law, Henry Schaeffer Jr.[77] Abraham did not move far, however. Appropriately enough, in 1814 he purchased the old Frederick Stump/Henry Valentine/Samuel Rex property on the southwest corner of the square and hired local workers to erect a grand new building on the site where his brother had first operated his store.[78]

Abraham did not keep a separate list of his building expenses; rather, he entered occasional payments to workmen in his store daybook. By September 1815 the new building was nearly finished; Abraham credited George Albright by "sundry smith work and locks for the new house" and mason John Smith for two days' work at the kitchen (porch?) and by "smearing" the window cases.[79] The new store was a two-story limestone Georgian building (partially visible in figure 5). Its main block was 44 × 38 feet (making it even larger than the Schaeffer hotel), and it had an integral ell extending another thirty-two feet to the rear of the building, along Main Street. With the sales area below and living space on the second floor (space that they would not have to share with guests, since he was not running an inn), it was a fitting venue for his expanding business and growing family, for he and Elizabeth were expecting their fourth child.[80]

As time went on Abraham added new features to his operation. Customers could deposit cloth at the store and have it picked up by fuller Michael Shepler, who washed and custom-dyed it.[81] With the completion of the Union Canal in 1828, Abraham found a cheaper and faster method of transportation than an overland trip with Conestoga wagons. In May 1828 he sent ten barrels of flour and two kegs of lard to Peter Schoch's store in Newmanstown "to be taken to Philadelphia on the canal." In May 1833 he instructed his son Abraham Jr., who was on a buying trip in Philadelphia, that he should hire a carter or have "our goods sent to the canal and forwarded with Miller's or Boslar's boat."[82]

Changes in financial institutions also affected Abraham. As more and more state and local banks emerged, well-to-do individuals such as the Rexes were no longer the sole source of local credit and loans. As a leading businessman of the community, Abraham became a founding board member of the Lebanon Bank in 1831.[83] But improvements brought new problems. With the increasing number of banks, Abraham saw a corresponding rise in paper currency drawn on regional institutions. This change brought with it the unpleasant possibility of receiving a bogus bill, something with which Samuel never had to contend. In May 1809 Abraham returned a bank note to Christian Hearnly of Indiantown, "being $5 on the Bank of Massachusetts. Doubtful of its being a counterf[ei]t."[84]

The Next Generation

Abraham's sons, Samuel Schaeffer (known as Samuel S. or S.S.) and Abraham Jr., were active in the family business; they worked in the store and made extended buying trips to Philadelphia for their father. In 1828 and 1829 Abraham Jr. spent a few months in Philadelphia going to school, but his father soon called him back in the belief that book learning was no substitute for practical experience in the store. By 1833 the young men were running their own store in Brickerville, a crossroads settlement seven miles south of Schaefferstown, not far from Elizabeth Furnace. Following the family tradition, they did a considerable trade with the furnace and even kept a separate ledger to record their sales there. In 1834 they bought out their father and took over the Schaefferstown store.[85] (When his sons assumed ownership of the business, Abraham moved his family out of the store building. He purchased the old Philip Erpff house on Market Street, a block south of the town square, and, as his brother had done before him, made a former tavern into his private home.)[86]

For the younger generation of Rexes, business changed even more dramatically as they expanded the store's services and worked actively to bring more commerce to their small village. They continued the practice of buying butter locally and selling it in Philadelphia, but they used the services of Lebanon resident John Ermentrout, who packed their butter professionally and sold it as far away as Boston.[87] Abraham Jr. and Samuel S. were also drawn to new manufacturing schemes. They flirted with the idea of establishing a silk industry in Schaefferstown and planted fifteen hundred mulberry trees that they guessed would support "probably a million" worms. The younger Rexes longed for an even faster means of sending their goods to market than the canal, and they lobbied to bring railroad lines through their village. They were dismayed when silk worms failed to thrive in the Pennsylvania climate and the rail companies chose Lebanon, not Schaefferstown, for the main depot.[88]

In 1839 the two brothers sold the store inventory to their former clerk, William M. Weigley, who two years later married their sister Anna.[89] Within a decade the store building itself came under Weigley's control when Abraham Sr. gave the property to Anna as a reward for "natural love and affection."[90] Like Samuel Rex's store in an earlier era, the Weigley store also had a competitor across the town square. In 1847 George F. Miller, who had previously clerked for Abraham Rex Sr., built a large limestone store on the southeast side of the square and moved his store business there. Miller's clerk, Joseph S. Lauser, purchased the business sometime around 1850, and he operated the store for the next fifty years (fig. 25).[91]

There was ample room for two stores in the village, however, and Weigley, who was as ambitious as his brothers-in-law, prospered. He opened two additional stores in nearby towns, and he purchased the Locust Grove flour mill, just south of Schaefferstown, in the hamlet of Waldeck. These ventures were successful enough to allow him to retire from storekeeping in 1856 at the age of thirty-eight. When the Panic of 1857 wiped out Weigley's investments, he returned to

FIG. 25. J. S. Lauser's Store, Market Square, c. 1880. George F. Miller built the store building in 1847, and Miller's former clerk, Joseph Lauser, took over the store in the 1850s. It operated as a store until the 1950s. Photo courtesy of Historic Schaefferstown, Inc.

business and, according to an admiring biographer, "retrieved his fortunes and again placed himself in the enjoyment of a comfortable independence."[92]

Weigley signaled the rise in his fortunes in his choice of housing. In 1875 he hired a Philadelphia architect to design a large Gothic-style brownstone mansion to be built on the vacant land behind the store but facing Main Street. The plans for the mansion were so impressive that *Godey's Lady's Book and Magazine* ran a short article on the "suburban residence" even before it was completed (fig. 26).[93] Erected at a cost of $30,000 and built with stones from Weigley's own quarry, the mansion boasted black marble fireplaces inside and an ornamental fountain on the lawn. Weigley's residence seems all the more ostentatious when compared to the old and venerable homes—both former inns and very much a part of the established village landscape—that Samuel and Abraham Rex occupied. His house contrasted dramatically with these and other older Germanic-style homes on Main and Market streets; if he wished, Weigley could literally look down on his neighbors from the lofty central tower of his home. The mansion showed plainly its owner's wish to set himself apart from and above other community residents, and it symbolized the changing business environment, and the increasingly impersonal relationship between the town storekeeper and his customers, that prevailed by the end of the nineteenth century.[94]

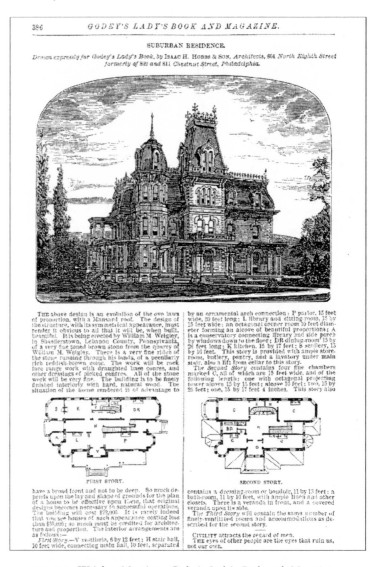

FIG. 26. Weigley Mansion, *Godey's Lady's Book and Magazine,* April 1875. Storekeeper William M. Weigley built his second empire brownstone home on Main Street just behind the store building his wife received from his father-in-law, Abraham Rex.

EPILOGUE:

REX'S NETWORK AND ITS SIGNIFICANCE

MODERN-DAY VISITORS TO SCHAEFFERSTOWN and the surrounding region find many reminders of the town's ethnic and commercial heritage and of Samuel Rex's network. Rex's home, the former Gemberling-Boyer tavern, remained in his family until 1974. Today it is known as the Gemberling-Rex House and operated as a museum by Historic Schaefferstown, Inc. Across the square the Franklin House continues to serve drinks and meals to locals and travelers, but it no longer rents out upstairs rooms to overnight guests. Other than the enormous arched cellar beneath the building where Rex and Valentine stored their perishables, there is little evidence left of the building's early use as a country store, but the old tavern is still a very busy place.

Across Main Street, the former Abraham Rex store remained a grocery store well into the twentieth century. Today it is an antique store whose owners continue the practice, common in earlier times, of living above their shop. Appropriately, Samuel and Abraham Rex would recognize not only this living arrangement but many of the objects in the first-floor sales space, although they would surely marvel at how their purposes have changed from utilitarian to decorative. Behind the former store, overlooking Main Street, the Weigley mansion remains an impressive suburban residence, and it is still a private home.

Numerous other buildings in the town date from Rex's day and earlier. The German Lutheran church, known since the early twentieth century as St. Luke Lutheran, was enlarged and its interior greatly altered in 1884, but the original configuration, built to demonstrate the solidarity of its loyal members in 1765, is clearly discernible. Although the interiors of most early houses have also been modernized over the years, the exteriors of these stone and log structures, with their small windows, center chimneys, and steep roofs, still exhibit a strong Germanic character and serve as a reminder of the village's Old World heritage. Extant buildings include several early stores and taverns besides Schaeffer's and Rex's establishments, including the former Erpff and Nathan stores on Market Street, as well as many smaller dwellings that were home to the craftsmen and craftswomen of Schaefferstown.

Outside town, a traveler will see reminders of the intermingled agricultural and commercial economy of the region in the many farms with large log and stone houses and the massive barns that are characteristic of south-central Pennsylvania. One of these farms, the Alexander Schaeffer farm, is also owned by Historic Schaefferstown, Inc., and is open to the public periodically for festivals and tours. Remnants of two whiskey stills in the basement of the Schaeffer farmhouse and an eighteenth-century pigsty and smokehouse on the property are tangible symbols of area farmers' production of spirits and pork for sale to local storekeepers.

A few miles southwest of Schaefferstown is the small hamlet of Rexmont, named for Samuel's nephew (Abraham's son) Cyrus Rex. Following in his family's footsteps, Cyrus built a large red brick mansion and opened a general store there in about 1875, Cyrus Rex & Company. After Cyrus's death, his niece, Susan Amanda Bucher, took over the store. The building stayed in the family's hands until 1941; until recently it was a bed-and-breakfast, and it is now a private residence.[1]

Evidence of the iron industry, which formed the second node of Rex's network, also survives in abundance. A short drive south from Schaefferstown takes the traveler to Elizabeth Furnace; along the way, small sandstone and log cottages, formerly homes to ironworkers, line the highway. The furnace mansion stands (well back from the road and hidden by a stand of trees) as a reminder of the wealth and power of the ironmasters and the great gap between the furnace owners and their workers. The Coleman family still owns Elizabeth Furnace; it is a private property and is closed to visitors. Further from Schaefferstown, George Ege's mansion, Charming Forge, is also a private home, but it is easily visible from the road for those who care to make the drive through the countryside north of Womelsdorf to find it. A number of auxiliary buildings and workers' homes are extant at the forge as well. Henry Grubb's property at Mount Hope, south of Lebanon, also survives; today it is a winery and home to an annual renaissance fair and other seasonal entertainment. Visitors who wish to glimpse the workings of an early iron furnace in a purer form may head to still another site where Rex did business, Cornwall Iron Furnace, which is maintained by the Pennsylvania Historical and Museum Commission and is open to the public.

Moving toward Philadelphia, the third component of Rex's network of relations, a visitor will find that the influence of the Rex family in Germantown is still apparent, most conspicuously in the street named Rex Avenue. The building that housed Abraham Rex's store still stands at 8031–8033 Germantown Avenue, but much has changed since the day of Rex's great store. Chestnut Hill and its neighboring three villages, once a haven for people escaping the heat and diseases in the city and separated from the city by ten miles of bad road, have long since become an extension of Philadelphia. The drive along Germantown Avenue today presents a study in extreme contrasts, with historic eighteenth-century structures such as Cliveden and Grumblethorpe, formerly bucolic country residences, now hemmed in by a decidedly urban landscape.

And what of the Philadelphia portion of Rex's network? Rex was just one of many small-town storekeepers who did business there in the early nineteenth century, so it will come as no surprise that he left no visible mark on Philadelphia. And, of course, the city has changed dramatically since the time when Rex delivered barrels of pork, lard, and butter to his agents. But a stroll through the historic district offers visitors views of some of the buildings (many restored or rebuilt to recapture their period look) that Rex would have passed on his excursions. Homes such as the Bishop White House (309 Walnut Street) and the Samuel Powel House (244 S. Third Street) are clear reminders of the city's wealth and prominence at the turn of the nineteenth century, but there are smaller row houses from Rex's era as well. Street numbers and even some street names have changed since their day, but Rex and his carters would recognize the city's orderly grids, its tall brick houses, and perhaps even such popular sites as the (reconstructed) City Tavern at Second and Walnut.

Locating the physical places where Rex and his customers lived, worked, and conducted business adds an important visual element and gives context to the fascinating stories that unfold from his copious business papers. But what do these trips into the past signify? The stories that emerge from Rex's reconstructed network put faces and names on the everyday people who drove the economy in one region of early America—the people who produced goods, moved those goods between markets, and made consumption of local and imported goods possible: craftsmen and craftswomen, farmers, ironworkers, country storekeepers and tavern keepers, carters, and Philadelphia shopkeepers and merchants.

Revealing details about the material lives of these people and the choices they made clarifies a number of historical issues, including the idea of a market revolution. Charles Sellers alleged that by the end of the eighteenth century most Americans still lived in a "distinctive subsistence culture removed from river navigation and the market world." According to Sellers, even in Pennsylvania, where residents may have sent as much as one-third of their crop to market, "the marketable surplus was not enough to push most of the Pennsylvania Dutch and their neighbors across the cultural divide into pursuit of wealth."[2] But Rex's business dealings reveal a more nuanced picture of the Pennsylvania Germans and show that their society was a complex, layered one. While they retained their Old World culture in their architecture, foodways, decorative arts, and language (as evidenced by their purchases of German books), they also produced goods specifically for the market, including enormous quantities of butter made by the women of the community, and they consumed the same imported goods that Rex's non-German customers purchased.

Likewise, the deals Rex made at the iron furnaces show the ironmasters and their diverse employees as real men and women who frequently visited the store to buy and sell goods, use his banking services, and arrange to have tailor work done. Rather than being self-contained, iron furnaces were very much a part of the local and regional economic network—and also a blend of community and market *mentalités*. Rex's transactions with the iron community were conducted with an air of deference for the powerful ironmasters, who lived in manorial splendor. He showed a similar respect to the managers at the furnaces, but he seems to have viewed them as his social and intellectual equals. Still, Rex had a business to run; despite the friendly terms of many of the deals he struck, neither farmers, nor craftsmen, nor ironworkers, nor ironmasters were immune to legal action for nonpayment of bills.

Reconstructing Rex's regular trips to Philadelphia conjures up the compelling image of the storekeeper and his men clattering down High Street with wagons loaded with barrels and tubs of produce. More specifically, though, these trips show precisely how goods moved between city and countryside, as well as the close interdependence of urban merchants and country storekeepers. Rex's papers also reveal something new—a relationship between country storekeepers and the city merchants who served as their agents. Philadelphia was closely tied to the market; lists of "prices current" dictated what one would have to pay for imported goods and produce, and payment terms were more stringent than in the countryside. But Rex and his associates in the city also relied on personal knowledge of each other and conducted face-to-face deals that were typical of a close community rather than an impersonal market milieu.

Finally, Rex's papers provide a new way to view the often hackneyed image of the country storekeeper. They reveal Rex's role as a culture broker and bring to light the important contribution storekeepers made in moving goods between seaports and inland communities and connecting rural people to the Atlantic world of goods. Later generations of storekeepers would have more transportation, communication, and business options than Rex and others like him enjoyed, although they would continue to expand on the culture-broker role by bringing new and innovative services to their customers. These developments would ultimately change the nature of storekeeping, render less personal the relationship of the storekeeper to the community, and decrease the need for an extended network of relations. In the early national years, though, storekeepers were integral players in complicated networks of relations. More than just proprietors of establishments where locals played checkers, warmed themselves by the stove, and bought some simple goods, storekeepers sold sophisticated imports as well as necessities and provided a market for local products. They linked country people with the national and international markets, and they enabled rural and urban residents alike to conduct traditional and long-distance exchanges that enhanced their material lives and helped them reach their economic goals.

APPENDIX A: REX AND VALENTINE FAMILIES

Samuel Rex's grandfather, Hans Jürg Rüx (Rüger, Rueger, Rieger) or George Rex (1682–1772), was a blacksmith who immigrated to America from a German-speaking part of Europe sometime before 1720. He and his wife, Barbara, settled in the Germantown area, north of Philadelphia. They had seven sons, including Samuel's father, Abraham; the sons anglicized the family name to Rex.[1] Samuel's father, Abraham Rex (November 7, 1735–February 7, 1793), married Anna Bastian (May 24, 1739–November 15, 1824), on July 26, 1759, at St. Michael's and Zion Lutheran Church, Philadelphia. They had thirteen children.

CHILDREN OF ABRAHAM AND ANNA BASTIAN REX[2]

1. John (February 10, 1760–August 10, 1827), m. Margaret Valentine
2. George (October 14, 1761 [1762?]–December 11, 1841), m. Susanna Riter (or Reiter)
3. Levi (February 25, 1763–September 28, 1828), m. Catherine Riter (or Reiter)
4. Mary (December 7, 1765–January 8, 1844), m., first, George Weiss; second, Wm. Hallman
5. Samuel (October 19, 1766–May 15, 1835), m. Anna Maria Valentine (Mary)
6. Enoch (April 5 [8?], 1768–March 14, 1832), m. Elizabeth Nice
7. Sebastian (October 18 [28?], 1770–February 7, 1786)
8. Jacob Martin (October 2 [5?], 1772–May 9, 1845), m. Mary Gorgas
9. William (October 13, 1774–April 11, 1778 [April 9, 1779?])
10. Anna Barbara (March 23 [August 29?], 1775–April 6, 1863), m. Jacob Hortter
11. Abraham (December 7 [12?], 1778–February 17, 1863), m. Elizabeth Schaeffer
12. Margaret (April 28, 1781–May 9, 1866), m. Joseph Bockius
13. Catherine (December 24 [25?], 1783–August 14, 1857), m. John Miller Bockius

CHILDREN OF ABRAHAM AND ELIZABETH SCHAEFFER REX[3]

1. Maria (Polly) (January 23, 1804–February 19, 1880), m. Peter Zimmerman
2. Samuel S. (April 5, 1806–October 3, 1878), m. Lucetta (Lucy) Schultz
3. Anna (November 16, 1808–April 1900), m. William M. Weigley
4. Franklin (April 8, 1811–November 8, 1833)
5. George (December 3, 1815–April 20, 1884), m. Henrietta Harper
6. Abraham (May 7, 1813–January 31, 1890), m. Amanda Melvina Hortter
7. Cyrus (August 22, 1822–January 21, 1904), never married

HENRY AND ANNA MARIA VALENTINE FAMILY[4]

Henry Valentine was born about 1726 in what is now Germany, perhaps in Baden-Württemberg. He arrived in Philadelphia on the ship *Ann Galley* in 1752 and married Anna Maria Weik (Weick, Wike). Henry died in November 1792.

CHILDREN OF HENRY AND ANNA MARIA VALENTINE

1. Philip (1753–1784), m. Mary (?)
2. Anna Maria (July 16, 1757–November 2, 1832), m. Samuel Rex
3. George (1758–November 27, 1838), m. Mary Grove
4. John (February 19, 1760–[1800?]), m. Eva Maria Zeller
5. Margaret (1761–May 18, 1850), m. John Rex
6. Catherine (January 12, 1763–May 6 or 27, 1840), m. Jacob Gass
7. John Michael (Feb. 6, 1767–?)
8. Michael (February 15 [25?], 1770–August 10 [19?], 1830), m. Magdalena Stiegel

CHILDREN OF MICHAEL AND MAGDALENA STIEGLE VALENTINE[5]

1. Samuel (August 20, 1795–?)
2. Henry (1797–sometime before 1850), m. Maria Haak
3. Salome (1800–May 23, 1866), m. William Reilly
4. Enoch (October 31, 1801–June 24, 1805)
5. Mary (October 6, 1803–April 22, 1889), m. Dr. Christian Bucher
6. Margaret (b. 1804, died young)
7. Eliza (1806–?), m. Dr. Carl (Corl)
8. Margaret (Polly) (January 30, 1809–April 9, 1897), m. Benjamin Mace (Mayes)
9. Martha (1811–?), m. ? Sellers
10. Benjamin (1813–?)
11. Lavina (March 18, 1815–?), m. John Staley
12. Susan (1816–?), m. Luther Kelker

APPENDIX B:
GOODS SOLD AT THE REX STORE,
1790-1807

ALCOHOL

Apple whiskey
Brandy
Cherry whiskey
French brandy
Lisbon wine
Peach whiskey
Port wine
Rum
Rye whiskey
Spirits
Tenerife wine
Whiskey
Wine

BOOKS

ABC books
Almanacs (German and
  English)
Bible history
Bibles (English and
  German)
Catechisms
Habermann prayer book
Hymn books
Large German Bible
Psalm books
Psalters
Ready Reckoners
Small books
Small history books
Spelling books
Testaments

GROCERIES

Allspice
Alum
Bohea tea
Cheese
Chocolate
Cinnamon
Cloves
Coffee
Fish
Flour
Ginger
Green tea
Licorice ball
Lisbon salt
Loaf sugar
Mace
Mackerel
Molasses
Mustard
Nutmegs
Pepper
Powder sugar
Raisins
Rice
Saffron
Salt
Sugar
Sugar Candy
Tea
Vinegar
Wheat
Young hyson tea

HABERDASHERY, CLOTH-
ING, PERSONAL ITEMS

Bandana handkerchief
Black silk handkerchiefs
Black worsted hose
Boots
Brass combs
Brass snuff box
Breeches
Broaches
Buckles
Camel's hair shawl
Caps
Case of razors
Castor hats
Children's hose
Chintz shawl
Coarse comb
Coats
Cotton caps
Cotton handkerchiefs
Cotton hose
Crooked combs
Fine aprons
Fine combs
Fine hats
Fur hats
Garters
Germantown hose
Gloves
Hair ribbon
Handkerchiefs
Hats
Heels
Hose

Knee buckles
Laces
Madras handkerchief
Mittens
Mitts
Morocco shoes
Pocket handkerchiefs
Purses
Razor strap and paste
Razors
Rib stockings
Shaving box
Shawl handkerchiefs
Shawls
Shirt buckles
Shirts—made
Shoe buckles
Shoe clasps
Shoes
Shoestrings
Silk gloves
Silk handkerchiefs
Silk ribbon
Silver watch
Slips
Snuff box
Spectacles
Spectacle cases
Stockings
String of amber beads
String of beads
String of white beads
Thick stockings
Trousers
Twilled hose
Umbrellas
Velvet ribbon
Velvet shoes
Vest coat, complete
Wammus (coat)
Watch
Watch chains
White aprons
Women's hats
Women's mitts
Women's shoes
Women's worsted hose

Wool hats
Worsted stockings

HARDWARE, TOOLS,
SUPPLIES

American steel
Antimony
Augers
Awl blades
Awls
Bar iron
Barlow knives
Bed screws
Black lead
Blister steel
Brass hinges
Brass knobs
Brass lock
Brass nails
Brass spigot
Brass wire
Brazil wood
Bridle bits
Brimstone
Butcher knives
Chalk lines
Chest lock
Chisels
Clasps
Coal baskets
Coffin screws
Compasses (by the pair)
Copperas
Curb bit
Curry combs
Double locks
Doubling nails
Drawer handles
English steel
Escutcheons
Files
Fish hooks
Fish line
Flints
Floor nails

French indigo
Gimlets
Girth buckles
Girth web
Glass paper
Grindstones
Hackles
Hand saws
Handles
Hat lining
Hat loops
Hinges
Hooks
Horse brush
Indigo
Iron
Key
Knives
Kumps (wet horns)
Lead
Locks
Logwood
Madder
Mill files
Nails
Nippers
Oil barrels
Oil cans
Padlocks
Paints
Panel saws
Panes of glass
Pearl ash
Pine boards
Plane bits
Plough lines
Potash
Powder
Prussian blue
Rakes
Rasps
Red chalk
Red paint
Redwood
Rope halters
Rosin
Rules

Saddle nails
Saddle tips
Saddlebag clasps
Saddlery ware
Sash saws
Scale beams
Screws
Scythes
Scythes, English
Sheet iron
Shingle nails
Shoe awls
Shoe nails
Shoemaker's hammer
Shoemaker's knife
Shoemaker's tongs
Shot
Shovels
Sickles
Side leather
Snaffle bits
Socket chisels
Spades
Spanish brown
Spanish white
Spigots
Spike borers
Spoonmaker's measure
Steel
Steel saws
Steel traps
Stirrups
Straw knives
Tacks
Tar pots
Tub nails (sold by the
    set)
Turkey red
Two-foot rules
Verdigris
Vitriol
Water barrels
Weavers' brushes
Weavers' reeds
Whetstones
Whips
White lead

Whitewash brush
Whiting
Women's stirrups
Wooden shovels
Worsted web
Yellow ochre

HOUSEHOLD GOODS

Barrels
Basins
Bed cord
Bellows
Blacking
Blankets
Bottles
Bowls
Brass ladles
Bread baskets
Brooms
Brushes
Buckets
Butter boats
Candles
Candle molds
Candlesticks
Chalk
Chamber pots
Cheese dishes
Cheese drains
China sets
Clothesline
Coffee mill
Coffeepot
Common teaware
Cords
Corks
Coverlids
Cream jugs/pots
Cups and saucers
Curtain rings
Decanters
Delft ware
Double barrels
Earthenware
Flasks

Flatirons
Frying pans
Gill glasses
Glasses
Graters
Green dishes
Green-edged dishes
Hair trunks
Hogsheads (some iron
    bound)
Indian blankets
Iron lamps
Japanned canisters
Japanned sugar boxes
Jars
Jugs
Kegs
Knives and forks
Ladles
Lamps
Lanterns
Large boxes
Looking glasses
Milk crocks/pots
Milk strainers
Mouse traps
Mustard bottles
Oil
Oil cloth
Oil kegs
Pepper boxes
Pepper cruets
Pewter basins
Pewter dishes, large, flat
Pewter plates
Pewter quarts
Pewter ware
Pipe/pepper box
Pitchers
Plates
Pots
Quart mugs
Rat traps
Red lead
Rope
Rose blankets
Salad dishes

Salt stands
Scissors
Scrubbing brushes
Shears
Shovel and tongs
Sling glasses (1½, 1 pint)
Small plates
Soap
Spoons
Sprinkling tins
Starch
Stone mugs
Sugar bowls
Sweeping brushes
Tablecloths
Tea boxes/canisters
Teaware
Teapots
Ten-plated stoves
Tierces
Tin bowls
Tin cups
Tin dishes
Tins
Titanium spoons
Tumblers
Twilled bags
Waiters
Wash/water bowls
Watering pots
Whitewashing brushes
Whiting
Wine glasses
Wine pipes
Wool cards

MEAT

Bacon
Beef
Gammon
Ham
Pork
Veal

MISCELLANEOUS

Allinton (by the ounce)
Asafetida
Bals de Malta
Balsam
Bergamot
Blackball
Box and snake (?)
Bristles
British oil
Calf skins
Camphene
Camphor
Cat gut
Cat skins
Conch ("kunk") shell
Cotton (by the pound)
Cotton bags
Cotton cords
Cotton rommel
Cow skins
Cover bag
Deerskins
Devil's Dung
Fine tobacco
Fish oil
Flat sets
Glue
Harlem oil
Heads and throats
Indian oil
Leather
Mems (?)
Pen knives
Plaster of Paris
Rabbit skins
Saltpeter
Sheep skins
Smoke pipes
Smoke tobacco
Snuff
Sticks of twist
Sweet oil
Tobacco
Turner
Two-bladed knife

Violin
Wafers (wax seals for
  documents?)
Ware crate

PATENT MEDICINES

Anderson's Pills
Bateman's Drops
Godfrey's Cordial
Golden Tincture

PROVISIONS (LOCAL)

Beeswax
Butter
Eggs
Flax
Flaxseed
Hay
Honey
Indian corn
Lard
Oats
Redstraw wheat
Rye
Rye straw
Tallow

SEWING NOTIONS

Beggar's lace
Binding
Buttons, large, small,
Darning needles
Hat binding
Hooks and eyes
Knitting pins
Lace
Molds (button)
Nonesopretties
Needles
Pins
Skeins of silk

Sleeve buttons
Steel knitting pins
Tape
Thimbles
Thread
Turkey yarn
Twist
Wilebone (whalebone?)

STATIONERY, WRITING
SUPPLIES

Blank books
Blank deeds
Bonds
Brass inkstand
Deck of cards
Flowered paper
Ink powder
Ink stand
Large docket
Lead pencils
Parchment
Paste board
Pewter ink stands
Quills
Sand
Slates and pencils
Writing books
Writing paper

TEXTILES

Baize
Beaver fustian
Bed tick
Black cloth
Black cord
Black lute string
Black muslin
Black nankeen
Black silk

Blue cloth
Blue nap
Brown velvet
Buckram
Calamanco
Calico
Cambric
Cassimere
Check
Chintz
Clouded jean
Coating
Constitution cord
Corduroy
Cotton
Cotton cassimere
Cotton stripe
Curtain calico
Dimity
Dowlas
Drab cloth
Durant
English nankeen
Fancy cord
Feather plush
Feather velvet
Ferret
Fine linen
Flannel
Flax linen
Flaxen stripe
Flowered flannel
Furniture cotton
Fustian
Galloon
German lawn
German stripe
Girdle
Green cloth
Green plush
Green serge
Grey coating
Grey napped cloth
Holland

Honeycomb
India calico
Irish linen
Jean
Joans spinning
Lawn
Linen
Linsey
Lutestring
Mixed cloth
Mode
Moreen
Mosail
Muslin
Nankeen
Osnaburg
Rattinett
Red baize
Red flannel
Red serge
Red silk ferret
Remnants of cloth
Ribbed cassimere
Royal rib
Rushy [Russian?] linen
Saddle cloth
Satin
Serge
Shalloon
Silk for a cap
Silk vest pattern
Spotted thickset
Sprigged muslin
Striped coating
Swansdown
Thickset
Toilanette
Torn stripe
Tow linen
Twilled velvet
Velvet
Vest pattern
White flannel
Yellow cassimere

APPENDIX C:
TRADESMEN AND CRAFTSMEN WHO USED THE REX STORE

Name	Craft or profession	Residence, if known
Arndt, Jacob	Hatter	
Baker, Frederick	Wheelwright	
Baker, George	Hatter	
Baum, Daniel	Tobacconist	
Baum, Henry	Cigar maker	Womelsdorf
Bear, George, Jr.	Cooper	
Beystol, Peter	Tailor	
Bladel, Conrad	Tinsmith	
Boyd, Thomas	Papermaker	
Boyer, David	Carpenter	
Boyer, Martin	Shoemaker	Schaefferstown
Boyer, Philip	Carpenter	Schaefferstown
Brecht, Peter	Shoemaker	
Brecht, Philip	Locksmith	Schaefferstown
Brown, John	Spinning wheel maker	
Buchter, Jacob, Jr.	Weaver	
Burkey, Henry	Shoemaker	Schaefferstown
Burkey, Jacob	Cooper	
Chalfint, James	Papermaker	
Cline, Jacob	Rake maker	
Cockley, David	Smith	The Swamp
Coller, Enoch	Papermaker	
Collier, Isaac	Hatter	
Debler, (unknown)	Hatter	
Densler, Christian	Potter	Heidelberg Township
Flower, John, Jr.	Potter	Heidelberg Township
Focht, Matthias	Cabinetmaker	
Folmer, Jacob	Tinsmith	Lebanon
Fornwalt, John	Egg merchant	
Garret, Christian	Hatter	Schaefferstown
Garret, Frederick	Tailor, innkeeper	Schaefferstown
Gass, Jacob	Cabinetmaker	Schaefferstown
Gettle, Lewis	Shoemaker	
Grumbine, Leonard	Shoemaker	
Harter, Jacob	(Weaver's) reed maker	Germantown?
Haverstick, Rudolph	Shoemaker	
Hoffer, Abraham and Philip	Hatters	Schaefferstown
Howser, Henry	Weaver	
Huston, James	Tailor, innkeeper	Schaefferstown
Iba, Henry	Shoemaker	Schaefferstown

Name	Craft or profession	Residence, if known
Kaley, John	Dyer	
Kinsell, Martin	Cabinetmaker	
Klein, Jacob	Rake maker	
Klein, John	Tanner	Schaefferstown
Krall, Abraham	Weaver	
Krall, Henry	Carpenter	
Kramer, David	Basket maker	Heidelberg Township
Kreech, Jacob	Tinsmith	
Lewis, John	Post rider	
Lewis, John	Weaver	
Leydich, Martin	Weaver	
Leydich, Peter	Blacksmith	
Longree, John	Papermaker	
Louser, Jacob	Weaver	
Lutz, Conrad	Weaver	
Mace, Benjamin	Cooper, joiner	Schaefferstown
Mace, Michael	Hatter	
Mace, Valentine	Joiner	Schaefferstown
Maddoch (Murdoch), James	Heel/shoemaker	Schaefferstown
Marshall, James	Weaver	
Marshall, William	Weaver	
Memmens, Conrad	Potter	
Mihl, Jacob	Brewer	
Miller, Frederick	Saddler	
Miller, Godfrey	Brush maker	The Swamp
Miller, Jacob	Brewer	
Miller, Jacob	Butcher	
Miller, Jacob	Silversmith	
Miller, John	Locksmith	
Miller, Martin	Brush maker	
Moore, Adam	Cooper	Schaefferstown
Moore, Benjamin	Cooper	Lebanon
Moore, Jacob	Cooper	Schaefferstown
Moore, Peter	Cooper, innkeeper	Schaefferstown
Mowrey, Daniel	Weaver	The Swamp
Moyer, Benjamin	Almanac salesman	
Moyer, Michael	Basket weaver	
Moyer, Michael	Brush maker	Cornwall
Muck, Philip	Locksmith	
Neaff, George	Millwright (also made kegs)	
Neaff, George, Jr.	Carpenter	
Neaff, Jacob	Tailor	
Neaff, John	Cooper	
Neip, John	Blacksmith/farrier	
Newman, Peter	Potter (also made clay pipes)	
Orndt, Charles	Hatter	
Orwrand, (unknown)	Smith	
Oves & Moore	Coopers	
Pattorf, George, Jr.	Shoemaker	
Peffer, Jacob	Shoemaker	Heidelberg Township

Name	Craft or profession	Residence, if known
Peters, John	Pump maker	
Peters, John	Hatter	
Philippi, Jacob	Brewer	Schaefferstown
Plank, Christ	Sickle maker	
Reidel (Reydel), John	Saddler	Schaefferstown
Richards, (unknown)	Hatter	
Salcheimer, William	Papermaker	
Seiler, Christian	Locksmith	Schaefferstown
Shindle, Peter	Tobacconist	
Shoeneman, Jonathan	Rake and brush maker	The Swamp
Shreiver, Widow	Seamstress	Schaefferstown
Shultz, H. M.	Weaver	Tulpehocken
Smith, Francis	Cooper	
Smith, John	Mason	
Smith, John	Weaver	Schaefferstown
Spyker, Jacob	Blacksmith	
Sterner, Jacob	Smith	Newmanstown
Stiegel, Widow	Seamstress	Schaefferstown
Stohler, Henry	Millwright, innkeeper	Schaefferstown
Stouch, Conrad	Shoemaker	Womelsdorf
Stover, Adam	Blue dyer	
Strickler, George	Weaver	Schaefferstown
Sunday, Jacob	Weaver	
Sweitzer, Casper	Nail smith	Schaefferstown
Sweitzer, John	Nail smith	Schaefferstown
Ulrich, John	Weaver	
Weitzer, John	Smith	
Wiest, Christian	Papermaker	
Winter, Michael	Saddler	
Wonnerly, John	Weaver	
Yeager, Daniel	Tinsmith	
Young, Matthias	Cabinetmaker	
Zimmerman, George	Mason	

APPENDIX D:
PHILADELPHIA MERCHANTS PATRONIZED BY REX

Merchant's name, dates did business with Rex	Type of business	Address, 1798 tax description, and value[1]	Clerk(s)
Allen & Clifford (1799)*			
Alsop & Clement (1800)*	Merchants	57 N. Front Street	Caleb Spencer
Anderson, Samuel V. (1795)			
Arrott, James (1805)*	Merchant	24 S. Front Street	Geo. Blaikie
Bacon & Longstreth (1802)*	Merchants	10 N. Third Street	
Baker, Godfrey, & Co. (1790–1801)	Booksellers	59 Sassafras Street[2]	
Baker, John R. (1801–5)*	Merchant	91 Race Street	Geo. Susman
Baker & Conegy (1794)	Merchants	28 Chestnut Street, "elegant brick" store, 4 stories, 14 × 15 ft., $4,000 (by 1801 they were at 60 North Front Street)	Saml. Harvey
Barth & Longstreth (1803)*			Thos. Bowman
Bartow, Thomas (1790–93)	Merchant	94 N. Second Street	Henry Hillegas
Bayley, Richard, & Co. (1795)	(calico)	136 Market Street[3]	
Beates, Barbara (1799–1806)	Tobacconist	209 Market Street	Wm. Beates
Beates, Conrad (1797–98)	Tobacconist	209 Market Street	
Benezet, Daniel (1792)	Merchant	Arch Street, 4 doors below Second Street[4]	

Merchant's name, dates did business with Rex	Type of business	Address, 1798 tax description, and value[1]	Clerk(s)
Berniard, Dumas & Jacques (1799)	China and glass dealers	19 S. Second Street	
Bickham & Reese (1798, 1802)	Merchants	152–154 High Street	M. Hollenbach
Bilsland, Alex., & Co. (1796–98)	Ironmonger	201 High Street	
Birhel, Elisha (1800)★	(sheet iron)		W. Brown
Blackfan & Ely (1798–1802)★	Merchants	42 N. Third Street	
Boller & Jordan (1794)	Grocers	122 N. Third Street	
Boyley, Richard (1797)	(calico, tablecloths)	36 High Street	
Branken, E. (1800)★			Jacob Foyce
Burton & Compsee (1791)	(ribbons, looking glass)		
Brooks, Samuel (1799)★			
Brown, Jacob (1798)	Iron store	161 & 167 N. Second Street	
Brugiere, Charles & ? (1804)★			
Bryan & Schlatter (1804–5)★			Chas. Foulke, William Morris
Bunting, Philip (1791)	Grocer	96 & 133 Sassafras Street	
Calbrath, James, & Co. (1791)	Merchants	31 Chestnut Street	
Canby, Ridgeway (1802)★	Flour merchant		Thos. Canby Jr.
Capper, Henry (1790)	Merchant	53 N. Third Street	G. McClarkson
Chancellor, William (1790, 1799)	Merchant	105 High Street	Zachary Evans, W. G. Govett
Chancellor & Davis (1796)	(cloth)		
Clark, William (1795)	Grocer	140 S. Front Street	
Clifton, Thomas & John (1798)	Merchants	39 N. Front Street	Jacob D. Dienik
Clifford, J. D. (1802)★			C. S. Raphinseque

Merchant's name, dates did business with Rex	Type of business	Address, 1798 tax description, and value[1]	Clerk(s)
Coe, Robert (1795)	Brush manufacturer, ironmonger	175 High Street	
Cohen, E. (1804)★			Robt. Wilson
Connelly, John (1800)★	Auctioneer	78 S. Front Street, brick store, 1 story, 21 × 48 ft.; accompting house, 10 × 15 ft., $3,500	Henry Connelly
Connor, John Jacob (1803)★			
Conrad, Elizabeth (1806)★			
Cooke, John (1801–4)★	Merchant	142 Race Street	Jos. Eves, Aaron Musgrave[5]
Cooke & Cresson (1804–6)★			
Cottringer, Elizabeth (1799)	Widow shopkeeper, china shop	189 High Street	
Daniel, Jorgen & Laughlin (1800)[6]			
Darroch, Henry (1790–93)	Grocer	130, 134 N. Third Street	Henry Andrews, Thomas Colbert
Davis, John, & Co. (1799)	Merchants	157 High Street, brick dwelling as store, $4,000	Jacob Old
Delacroix, Joseph (1791)	Distiller/ confectioner	59 High Street	
Delecorth, Jos. (1799)★	(grass scythes)		
Denckla, Christian (1799)	Merchant	70 N. Third Street	
Dilworth, Joseph (1799)★	Ironmonger	201 High Street	
Dorsey, Benedict, & Son (1795–99)[7]	Grocers	3 & 5 S. Third Street, 4-story brick store, 20 × 25 ft., $3,000	Ben Hannson, Thomas Pope
Douglas, Andrew (1790, 1794)	Iron merchant	56 & 58 N. Third Street	J. Pevisol
Drinker, Daniel (1790)	Merchant	149 High Street	

Merchant's name, dates did business with Rex	Type of business	Address, 1798 tax description, and value[1]	Clerk(s)
Drinker, Henry, Jr. (1796)	Merchant	30 N. Front Street	
Dubarry & Co. (1799)★	Merchants	25 S. Third Street	
Dubois, Abm., Jr. (1800)	Gold- & silversmith	65 N. Second Street	
Dubs, Martin, & Co. (1797–1806)	Merchants		Geo. Spangler
Dubs & Earl (1797–1800)[8]	Merchants	37 N. Seventh Street (may be Dubs residence); 247 High Street, 22 × 40-ft. frame store, $1,600	P. Mahoney
Dubs & Marquedant (1794–95)	Grocers	245 Market Street	
Duvall, James S. (1803)★	Merchant	80 N. Second Street	
Edwards & Maddock (1794)★	Grocers	72 Market Street, 2-story brick store, 20 × 27 ft., $2,000	
Eigelberner, Peter (1793)	Tobacconist	Sassafrass betw. Eighth & Ninth	
Eldredge, Samuel[9] (1797–1804)	Merchant	139 High Street, brick dwelling as store, 60 × 24 ft., 2 stories, $4,500	J. Dull, Chas. Foulke, C. Schlatter
Ellett, John & Charles (1800)	Merchants/ Ironmongers	193 High Street	James Roger
Emlen, Caleb (1802)★			Chas. Rogers
Evans, John B., & Co. (1795)	Merchants	54 S. Second Street	Wm. H. Jack
Eves & Wistar (1803)★			
Fider & Thomas (1805)★			
Fisher, Samuel (1797)	Merchant	5 Dock Street, brick store, 60 × 24 ft., 2 stories, $2,680	Thos. Fisher, Joshua Fisher
Fisher, Samuel & Miers (1797)	Merchants	27 Dock Street	Thos. M. Fisher
Folwell, John (1790, 1795)	Merchant	52 N. Front Street	Thos. Folwell

Merchant's name, dates did business with Rex	Type of business	Address, 1798 tax description, and value[1]	Clerk(s)
Folwell, Nathan (1799)	Shopkeeper	44 N. Second Street	
Footman, Richard, & Co. (1798)	Auctioneers	65 S. Front Street	
Foulke, Caleb, Jr., & Co. (1798)★	Merchant	37 N. Eighth Street	
Foulke, Owen & Charles (1800–1801)★	Merchants	275 High Street	
Freeman, B. (1806)★			Abm. Sonntagg
Fricke, Augustus (1795)	Woolen draper	7 S. Third Street, house & outbuilding, $2,000	John Saulnier
Friend, John (1790)	Shopkeeper	93 N. Third Street	
Fries, John (1797–98)	Merchant	90 High Street	B. Marshall, ? Klahr, Sam. Chambers
Fromberger, William (1795)	Merchant	34 N. Second Street, 16 × 33-ft. brick store, 3 stories, $3,000	
Gallagher, James (1790–95, 1800)	China merchant	5 S. Second Street, 18 S. Front Street (1800)	J. Gallagher Jr., Hugh Green
Garrett, William & Levi (1796)	Tobacconists	120 S. Front Street	
Gaull, Martin (1791)	(snuff boxes, testaments)		
Gibbs, Jos. & William (1790–1804)	Merchants	92 N. Front Street, 43 S. Eighth Street	
Gimkle, Michael (1799)★			J. Mattson
Guist & Bauker (1803)★			Geo. Morris, Robt. Coe Jr.
Gulbert, James, & Co. (1801)★	Merchant	89 Market Street	
Guyer, John (1791)	Grocer	193 & 195 High Street	
Hagenau, John (1798)	Merchant	158 High Street	
Haga, Godfrey, & Co. (1803)★	Merchant	87 Sassafras Street	
Hamilton, G. & W. (1802)★			Geo. Patton

Merchant's name, dates did business with Rex	Type of business	Address, 1798 tax description, and value[1]	Clerk(s)
Hamon, W. (1798)			Robt. Poalk
Hart, John (1791–96)	Apothecary and druggist	37 High Street (1791), 8 S. Second Street (1794)[10]	Evan Evans
Harwood, W. (1798)★			John Hudson
Hass, M. (1791)	(men's hose)		
Henry, Alexander, & Co. (1805)★	Merchant	225 High Street	John Magerfair
Herbert, Laurence (1799–1801)	Shopkeeper	161 Market Street	
Hockley, Thomas (1799)	Ironmonger	82 High Street	H. Jamison
Hofringer, J. (1805)★	(Dutch scythes)		John McQuinn
Holland, Benjamin (1791)	Merchant	3 N. Front Street	Edward Rowley
Hollewell, John, & Co. (1804)★			Hugh Fell
Hubley & Co. (1791)	Auctioneers	285 S. Front Street	
Hunt, Wilson (1798)	Merchant	16 S. Front Street	Philip Habuck
Hutton, James (1802)★	Ironmonger	53 High Street	Thos. Shipley
Immel, Michael (1800)★[11]	Innkeeper/ bookseller?	76 N. Third Street	
Israel, Samuel (1800–1801)★[12]	Auctioneer	55 N. Second Street	P. Potter
Jackson, Hugh & John (1799)★	Merchants	Corner of Sixth & High streets	
Jacoby, Leonard (1790)	Merchant	145 N. Second Street	
Johnson, Robert, & Co. (1798–1803)	Booksellers	147 Market Street	John Taylor, James Moore
Jones, H. (1803)★			
Jones, Owen (1791)[13]	Merchant	154 S. Second Street	
Jones & Parson (1799)★			
Justice, J., & Co. (1802)★			W. M. Howell
Keigart, Adam (1798)	(coffee)		
Kelly, Thomas & Philip (1804)★	Shoe and trunk store		G. Beckel, Wm. Rayfield
Kennedy, Alexander (1794)★			Thos. MacCoffer

Merchant's name, dates did business with Rex	Type of business	Address, 1798 tax description, and value[1]	Clerk(s)
Keppele, George (1791–95)	Merchant	98 High Street	
Keppele & Zantzinger, Hy. (1795)	Merchants	98 Market Street	
Kibler, Joseph (1798)	Brush maker		
King, Reay (1797)	Ironmonger	27 N. Second Street	
Knight, J. M. (1795)★			
Knorr, Jacob (1798)★	Ironmonger	80 Carters Alley, 50 N. Third Street	
Kratz & Buehler (1796)	(knives and forks)		
Krouse, David (1790)	(tobacco)		
Longstreth, Joseph, & Co. (1801)★	Merchants	28 N. Third Street	
Longstreth, Morris (1802)★			
Maris, Richard (1799)★	Merchant	157 High Street	Jacob Donnech
Marshall, John (1794–96)	(glass)	11 Second Street[14]	Shel. Marshall
Martin, John (1795)	(oysters)	27 S. Wharves	
Matthew, John (1802)★			
McMann, John (1791)	(linen)		
Meissen, Joseph (1794)	Grocer	62 High Street	
Millberg, Peter (1803)★			Rees Harry
Miles, Samuel, Jr. (1796–97)	Merchant	191–193 High Street, 14 × 30-ft. brick store, $2,800	
Miller, John, Jr. (1794)	Merchant	8 Chestnut Street	
Miller, Thomas (1790)	Grocer	72 N. Second Street	
Morgan, Douglas & Schaffer (1800, 1803)★	Sugar refiners	88 N. Second Street	
Mousel, Robert (1805)★			
Myers, John (1802)	Silversmith and shopkeeper		

Merchant's name, dates did business with Rex	Type of business	Address, 1798 tax description, and value[1]	Clerk(s)
Naldergin, Jos. (1799)★			J. N. Hagenau
Neal & Smith (1800)★		131 Market Street, 15 × 35-ft. brick store, $4,500	
Nottnagel, Montmollen (1794, 1799)	Merchants	22 S. Front Street, $5,000/$7,500[15]	Jas. Brown Jr.
Orth, Henry (1804)	(china)		John Berryhill
Orth & Boyd (1805–6)★			
Panwart & Walker (1796)	Ironmongers	148 High Street	
Parry, Thomas (1798)★	Shopkeeper	5 N. Second Street	
Parson, Isaac & Wm. (1801)★	(window glass)		
Patton, John (1791, 1796)	Vendue master	78 S. Front Street[16]	
Peacock & Wunston (1794)★			
Pennington, Edward (1801)★		159 Sassafras Street	G. Handon, T. Mendenhall
Pennock, George (1798)★	Merchant	103 Market Street	Thos. Gileson
Piesch & Mayerhoff (1798)	Merchants	71 Race Street	
Pinnset, George (1798)	(knives, combs, cloth)		
Poalk, S. V. (1799)★			
Potter, Page & Price (1798–99)	(cloth)	31 Chestnut Street	David Dewey
Poultney, John & James (1796)	Ironmongers	124 Market Street[17]	
Poultney & Wistar (1790, 1796)	Ironmongers	96 High Street	Richard Waln
Preisel & Mayerhoff (1798)★			Geo. Beckel
Price, John M. (1796–97)	Merchant	177 High Street	Jos. B. Davis, Jn. Greenfield, Jos. Blare

Merchant's name, dates did business with Rex	Type of business	Address, 1798 tax description, and value[1]	Clerk(s)
Puir, William, & Co. (1803)★	(steel)		
Reichmen, George (1791)	(tobacco)		
Rice, Henry & Patrick (1795)	Booksellers	30 High Street, 16 S. Second Street	
Richards, John (1802, 1805)★			Wm. Wayne
Riehl, John & Jacob (1794–1802)	Tobacconists	150 High Street	Jos. J. Walter
Rizer, Martin (1790)	Tin plate worker	97 N. Third Street	
Roberts & Swamby (1790)	Wholesale ironmongers	83 High Street	
Roland & Denkla (1791)	Shopkeepers	110 N. Second Street	
Rose, Thomas (1802)★	Merchant	47 High Street	
Roush, Mathias (1796)	(skins, gloves)	124 N. Second Street	
Rugen & Rhoads (1798)★	Grocers	259 Market Street	
Russel, Francis (1796)	Grocer	184 S. Second Street	
Schoefield & Tyson (1798)★			George Jones
Schoefield, Samuel (1800)★			Jos. Wilson
Sellers, N. & D. (1804)★			Coleman Sellers
Shannon William (1797–98)	Auctioneer	183 High Street	W. Weissman
Shannon & Poalk (1801)★	Auctioneers	177 High Street	W. Weissman
Shatter, Richard (1800)★			
Shields, John, & Sons (1794)	Broker, commission merchant	22 Chestnut Street	Henry Howell Jr.
Shoemaker, Edward (1795, 1800)	Merchant	127 High Street	Matt. Ludwig, Benj. Shoemaker
Shoemaker & Dull (1802)★			

Merchant's name, dates did business with Rex	Type of business	Address, 1798 tax description, and value[1]	Clerk(s)
Simmons, Joseph (1799)	Ironmonger	91 High Street	Wm. Gardener
Singer, John (1805)★			Henry Erben
Singer, John and Abraham (1798)	Merchants	137 High Street	
Smith, B. (1799)★			
Smith, James (1791)	(wool cards, cotton)		
Smith, Lewis (1790)	(balsam, tincture)		
Smith, Sam. (1800)	(camphor)		
Smith, T. (1799)	(corn scythes)		
Snail, Lawrence, & Co. (1802)★			
Somerkomp, Philip (1790)	Druggist and apothecary	45 High Street	
Sommers, John Jacob (1805)★	Merchant	61 Sassafras Street	
Sperry, Jacob & Co. (1800)★[18]	Merchants	195, 197 High Street, two brick stores, 15 × 30ft., $1,800, and 15 × 20 ft., $2,000	Fred. Langmayer, Jos. Huffnagle
Sperry & Huffnagle (1803)			Dav. Muhlenberg
Stahl (Jacob) & Wilhelm (1798)	(watch keys)		
Starr & Thomas (1802)	(salt)		
Steinamer, A. (1799)★			
Stein, Abraham (1801)	Dealer in watches	86 N. Third Street	
Stoddard, John (1801, 1804)★			
Sweitzer, Henry (1797)	Printer	Race & N. Fourth streets	Anthony Myer
Taggert, John (1794)	Merchant	51 N. Water Street, 27 × 39-ft. brick store, $4,000	Philip Toner
Taylor & Newbold (1800)★	Merchants	20 Chestnut Street, 2 stories, 12 × 60-ft. brick store, $2,250	Robt. Harr/Hurr
Thomson, Edward (1799)★	Merchant	Next to 86 Arch Street	Enoch Price

Merchant's name, dates did business with Rex	Type of business	Address, 1798 tax description, and value[1]	Clerk(s)
Thomson, Ries, & Co. (1798)★	Merchants	193 High Street	
Thomson & Maris (1805–6)★			
Thomson & Price (1801)★	Merchants	131 High Street	
Truchel & Fruike (1792)★			
Turnbull, William (1798)★	Merchant	26 S. Front Street	
Underwood, Thomas (1801)★	Merchant	205 High Street	
Waddington & Harwood (1799–1801)★	Merchants	30 S. Front Street	Joshua Hamill
Wells, Gideon, & Co. (1798)★	Merchants	135 Market, 108 Arch Street, 3 stories, 14 × 50-ft. brick store, $3,000	Wm. Nekerris
Wells & Morris (1791)	Ironmongers	135 High Street	
West & Nanikin (1802)★			
Wetherill, Samuel, & Son (1804–6)★	Colorman[19]	61 N. Front Street[20]	
White & Conrad (1797)	Merchants	6 N. Front Street	
White, Solomon, & Co. (1790)	Shopkeepers	94 High Street	
White, Webster A. (1794)	(wool cards)		
Wilson, James (1790)	Merchant	16 N. Second Street, 97 Mulberry Street	
Wiltburger, Peter (1803, 1805)★	Merchant	101 High Street, 3-story dwelling, 13 × 42 ft., occupied as store, $2,300	Israel Wiltburger
Wistar & Cooke (1794–99)	Merchants	133 High Street	
Wistar & Konigmaker (1798–1805)	Ironmongers	117 High Street	
Wistar, Richard (1795–98)	Ironmonger	Corner High & Third Streets, 30 × 30-ft. brick store, 4 stories, $7,500	

Merchant's name, dates did business with Rex	Type of business	Address, 1798 tax description, and value[1]	Clerk(s)
Wistar, Thomas (1791)	Dry goods merchant	119 Chestnut Street	Richard Waln Jr.
Wister & Aston (1791)		143 High Street	
Wister, John & Charles (1805)★			Peter Muhlenberg
Wister, Price & Wister (1798)	Merchants	143 High Street	
Wister, William (1792–98)	Merchant	143 High Street, 18 × 28-ft. brick store, $1,500	Daniel Windez
Wister, William & John Jr. (1795)	Merchants	143 High Street	Saml. Eldredge, Jos. Warner
Wood, Catherine (1799)★	Widow shopkeeper	8 N. Second Street	Thos. Long
Wood, William (1795–97)	(cloth, baize, etc.)		Joseph Shaw
Woodington & Flouvard (1803)★			? Smith
Worstall, James (1790)	Ironmonger	50 N. Third Street, 36 Broad Street	Lawrence Allman
Wotherspoon, Thomas (1801)★	Merchant	56 S. Front Street	Jas. Spencer
Zantzinger, Adam (1799)	Merchant	53 High Street	

★ These people are listed in Rex's receipt books, but there are no bills to indicate what he bought from them.

1. Addresses and business listings are found in city directories; where I could not locate the business in a directory I include the item sold in parentheses. The street-numbering system has changed over the years; street numbers do not correspond to the current system. There are also minor discrepancies between the addresses listed in the city directories and those in the 1798 direct tax list. For lists of residents of Market Street in the years 1785, 1801, and 1918, see Jackson, *Market Street,* 203–10.

2. Sassafras Street was also known as Race Street.

3. Market Street was also known as High Street. Bayley's address appears on the bill he gave Rex on May 26, 1797, LEL, roll 6: AS106.

4. Arch Street was also known as Mulberry Street. Benezet advertised goods for sale at this address in the *Pennsylvania Gazette,* April 14, 1790.

5. Aaron Musgrave Jr. was one of the assessors of the 1798 direct tax; by 1801 he was a "conveyancer" with a shop at 195 S. Second Street.

6. Bill written in German.

7. Dorsey sold seed, dyestuff, chocolate, raisins, sugar, and "other groceries as usual" at his shop "between the Harp and Crown Tavern and Market Street." *Pennsylvania Gazette,* March 12, 1788.

8. The first name of Dubs's partner is not given in Rex's papers, but it may have been Clayton Earl, a merchant who lived at 309 High Street, between Eighth and Ninth streets.

9. Eldredge signed a receipt for Rex's purchase from Wister in August 1795; by May 1797 Eldredge was on his own and selling goods to Rex.

10. Hart advertised from this address on July 16, 1794, offering a penny reward for the return of his boy, Silas Lewis, age fourteen. A week later Hart placed a second ad announcing that the boy had been brought back but had run away on the same day, taking with him a $10 bank note and other money. This time Hart offered a $5 reward for his apprehension. *Pennsylvania Gazette,* July 16 and July 23, 1794.

11. City directories list Immel as an innkeeper, but a Michael Immel was also a merchant bookseller (1787–1803) according to Cazden, *Social History of the German Book Trade,* 15.

12. Israel's ad in the March 4, 1801, edition of *Poulson's American Daily Advertiser* gives the address of his "auction store" and announces upcoming dry goods auctions.

13. Owen Jones was in partnership with Daniel Wister and went bankrupt in 1761. Doerflinger, *Vigorous Spirit of Enterprise,* 96–97.

14. Marshall receipt, October 28, 1796, LEL, roll 2: B1.

15. Schedule A, Chestnut Ward, Philadelphia County, Pennsylvania, shows the assessed value as $5,000, while the recapitulation lists the property at $7,500.

16. Patton advertised that he had been appointed auctioneer for the city and was ready to receive goods for sales to be held Tuesdays and Thursdays (dry goods) and Wednesdays (furniture) from 9:00 A.M. till noon. *Pennsylvania Gazette,* January 16, 1788.

17. Address from Poultney receipt, October 26, 1796, LEL, roll 2: B1.

18. In March 1801 Jacob Sperry & Co. announced the removal of the "compting house" to 10 Walnut Street wharf and advertised the store and house at 195 Walnut Street for rent. The firm's ad shows that it sold textiles, scythes, coffee mills, glassware, and Madeira wine. *Poulson's American Daily Advertiser,* March 4, 1801.

19. Doerflinger, *Vigorous Spirit of Enterprise,* 52.

20. In 1798 Wetherill lived at 65 Water Street; he had a frame workshop (15 × 41 feet) and a brick laboratory (15 × 30 feet) in the alley back of and adjacent to his home.

APPENDIX E: SAMUEL REX'S CARTERS

Name	Occupation	Dates Drove for Rex
Allison, Hugh (Mr. Pfouts's team)		March 1803
Bowen, William		September 1803
Bullein, William		March 1804 (one way from Philadelphia)
Deal (tenant at Shell's place)		November 1801
Detweiler, John		May 1800
Ellinger, Casper		August, November 1799; June 1800; November 1802; February, July, August, October 1804; June 1805
Ellinger, George		June 1807
Ellinger, John (Casper's son)		November 1802; July, October 1804; June 1805
Foorman, Peter		March 1797
Funk, Martin		November 1801
Garret, George	Farmer	February 1799
Garret, Jacob	Farmer	May 1806
Gingrich, Peter		June 1797
Gockley, Dietrich		May 1806
Grabill, [Michael]	Oil miller	June 1792
Hawk, John & Jonas		February 1804
Hawk, Michael	Farmer/Miller	November 1801; January 1802
Hipchman, Henry, Jr.	Farmer	January 1798; January 1806
Hurst, Peter	Farmer	November 1803
Klein, John	Tanner	June 1802
Krall, Christian	Farmer	February 1795
Krall, Henry	Farmer	May 1805
Kratzer, Joseph	Farmer	October 1804
Kreider, John		January 1800
Kring, H.		December 1794

Name	Occupation	Dates Drove for Rex
Lesher, (unknown)		November 1801
Leydig, Michael	Farmer	February 1807
Lowrey, William	Ironworker	June 1805
Mace, Jacob	Farmer	June 1798; May 1805
Meese, John		August 1803 (three trips)
Miley, Philip		February 1800
Montgomery, Alexander	Ironworker	1791 (no month and day listed on receipt)
Moore, Peter	Cooper	February, July, August 1802; September 1803; April 1804; April 1805; May, September 1806; January 1807
Nare, Adam		December 1803 (one way from Philadelphia)
Newman, Benjamin	Farmer	December 1803 (Baltimore)
Newman, John		February 1802
Pekins, Thomas	Farmer	June 1802 (hauled whiskey locally)
Pitner, Mathias	Farmer/ 1798 tax collector	December 1798; June 1799; May 1804
Prusman, Peter	Farmer	May 1801; April 1802
Sanders, Jacob		May 1805; May, September, December 1806
Sechrist, John		May 1801
Shaw, John		May 1802
Sheafer, George		January 1803 (one way from Philadelphia
Sheaffer, John		November 1806
Sheetz, Peter	Farmer	May 1796; June 1800; May 1806
Shultz, Christian		May 1806
Snavely, John		October 1801
Snyder, Jacob	Laborer	February, July, August 1802
Stager, (unknown)		December 1791
Stoner, Philip		September 1799
Stouch, Conrad	Shoemaker/ Tavern keeper	June 1800
Stover, John	Farmer	December 1797; August 1799; April, May 1800; January, April, May, November, 1802
Strock, Henry	Farmer	June 1799; July 1800

Name	Occupation	Dates Drove for Rex
Swanger, Nicholas	Farmer	May, August, November 1799; January, May 1800; March, November 1801; May 1802; April 1805
Thomas, Jacob	Miller	September 1796
Trosill, George		April, May 1802
Troutman, Jonas	Farmer	August 1801
Valentine, Michael	Innkeeper	September 1792
Weaver, John	Farmer	February 1798; August 1799; July, August 1802; June 1804
Weaver, (unknown)		April 1791
Weiss, Henry	Farmer/ 1798 tax collector	February, August 1799; September 1802; July 1803
Weiss, Jacob		May 1802; December 1803
Wolfesberger, John		March 1803
Yeager, Earhart		January 1795

APPENDIX F:
LOCATION OF SAMUEL REX DOCUMENTS

Documents	Dates	Repository
Bills and receipts from Philadelphia merchants	1790–1802	LEL, roll 1: AB1; roll 2: B1; roll 5: AS100, 103; roll 6: S104–10; and HSI
Daybook or blotter[1]	December 22, 1790–November 28, 1791	JDC, Collection 417, box 1
Daybook(s) or blotter(s)	1791–93	Missing
Daybook or blotter	May 21, 1793–March 1, 1795	LEL, roll 1: AB2
Index (?) for daybook 3	1795	LEL, roll 1: AB3
Daybook 1	March 4–December 1, 1795[2]	HSI
Daybook (2)	January 23–June 4, 1796	LEL, roll 1: AB5
Daybook 3	July 23, 1796–May 6, 1797	JDC, 417, box 1
Daybook (4)	May 12–November 29, 1797	LEL, roll 1: AB6
Daybook (5)	December 1, 1797–May 25, 1798	LEL, roll 1: AB7
Daybook 6	May 28–December 10, 1798	HSI
Daybook (7)	January 18–April 1, 1799	LEL, roll 1: AB8
Daybook 8	April 18–August 13, 1799	JDC, 417, box 1
Daybook 9	August 15–November 29, 1799	HSI
Daybook (10)	November 29, 1799–February 8, 1800	LEL, roll 1: AB9
Daybook 11	February 10–June 4, 1800	HSI
Daybook 12	June 10–August 23, 1800	JDC, 417, box 1
Daybook (13)	September 6–November 5, 1800	LEL, roll 1: AB10
Daybook 14	November 12, 1800–January 24, 1801	JDC, 417, box 1
Daybook (15)	January 24–May 21, 1801	LEL, roll 1: AB11
Daybook 16		Missing
Daybook (17)	September 1–November 28, 1801	LEL, roll 1: AB12
Daybook 18	December 1, 1801–March 17, 1802	HSI
Daybook 19	March 18–June 18, 1802	JDC, 417, box 1
Daybook 20	June 30–October 9, 1802	HSI
Daybook 21	October 12, 1802–January 23, 1803	JDC, 417, box 1
Daybook 22	January 22–June 3, 1803	HSI
Daybook 23	June 4–September 8, 1803	JDC, 417, box 1

Documents	Dates	Repository
Daybook 24	September 12–December 5, 1803	HSI
Daybook (25)	December 6, 1803–March 10, 1804	LEL, roll 1: AB13
Daybook 26	May 12–June 7, 1804	LEL, roll 1: AB14
Daybook 27	June 17–August 23, 1804	HSI
Daybook 28	August 25–November 12, 1804	HSI
Daybook 29		Missing
Daybook (30)	February 13–May 9, 1805	LEL, roll 1: AB15
Daybook 31	May 11–July 19, 1805	HSI
Daybook 32		Missing
Daybook 33	September 30–December 3, 1805	JDC, 417, box 1
Daybook 34	December 4, 1805–February 22, 1806	LEL, roll 1: AB16
Daybook 35	February 22–May 3, 1806	HSI
Daybook 36	May 3–June 21, 1806	HSI
Daybook 37	June 21–August 19, 1806	HSI
Daybook (38)	August 21–October 11, 1806	LEL, roll 1: AB17
Daybook (39)	October 11–December 6, 1806	LEL, roll 1: AB18
Daybook (40)	December 6, 1806–February 14, 1807	LEL, roll 1: AB19
Daybook 41	February 16, 1807–September 1, 1810	HSI
Daybook (42)	September 15, 1810–August 6, 1823	HSI
Daybook (43)	December 9, 1831–June 29, 1836	HSI
Ledgers 1–4		Missing
Ledger 5	1798–1808	HSI
Ledger 6		Missing
Ledger 7	1804–7	LEL, roll 2: AB21
Ledger 8	1806–33	LEL, roll 2: AB22
Receipt book 1	May 5, 1791–May 18, 1802	HSI
Receipt book 2	July 27, 1802–April 6, 1835	LEL, roll 5: AS 80
Store inventory	June 1, 1807	HSI

1. Rex numbered some but not all of his daybooks. Parentheses indicate that I have inferred the daybook number. He did not number the daybooks he used before moving to the Schaeffer hotel.

2. The gap of several days or weeks in some cases between the end of one daybook and the beginning of another is a mystery.

NOTES

INTRODUCTION

1. La Rochefoucauld-Liancourt, *Travels Through the United States,* 2:583. Thanks to Cindy Falk for suggesting this and other travelers' accounts of this period.

2. I am indebted to Cathy Matson for suggesting the network-of-relations approach.

3. See Rutman, "Social Web"; Rutman and Rutman, *Place in Time,* 27–29; Bender, *Community and Social Change in America,* 112.

4. Sellers, *Market Revolution.*

5. Ibid., 15.

6. On the power and prevalence of this myth, see Shammas, "How Self-Sufficient Was Early America?"

7. Most monographs on country stores and storekeepers are antiquarian or outdated. See Carson, *Old Country Store;* Clark, *Pills, Plows, and Petticoats;* Johnson, *Over the Counter;* and Long, "General Store." Atherton, *Southern Country Store, 1800–1860,* is the best of the older works. Newer and/or more scholarly treatments of the storekeeper that have influenced this study are Clark, *Roots of Rural Capitalism;* De Cunzo, "Culture Broker Revisited"; Engel, "Strangers' Store"; Fanelli, "William Polk's General Store"; Friend, "Merchants and Markethouses"; Lewis, *Artisans in the North Carolina Backcountry;* Martin, "Makers, Buyers, and Users" and "Buying into the World of Goods"; Nobles, "Rise of Merchants in Rural Market Towns"; Perkins, "Consumer Frontier"; Rothenberg, *From Market Places to a Market Economy;* Sweeney, "Gentlemen Farmers and Inland Merchants"; and Thorp, "Doing Business in the Backcountry."

8. Schlereth, "Country Stores, County Fairs," 349.

9. Tönnies, *Fundamental Concepts of Sociology.* On Tönnies' theories and the transformation from a community to market society in early America, see Bender, *Community and Social Change,* 17, 110–15.

10. Taylor, *Transportation Revolution.*

11. Clemens, "Rural Culture and the Farm Economy," 1–2.

12. See, for example, Lockridge, *New England Town.*

13. Pennsylvania studies include Becker, "Diversity and Its Significance"; Lemon, *Best Poor Man's Country;* Wolf, *Urban Village;* and Wood, *Conestoga Crossroads.*

14. Lemon, *Best Poor Man's Country,* xv, 6–7.

15. Henretta, "Families and Farms." The body of literature on the transition to capitalism is enormous. Paul A. Gilje provides a summary of the various positions as well as a comprehensive bibliography in "The Rise of Capitalism in the Early Republic." For another summary that has itself become a classic, see Allan Kulikoff, "Transition to Capitalism in Rural America." Among the most influential of the early works on the debate are Clark, "Household Economy, Market Exchange"; Merrill, "Cash Is Good to Eat"; Mutch, "Yeoman and Merchant in Pre-industrial America"; Pruitt, "Self-Sufficiency and the Agricultural Economy"; and Shammas, "How Self-Sufficient Was Early America?"

16. Henretta, "Families and Farms," 25.

17. On the Mid-Atlantic region, see Bodle, "Themes and Directions in Middle Colonies Historiography."

18. For more on this opposition, see Kulikoff, "Transition to Capitalism," 122–23.

19. Rothenberg, *From Market Places to a Market Economy;* see also Rothenberg, "Market and Massachusetts Farmers, 1750–1855."

20. Clark, *Roots of Rural Capitalism,* 164–67.

21. See Ellis et al., "Symposium on Charles Sellers"; Wilentz, "Society, Politics, and the Market Revolution"; and Stokes and Conway, *Market Revolution in America.*

22. Clark, "Consequences of the Market Revolution," 30.

23. Barron, "Reaping What Has Been Sown," 287.

24. Vickers, "Competency and Competition," 4; McMurry, *Transforming Rural Life,* 52.

25. Clemens, "Rural Culture and the Farm Economy," 3–4.

26. Bushman, "Markets and Composite Farms in Early America."

27. Lamoreaux, "Rethinking the Transition to Capitalism."

28. Bruegel, *Farm, Shop, Landing,* 42–43, 54; Wermuth, *Rip Van Winkle's Neighbors,* 140–41.

29. Appleby, "Vexed Story of Capitalism," 16–17; Barron, "Reaping What Has Been Sown," 288.

30. Classic works on consumption include Breen, "'Baubles of Britain,'" and Carson, Hoffman, and Albert, *Of Consuming Interests.*

31. Martin, "Buying into the World of Goods," 187–257; Perkins, "Consumer Frontier," 510.

32. Carson, "Consumer Revolution in Colonial America," 672; Falk, "Constructing Identity with Belongings and Buildings," 47–55. Falk's book on the same subject, *Architecture and Artifacts of the Pennsylvania Germans,* is forthcoming from the Pennsylvania State University Press.

33. Richard Bushman bemoans our lack of knowledge about inland trade in "Shopping and Advertising in Colonial America," 234. Ann Smart Martin urges a shift in interest from ownership to the study of exchanges that made acquisition (and hence consumption) possible in "Makers, Buyers, and Users," 156.

34. For the argument that goods were not moved great distances, see Doerflinger, "Farmers and Dry Goods," 170; for the opposing view, see Thorp, "Doing Business in the Backcountry," 402; Tooker, *Nathan Trotter,* 120.

35. On Pennsylvania German material culture, see Garvan and Hummel, *Pennsylvania Germans;* Hess, *Mennonite Arts;* Richman, *Pennsylvania German Arts;* and Swank et al., *Arts of the Pennsylvania Germans.*

36. On storekeepers as culture brokers, see De Cunzo, "Culture Broker Revisited," 185–86; Nobles, "Rise of Merchants," 5. On German-American culture brokers, see Roeber, "'Whatever Is Not English Among Us," 264. On Germantown, see Wolf, *Urban Village.*

37. On butter production, see Jensen, *Loosening the Bonds.* Other works on women's economic contributions include Boydston, "Woman Who Wasn't There"; Ulrich, "Martha Ballard and Her Girls."

38. On the importance of Pennsylvania's iron industry, see Paskoff, *Industrial Evolution,* xv. For a community study of iron making, see Walker, *Hopewell Village.* On slavery and ironworking, see Bezís-Selfa, "Tale of Two Ironworks."

39. On the city in general, see Dunn and Dunn, *World of William Penn;* Eberlein and Hubbard, *Portrait of a Colonial City;* Mease, *Picture of Philadelphia;* Miller, "Federal City, 1783–1800"; Nash, *Forging Freedom* and *Urban Crucible;* Hiltzheimer, *Diary of Jacob Hiltzheimer;* Riley, "Philadelphia, the Nation's Capital," Schweitzer, "Spatial Organization of Philadelphia"; *Historic Philadelphia from the Founding;* Siegel, *Philadelphia;* Smith, *"Lower Sort";* Thompson, *Rum Punch and Revolution;* Wainwright, *Colonial Grandeur in Philadelphia;* Warner, *Private City;* and Webster, *Philadelphia Preserved.* On Philadelphia's business community, see Berg, "Organization of Business in Colonial Philadelphia"; Cole, "Tempo of Mercantile Life"; Lindstrom, *Economic Development in the Philadelphia Region;* Ritter, *Philadelphia and Her Merchants;* and Simpson, *Lives of Eminent Philadelphians.* On interregional trade, see Dauer, "Colonial Philadelphia's Interregional Transportation System"; Faris, *Old Roads Out of Philadelphia;* and Walzer, "Colonial Philadelphia and Its Backcountry."

40. On agent-client relationships in the international business community, see Hancock, *Citizens of the World,* 124–28.

41. On merchants, see Bruchey, *Robert Oliver and Mercantile Bookkeeping;* Dalzell, *Enterprising Elite;* Guffin, "'Satisfaction of Arriving to a Good Market'"; Hancock, *Citizens of the World;* Martin, *Merchants and Trade;* Matson, *Merchants and Empire;* Papenfuse, *In Pursuit of Profit;* Tolles, *Meeting Houses and Counting Houses;* and Tooker, *Nathan Trotter.*

42. Dublin, "Rural Putting-Out Work"; Wermuth, *Rip Van Winkle's Neighbors,* 112.

43. Appleby, "Commercial Farming and the 'Agrarian Myth,'" 838.

44. Rex family records are scattered among local archives and private collections. Many manuscript documents are in the archives of Historic Schaefferstown, Inc., Schaefferstown, Pennsylvania (hereafter HSI). Others are in the Joseph Downs Collection of Manuscripts and Printed Ephemera at the Henry Francis du Pont Winterthur Library, Winterthur, Delaware (hereafter JDC.) In addition, many papers remain in the family's possession but have been microfilmed as the Leon E. Lewis Collection (hereafter LEL, followed by microfilm roll and item numbers), with copies in the Joseph Downs Collection and the Lebanon County Historical Society, Lebanon, Pennsylvania.

CHAPTER I

1. The exact date was August 28, 1763; Muhlenberg preached on Acts 10. Muhlenberg, *Journals of Muhlenberg,* 1:666. The more favorable comment is in the entry for May 13, 1770, 2:434.

2. Persistent lore claims that the earliest European arrivals were Jews who established a synagogue and cemetery; if this were true, the Schaefferstown settlement would have been one of the earliest Judaic communities in America. See Zerbe, *Annals of Schaefferstown,* 149–68; and Mays, *Jewish Colony at Tower Hill.* While most historians now reject the story of a sizable early eighteenth-century Jewish community, they stress that by the mid-eighteenth century a few Jewish store-keepers were working in Schaefferstown. See, for example, Hoover, "Questions Regarding the Early History of Schaefferstown"; Brener, "Lancaster's First Jewish Community," 297–99. On the origins of the village, see Brendle, *Brief History of Schaefferstown,* 11–13; Huber, *Schaefferstown, Pennsylvania, 1763–1963,* 17–19.

3. *Pennsylvania Gazette,* November 12, 1761, Accessible Archives, http://www.accessible.com (item 237633).

4. Brendle, *Brief History of Schaefferstown,* 13.

5. Wolf, *Urban Village,* 21.

6. Huber, *Schaefferstown,* 24–35.

7. Lemon, *Best Poor Man's Country,* 122.

8. Market house documents, LEL, roll 5: AS52, roll 13: M5.

9. Reward arbitration for apprehension of Francis Sheetz murderer, 1799, LEL, roll 7: TR3. The petitioners shared a $250 reward, but the arbitrators assessed them for their trouble. Each man had to contribute 3s. 9d. to cover the costs of writing the document and the "tavern charge while sitting on this business."

10. On townships, see Simler, "Township." One cannot, of course, equate these political divisions with the geographical distribution of patrons of Schaefferstown businesses, which drew customers from the town, township, and beyond, especially from Elizabeth Township, Lancaster County, immediately to the south.

11. Egle, *Pennsylvania Archives,* 670–72. My estimates are based on the number of taxable heads of household multiplied by six.

12. When Lebanon County was divided from Dauphin County in 1813, Heidelberg gave some land to the newly created Jackson Township; in 1844, when Millcreek Township was formed out of Heidelberg and Jackson, Heidelberg took on its current size, 24.4 square miles. The township's current population is about four thousand. *Comprehensive Plan, Heidelberg Township, Lebanon County, Pa.,* 52, 55, 67; Brown, *Lebanon County,* 51, 67, 94.

13. Tavern keepers also sold goods, and Schaefferstown had six taverns in 1779. Egle,

Pennsylvania Archives, 670–72. On the city of Reading, see Becker, "Diversity and Its Significance," 196–221. On Lancaster, see Wood, *Conestoga Crossroads,* 160, 171.

14. In Lancaster, Joseph Simon and gunsmith William Henry both sold hardware, James Burd had a wine store, Widow Moore dealt in china and earthenware, and Henry Stuber sold medicine and drugs at the sign of the Golden Pestle and Mortar. Wood, *Conestoga Crossroads,* 93–156.

15. Egle, *Pennsylvania Archives,* 670–72, 879–80. The town had a brew house early on; in 1765 ironmaster Henry William Stiegel advertised for sale a property "two stories high, built of Stone, with all the Utensils necessary for a compleat Brew house. The Malt Floor is one of the best in the Country . . . being cast of iron." *Pennsylvania Gazette,* February 7, 1765, Accessible Archives, item 35138.

16. Becker, "Diversity and Its Significance," 199, 211.

17. Winpenny, *Bending Is Not Breaking,* 9, 44. Peter Getz's advertisement for making and repairing fire engines appeared in the *Lancaster Journal,* December 2, 1796, microfilm, Lancaster County Historical Society, Lancaster, Pennsylvania.

18. Becker, "Diversity and Its Significance," 197–98; Wood, *Conestoga Crossroads,* 181–203.

19. Public transportation came through the town later, but only briefly, in the form of a trolley line that ran from Lebanon to Ephrata via Schaefferstown from 1910 to 1939. Huber, *Schaefferstown,* 176–85.

20. Mays, 'Battalion,' Brendle, *Brief History of Schaefferstown,* 25–26, 30–31. On battalion days in general, see Garrison, "Battalion Day."

21. *Schaeffersschteddel* is the Pennsylvania German dialect name for Schaefferstown. Weiser, "Fraktur," 233.

22. Fogleman, *Hopeful Journeys,* 21–24, 37.

23. Lemon, *Best Poor Man's Country,* xiii–xvi, 1–41; Wolf, *Urban Village,* 329–30; Swank, "Germanic Fragment," 10.

24. Fogleman, *Hopeful Journeys,* 31–34.

25. Ibid., 152; Nolt, *Foreigners in Their Own Land,* 7, 47–65.

26. Nolt, *Foreigners in Their Own Land,* 14; Fogleman, *Hopeful Journeys,* 93–99. For a list of early Schaefferstown residents and the ships they arrived on from 1727 to 1787, see Brendle, *Brief History of Schaefferstown,* 193–95.

27. Cazenove, *Cazenove Journal,* 45.

28. Muhlenberg, *Journals of Muhlenberg,* 2:515.

29. The dialect is spoken mostly by older people and among social groups known as *Grundsau* (Groundhog) Lodges that meet annually to speak "Dutch" and celebrate Groundhog Day. The dialect is also spoken by Amish people of all ages.

30. Egle, *History of the Counties of Dauphin and Lebanon,* 261; *History of St. Paul's Church, Schaefferstown,* 186.

31. Day, *Historical Collections of the State of Pennsylvania,* 417.

32. *History of St. Paul's Church, Schaefferstown,* 53–54.

33. Reference to afternoon services and language is found in Abraham Rex's treasurer's reports, St. Luke Lutheran Church Archives, Schaefferstown, and also in the minutes of St. Luke Church Council from May 14, 1894, A. R. Wentz Library, Gettysburg Theological Seminary, Gettysburg, Pennsylvania.

34. Council Minutes, May 1918, St. Luke Archives. It seems that the German services were discontinued shortly after this, as older Schaefferstown residents have no memory of German services.

35. Nolt, *Foreigners in Their Own Land,* 16, 71.

36. Brendle, *Brief History of Schaefferstown,* 27–28. Samuel Rex bequeathed additional land to the cemetery in his will of 1833, and he stipulated that part of the land go to the Lutherans and part to the Reformed congregation, with a third area reserved for strangers and paupers. Samuel Rex will, will book B, p. 333, Lebanon County Courthouse, Lebanon, Pennsylvania, and LEL, roll 6: AS128.

37. Muhlenberg wrote that the "rightminded and somewhat prosperous" church members "became afraid [of their large debt]. Some moved away; others died, and the rest hit upon the idea of attempting a lottery" to pay for the new building. Muhlenberg, *Journals of Muhlenberg*, 2:468–69.

38. The other committee members were John Nicholas Ensminger and Jacob Seltzer. On George "Swingle's" land holdings in 1764, see Egle, *Pennsylvania Archives*, 154. Schwengel, Ensminger, and Seltzer may have moved out of the area early on, as they are not buried (at least not in marked graves) in the town cemetery.

39. Muhlenberg, *Journals of Muhlenberg*, 2:466–67.

40. Nolt, *Foreigners in Their Own Land*, 51.

41. Huber, *Schaefferstown*, 197–98. Bricker is listed as a member of the Schaefferstown Reformed Church in Brendle, *Brief History of Schaefferstown*, 16. See also Yeakel, *Jacob Albright and His Co-Laborers*, 80–81.

42. Nolt, *Foreigners in Their Own Land*, 34–39; Newman, *Fries's Rebellion*, 72–141.

43. *Oracle of Dauphin*, January 9, 16, and 23, February 6, and March 6, 13, and 20, 1799, quoted in Newman, *Fries's Rebellion*, 93.

44. *General Advertiser*, October 18, 1799, quoted in Nolt, *Foreigners in Their Own Land*, 39.

45. Ibid., 39. Nolt describes Ross and McKean as Irish Protestants. There were other issues involved in the election besides the tax. German speakers were attracted to the Republican Party's reform proposals, which would allow hearings by justices of the peace in German communities to be conducted in German.

46. *Ein ernstlicher Ruf an die Deutschen in Pennsylvanien*, Lancaster, 1799, quoted in Newman, *Fries's Rebellion*, 193.

47. Samuel Laird, William Wallace, William Gayda, Christ. Schenkel, George Lechy, Frederick Young, Conrad Hambaugh, and J. Denzel to Henry Schaeffer et al., August 12, 1799, LEL, roll 13: P16. Other recipients were innkeepers or former innkeepers Michael Valentine, Anthony Seyfert, and Philip Erpff; miller John Shenk; and farmers Joseph Bomberger, George Dissinger, Nicholas Swanger, George Weyman, and Jacob Bricker.

48. Newman, *Fries's Rebellion*, 194; Cox, "Pennsylvania Gubernatorial Election Returns, 1799."

49. Election tally, 1799, Heidelberg Township, LEL, roll 14: VI.

50. Cox, "Pennsylvania Gubernatorial Election Returns, 1799."

51. Noble, *Touch of Time*, 9. Coleman, a supporter of John Adams, was an unsuccessful nominee for presidential elector in 1800. Cox, "Pennsylvania Presidential Election Returns, 1800," *Pennsylvania Election Statistics, 1789–2004*. On Ege, see Newman, *Fries's Rebellion*, 27–28.

52. Bergengren, "From Lovers to Murderers," 48–49. See also Bergengren, "Transformations in the Houses of Schaefferstown"; and Swank, "Architectural Landscape."

53. Schoepf, *Travels in the Confederation, 1783–1784*, 1:125.

54. There were other floor plans in early Schaefferstown houses besides the *Flurkuchen*. See Bergengren, "Transformations in the Houses of Schaefferstown," 62–108. Early residents would not have known the term *Flurkuchen*; this is a modern word applied by some folklorists and historians.

55. In standard or "High" German the three rooms would be *Küche*, *Kammer*, and *Stube*. I am indebted to Christopher Witmer for providing the Pennsylvania Dutch and standard German terms.

56. Bergengren, "Transformations in the Houses of Schaefferstown," 537–39.

57. I computed the average farm size from acreages listed in U.S. direct tax returns, 1798 (hereafter USDT), Heidelberg Township, Dauphin County, Pennsylvania, schedule II, microfilm, Center for Historic Architecture and Design, University of Delaware, Newark. On farm size and the number of workers needed, see Miller, *Rise of an Iron Community*, 25.

58. On indentured servants, see Salinger, *"To Serve Well and Faithfully"*; on tenants, see Clemens and Simler, "Rural Labor and the Farm Household." The direct tax assessors recorded a number of "occupants" who lived in tenant houses on farms, and Rex often noted that his customers lived on another's farm (e.g., "at Eckert's place").

59. Slave owners in 1771 were George Holstoner, Simon Koppenhefer, the widow of Isaac Meyer (who owned two), Nicholaus Schwengel, Christopher Stump, Peter Shitz, and Philip Wolfersberger. Sowers, *Colonial Taxes, Heidelberg Township,* 22–29; Weiser and Neff, *Purchases of the King George Hotel,* 199–205. The 1780 slave owners were Widow Meyer, Peter Shitz, Philip Wolfersberger, and possibly Thomas Bassler. There were two returns for September 1780; Bassler is listed as a slave owner on one but not on the other. Sowers, *Colonial Taxes,* 71–90.

60. He may have been the same David "Kramer" who wove the baskets that Rex bought for resale to the ironmasters. If so, he was one of the few farmers who sold craft goods to Rex and was apparently offsetting his lack of good farmland with a second occupation.

61. All property information comes from USDT, Heidelberg Township. The $101 value of Gromer's house was just high enough to put the property on schedule I rather than schedule II, which was reserved for farm buildings, wharves, mills, land more than two acres in size, and smaller lots with houses valued at less than $100. Tax assessors in Heidelberg valued only two houses at less than $100, and these were apparently in extremely bad shape.

62. Bartram, Evans, and Weiser, *Journey from Pennsylvania to Onondaga in 1743,* 107. On the geography and fertility of this part of Pennsylvania, see Lemon, *Best Poor Man's Country,* 32–41.

63. Rush, *Account of the Manners of the German Inhabitants,* 64. The decision to sell the best produce is the reverse of the tendency in New England, where farmers sent the poorest stuff off to market. Clark, *Roots of Rural Capitalism,* 95.

64. Cazenove, *Cazenove Journal,* 34, 82–83. Travelers' descriptions, of course, reflect their own political and cultural biases and need to be understood within that framework. On this point, see Falk, "Constructing Identity with Belongings and Buildings," chapter 2.

65. Miller's house, known as the House of the Miller, is still standing; in the 1920s the Pennsylvania Museum of Art (now the Philadelphia Museum of Art) acquired two rooms from the house and put them on display. Downs, *House of the Miller at Millbach;* Garvan, *Pennsylvania German Collection,* 6–7.

66. Pendleton, *Oley Valley Heritage,* 38.

67. Kline owned twenty-three and one-half acres of land in addition to the town properties; altogether his real estate was worth $852. His log house is still standing on Lancaster Avenue in Schaefferstown.

68. Probably the same brew house once owned by Stiegel. See note 15 above.

69. On this point, see Swank, "Germanic Fragment," 14.

70. In June 1819 Flower's widow advertised that the Westmoreland County pottery was for sale. Whisker, *Pennsylvania Potters, 1660–1900,* 107.

71. Lewis, *Artisans in the North Carolina Backcountry,* 22–23; Rothenberg, "Invention of American Capitalism," 91; Bruegel, *Farm, Shop, Landing,* 44; and Fogleman, *Hopeful Journeys,* 189n37.

72. Swank, "Germanic Fragment," 18.

73. The farmers were John Krum, John Moyer, Peter Ream Sr., and Jacob Kapp.

74. Clemens and Simler, "Rural Labor and the Farm Household," 106, 122.

75. One such community exchange is revealed in a legal document from 1780. When an arbitration team ruled on a dispute between Schaefferstown residents and erstwhile lovers Durst Thoma and Sophia Fried regarding household expenses and care for the couple's children, they stipulated that among Thoma's responsibilities was the "weaver's wage" of four and one-half bushels of rye in exchange for a length of linen the couple had ordered. LEL, roll 7: TR17.

76. Moore purchase, December 10, 1799, Rex daybook 10, LEL, roll 1: AB9. Mace exchanged butter kegs for a watch on October 10, 1806. Rex daybook 38, LEL, roll 1: AB1.

77. These probate inventories, on file at the Dauphin County Courthouse, Harrisburg, are much more extensive than the selected items mentioned here.

78. Sheetz owned an eighteen-year-old slave in 1771 and a fifty-year-old slave in 1780, according to the tax records. Sowers, *Colonial Taxes,* 27, 76. The Sheetz farm gained notoriety as the scene of the violent murder of Francis Sheetz, son of Peter Sheetz Sr., on December 28, 1787. Brendle, *Brief History of Schaefferstown,* 33–35.

79. It was common for people, including businessmen, to use the old pound system for years after the United States switched to the dollar. McCusker, *Money and Exchange in Europe and America*, 120–21, 175; Hammond, *Banks and Politics in America*, 48–53.

80. Tall clocks were common in Pennsylvania German inventories of this era; they were usually the most expensive piece of furniture in the house and served as a sign of one's success. Foreman, "German Influences in Pennsylvania Furniture," 148.

81. Cazenove, *Cazenove Journal*, 84.

82. Smith inventory, photocopy, HSI. The exact location of his house is unknown, but he owned thirty-two acres in 1780. Smith is listed as a tanner in the 1771 and 1780 tax lists, but in his inventory he is described as a farmer. Sowers, *Colonial Taxes*, 28, 76.

83. The Albrecht genealogy is recounted in Brendle, *Brief History of Schaefferstown*, 196.

84. While combining a tavern and store was common in the countryside, taverns and stores were usually separate enterprises in cities. Thorp, "Doing Business in the Backcountry," 391.

85. Brendle, *Brief History of Schaefferstown*, 13–14. Apparently the name "King George" was handed down in oral history. It does not appear in primary documents; rather, the custom seems to have been to refer to a hotel or inn by the proprietor's name.

86. Such buildings are known as *durchgangigen* in recent studies; see Bergengren, "Transformations in the Houses of Schaefferstown," 19, 89, 146, 179. The building was enlarged and remodeled in 1883, but it still retains a center passage plan with a barroom on the south side of the building.

87. Ibid., 146.

88. Details about Schaeffer's store come from Weiser and Neff, *Records of Purchases at the King George Hotel*. Reference to the old Irisher is on p. 94.

89. Alexander Schaeffer died on April 10, 1786; his will is on file in the Lancaster County Courthouse. Henry's inheritance (for which he paid £1,800) included several plantations and tracts of land, as well as the tavern house. His will is filed in the Dauphin County Courthouse, Harrisburg. For disposition of Henry Jr.'s inventory, see "Abraham Rex's account of store goods of Henry Schaeffer Jr.," HSI.

90. *Pennsylvanische Berichte*, June 22, 1759, photocopy, HSI. I am indebted to Robert C. Bucher for providing this citation and the English translation.

91. Transfer by deed poll from Bartholomew Lobach to Lyon Nathan and Benjamin Nathan, who sold it to Henry Harrison, David Franks, Charles Woodham, and James Young, merchants of Philadelphia, and Joseph Symonds of Lancaster, on August 7, 1763; this deed is in the HSI archives.

92. Quoted in Brener, "Lancaster's First Jewish Community," 253–54; on the *Staatsbote*, see Miller, *Early German American Newspapers*, 27. Simon and Nathan's ad is reproduced along with a slightly different translation in Sowers, *Colonial Taxes*, 37.

93. Edwin Hocker, *Genealogical Data Relating to the German Settlers of Pennsylvania*, 85.

94. Stern, "Two Jewish Functionaries in Colonial Pennsylvania," 29.

95. Cited by Guice in *Frederick Stump*, 23. The same notice must have run for several months; Hocker, *Genealogical Data*, 81, refers to a similar ad dated October 12, 1759. On Sauer's newspaper, see Miller, *Early German American Newspapers*, 34–41.

96. Stump's career was checkered after leaving Schaefferstown. In 1768 he was jailed for the massacre of ten peaceful Native Americans near Selinsgrove, Pennsylvania. An angry mob released him from jail; he fled south and started life anew in the backcountry. He served under Francis Marion during the Revolution, was captured by the British, and by 1789 was keeping a tavern in Tennessee. At the age of ninety-three he married his second wife, a twenty-five-year-old barmaid. Guice, *Frederick Stump*, ix, x, 23–24, 67, 83. Stumpstown is now known as Fredericksburg.

97. Jacobs advertised in Sauer's newspaper, May 11, 1759, that he had opened a store in company with Jacob Levi "on Muehlbach road, five miles from Conrad Weiser's inn and one mile from Saltzgeber and two miles from Tulpehocken." His advertisement specifically warned customers that he did not do business on Saturday or Sunday because he was Jewish. A second ad for the store appeared on February 13, 1761. Hocker, *Genealogical Data*, 77.

98. Wood, *Conestoga Crossroads*, 101.

99. Stern, "Two Jewish Functionaries in Colonial Pennsylvania," 29–35. There were some questions about his management of the lottery, but he was exonerated. By 1780 he had moved on to Lancaster and opened a store there.

100. Hoover, "Questions Regarding the Early History of Schaefferstown," 48. For more on Jacobs and the other Jewish storekeepers discussed in this section, see Pencak, *Jews and Gentiles in Early America*, 191–99.

101. It is only through Rex's papers that we learn about Kreider's Schaefferstown store, as it has otherwise disappeared from the records. The location of the store is unknown; an invoice from potter Peter Newman dated August 10, 1791 (LEL, roll 2: B1), refers to "earthenware left in the hands of Hy Valentine" on September 14, 1790, hinting that Kreider may have rented space in Henry Valentine's tavern, as Samuel Rex would do later.

102. A letter from a mutual acquaintance shows that Rex worked among a group of young scriveners in the city and that he left town suddenly. N. Hammond to Rex, October 28, 1790, LEL, roll 12: L53. Rex wrote the terms of his employment agreement in a small notebook of wages and expenses, LEL, roll 6: AS111.

103. *Lancaster Journal*, August 25, 1798, microfilm, Lancaster County Historical Society.

104. Rex's grandfather, Hans Jürg Rüger, was an immigrant from a German-speaking region of Europe and an early settler in the area that became Germantown. In the next generation the family anglicized its name to Rex. Schutte, "George Rex (1682–1772)." (For more on the Rex family, see Appendix A.) Chestnut Hill was also known as Sommerhausen; it was one of four villages (the others were Germantown, Cresheim, and Crefeld) situated along the road leading into Philadelphia that now make up Germantown. In 1790 Sommerhausen contained about a hundred families; residents commonly described themselves as being from Germantown. Wolf, *Urban Village*, 23.

105. Contosta, *Suburb in the City*, 14–15; 19–20; MacFarlane, *History of Early Chestnut Hill*, 53, 70.

106. Lewis Kreider to Samuel Rex, n.d., LEL, roll 6: AS116. "Mr. Boyers" almost certainly refers to the inn, built by Paul Gemberling and owned by George Boyer from 1787 to 1792, on the northeast corner of the town square; this is the same building that Samuel Rex later purchased for his home. The earlier chain of ownership is recited in the deed transferring ownership from George and Anna Maria Boyer to George Weidman, March 30, 1792, LEL, roll 9: 118, and Dauphin County deed book E, vol. 21, p. 294.

107. Kreider to Rex, LEL, roll 5: AS79. Store daybooks were the chronological record of daily business; entries in daybooks were crucial because they were the only admissible evidence in litigation over a store bill. Coffin, *Progressive Exercises in Bookkeeping*, 29, quoted in Fanelli, "William Polk's General Store," 214.

108. Carson, *Old Country Store*, 15, 66.

109. Rex's small notebook of wages and expenses, LEL, roll 6: AS111.

110. Ibid. By 1796 Rex had done well enough at storekeeping to buy himself a gold watch for £9 15s. Receipt from Roger Caulet, October 25, 1796, LEL, roll 8: C17.

111. Kreider was issued a license to operate a tavern in Jonestown in 1795. Fox, "Our Old Taverns," 132. In 1792 and 1793 Kreider ran for the Pennsylvania Assembly. In 1793 he wrote to ask Rex to drum up support in Schaefferstown for him and the largely German ticket, headed by F. A. C. Muhlenberg as candidate for governor. Kreider to Rex, LEL, roll 6: AS153. Muhlenberg, although well known in Pennsylvania, lost to the incumbent, Thomas Mifflin. Tinkcom, *Republicans and Federalists in Pennsylvania*, 136–38.

112. Kreider to Rex, February 23, 1795, LEL, roll 5: AS79.

113. Kipplinger store ledger, 1799, kept by Martin Meily; Lebanon County Historical Society.

114. On November 15, 1791, Rex paid Valentine £1 8s. for room and board; two days later, he paid £3 for a "half year's house rent." Rex receipt book, HSI. While Rex did not state to whom he paid the second sum, his correspondence shows that his store was in the Valentine tavern. In

July 1791 Rex's brother John wrote to him about leaving the store in the care of "the people of the house"; in a second letter, dated October 1791, John specifically advised Rex to ask Michael Valentine or his sister to tend the store. John Rex to Samuel Rex, LEL, roll 6: AS188, and roll 5: AS101.

115. "I do acknowledge to have rec'd of my Father the following sums of money and goods viz.: about the month of Nov 1790 £25 [and] 2 doz. Germantown stockings . . . £6." Receipt, LEL, roll 6: AS175.

116. In 1763 Erpff listed his occupation as "innkeeper." Property deed, George Swengle, blacksmith, to Philip Erpff, innkeeper, LEL, roll 9: TR139. In 1796, in a legal document concerning guardianship of a friend's children, Erpff listed himself as a "storekeeper." LEL, roll 12: G31.

117. The other link to the war involves the town's Lutheran church, which was used as a hospital for wounded soldiers and was badly damaged in 1778. Gillett, *Army Medical Department, 1775–1818*, 109, 210. In 1779 the congregation petitioned the Continental Congress to help pay for the damages. A copy of the letter is in the St. Luke Archives; the text is quoted in Brendle, *Brief History of Schaefferstown*, 230.

118. In January 1799 Erpff sold Rex seventeen yards of linen, two dozen scissors, two quires of paper, and thirty-six pounds of ginger. In return, Rex sold Erpff ten pounds of loaf sugar and a bushel of salt and hauled half a barrel of rum for him. Erpff receipt book, HSI; receipt, "Samuel Rex bo't of Philip Erpff," January 7, 1799, LEL, roll 2: B1. By 1800 Erpff was no longer in business, and he was renting the part of his house that was the store to a lodger, Dr. Jacob Grubb, for £9 a year. Erpff-Grubb lease, LEL, roll 11: A15. Erpff's will, Dauphin County Courthouse, Harrisburg, and LEL, roll 9: EE1.

119. The Kapp (Capp) family arrived from Europe in 1750; by 1765 they had warranted land in Heidelberg Township (Brendle, *Brief History of Schaefferstown*, 189, 195). Michael Kapp is listed as a shopkeeper in the 1779 tax returns (Egle, *Pennsylvania Archives*, 670–72). From 1786 to 1788 Michael had a tavern license; his kinsman Andreas, who had a tavern license in 1795 and 1796, apparently succeeded him in storekeeping. Dauphin County Tavern License Petitions, microfilm, Pennsylvania State Archives, Harrisburg.

120. The 1798 direct tax assessors specifically described the Rex and Kapp buildings as stores, but they did not list Erpff's building as an inn or store, perhaps because it was also his dwelling, or perhaps because he had recently gone out of business.

121. Kapp's personal inventory includes the value of the store inventory but does not give a breakdown of goods. Kapp will and probate inventory, Dauphin County Courthouse, Harrisburg.

122. "Inventory and Amount of Store Goods Sold to Abraham Rex by Samuel Rex, June 1, 1807," HSI.

123. Rex commission as justice of the peace, LEL, roll 8: TR68; Kapp's appointment is cited in Egle, *History of the Counties of Dauphin and Lebanon*, 282. In 1815 Henry Schaeffer Jr. described Kapp as a "storekepir" in an entry in his store ledger; Schaeffer ledger, private collection of Dr. Robert Kline.

CHAPTER 2

1. Rex ledger 8, 1806–1833, LEL, roll 2: AB22.

2. Rex to Frederick Seylor, August 17, 1833, LEL, roll 5: AS55.

3. On November 17, 1789, Kreider wrote Rex to tell him not to hurry back (from Germantown to Philadelphia?) and that the delay in getting cash would give Rex more time to get his things together. Kreider to Rex, LEL, roll 6: AS117.

4. Many historians define the early republic as the years between the ratification of the Constitution and the election of Andrew Jackson in 1828. See Wood, "Significance of the Early Republic"; Hutchins, *Everyday Life in the Early Republic*, 1. Jack Larkin considers a slightly longer period in *Reshaping of Everyday Life*.

5. McCoy, *Elusive Republic,* 101.

6. Gilje, "Rise of Capitalism in the Early Republic," 2–6. Rothenberg also stresses the importance of the federal period in "Invention of American Capitalism," 68.

7. On traditional business methods, see Chandler, *Visible Hand,* 15–49.

8. Cazenove, *Cazenove Journal,* 44. Cazenove was referring to the countryside between Sinking Spring and Womelsdorf, Pennsylvania. While he approved of the farmers' enterprise, he thought they used their money unwisely.

9. The Rexes were married on December 13, 1791, at Christ Lutheran Church, Stouchburg, Pennsylvania. "Records of Christ Lutheran, Stouchburg," Lebanon County Historical Society. Anna Maria Rex's birth date is listed in Brendle, *Brief History of Schaefferstown,* 172.

10. "Brief of Title to Lot #17 in Schaefferstown, Lebanon County, Pennsylvania," HSI. Michael Valentine's tavern license is listed in Dauphin County Tavern License Petitions, microfilm, Pennsylvania State Archives, Harrisburg.

11. Alexander Schaeffer died in 1786; Valentine and Rex rented the building from Alexander's son Henry. They are listed as "occupants" of Henry Schaeffer's tavern and store in USDT, Heidelberg Township, Dauphin County, schedule I.

12. *Pennsylvania Gazette,* February 17, 1787, Accessible Archives, item 73646. Lebanon is seven miles west of Schaefferstown. Leasing a property for business was also common in Philadelphia. See Salinger, "Spaces, Inside and Outside," 6.

13. USDT, Heidelberg Township, Dauphin County, schedule I.

14. The dates, numbers, and current locations of Rex's daybooks are shown in Appendix F.

15. The Valentines' son, Samuel, was born August 20, 1795; Samuel and Mary Rex were godparents at the child's baptism. Brendle, *Brief History of Schaefferstown,* 110.

16. The occupants of the property are shown in USDT, Heidelberg Township, Dauphin County, schedule I.

17. Rex's purchase of the property is shown in the deed from Henry Stohler to Samuel Rex, March 5, 1799, LEL, roll 5: AS48. Garret is listed as an occupant of the hatter shop in USDT, Heidelberg Township, Dauphin County, schedule I.

18. Seyfert's sales of sundries appear in his two extant tavern books. Seyfert, who was formerly the Dauphin County coroner, wrote tavern records in the back of his old coroner's docket, LEL, roll 7: GM6. A second (manuscript) tavern book is in the Joseph Downs Collection at the Winterthur Library. Though the latter is not identified as Seyfert's, comparison of the dates and handwriting in the two books shows that he wrote them both.

19. On scrivening, see Thornton, *Handwriting in America,* 6–12.

20. On Harris, see Shammas, *Pre-Industrial Consumer in England and America,* 283; on Polk and combining storekeeping with other enterprises, see Fanelli, "William Polk's General Store," 213, 215. Jeremiah Brown's account books are at the Hagley Museum and Library, Wilmington, Delaware. Doerflinger describes similar activities among New Jersey storekeepers in "Farmers and Dry Goods," 190.

21. Taylor, "'Where Humbler Shop-Men from the Crowd Retreat.'" Ann Smart Martin describes two different store configurations in Virginia in "Buying into the World of Goods," 203.

22. Henry Valentine probate inventory, 1792, Dauphin County Courthouse, Harrisburg.

23. On heating stores, see Bergengren, "Transformations in the Houses of Schaefferstown," 511, and Martin, "Buying into the World of Goods," 201. Rex paid Valentine 7s. 6d. for a stove in November 1791. Rex receipt book, HSI.

24. Henry Schaeffer probate inventory, 1803; Dauphin County Courthouse, Harrisburg.

25. Rex made a note in his daybook that a customer left cash "on the counter" in July 1806. Rex daybook 37, HSI.

26. Martin, "Buying into the World of Goods," 207.

27. Kuhn and Risberg to French and Co., August 17, 1786, Kuhn and Risberg letter book, Kuhn and Risberg papers, Bucks County Historical Society, Doylestown, Pennsylvania, quoted in Doerflinger, "Farmers and Dry Goods," 170.

28. Martin, "Buying into the World of Goods," 205, 207.

29. Letter book of Michael Hillegas, 1757–1760, Am.0803, letter to P. Clopper, July 1757 (illegible), Historical Society of Pennsylvania, quoted in Roeber, "'Whatever Is Not English Among Us,'" 260.

30. Adrienne D. Hood argues that such terms as Irish linen, British sail cloth, etc. were generic by the eighteenth century. Hood, *Weaver's Craft*, 137.

31. Some writers suggest that English firms produced particularly "gaudy" dishes for the German American market, but this has not been proved. See Schwind, "Pennsylvania German Earthenware," 181.

32. Among the specific devotional titles that can be identified from Rex's receipts and daybooks are *Das kleine Davidische Psalterspiel der kinder Zions* . . . (Chestnut Hill, Pa.: Samuel Saur, 1791); Johann Philip Schabalie, *Die Wandlende Seel* . . . (Germantown, Pa.: Peter Leibert, 1794); Rudolph Zacharias Becker, *Noth- und Hülfs-Büchlein* (Gotha: In der Expedition der Deutschen Zeitung, 1793); Gerhard Tersteegen, *Geistliches Blumen-Gärtlein inniger Seelen* . . . (Germantown, Pa.: Michael Billmeyer, 1800); and Johann Habermann, *Christliche Morgen und Abend-Gebäter* (Germantown, Pa.: Peter Leibert, 1788).

33. The editions of Starck and Zollikofer that Rex sold must have been European imports since the American editions came slightly later. Johann Friedrich Starck, *Tägliches Hand-Buch in guten und bösen Tagen* (Philadelphia: Gedrickt für Conrad Zentler und George Mentz, 1812); Johannes Zollikofer, *Himmlischer Weihrauchschatz,* 6th ed. (New York: Martin, Lambert & Co., 1839). I am deeply indebted to Alan Keyser for his help in identifying the German-language books that Rex sold.

34. The ABC books Rex sold were published by Germantown printers Christopher Saur and Michael Billmeyer. Rosalind Remer describes Billmeyer as "the major source for German books"; he had a "virtual monopoly on the German book market." Remer, *Printers and Men of Capital,* 86.

35. Rex sold almanacs distributed by Philadelphia printers Steiner and Cist; he also obtained German almanacs from Lancaster printers Albrecht and Lahn. The latter partner, Jacob Lahn, trained under Christopher Saur; he and Albrecht produced Lancaster's first German newspaper. On Lahn, see Wood, *Conestoga Crossroads,* 236–38; Cazden, *Social History of the German Book Trade,* 15.

36. Rex's book purchases were as follows: in November 1794, three dozen German almanacs and one dozen English almanacs; in January 1795, six German Bibles, six Lutheran hymnals, a dozen each German testaments and ABC books, and three English Bibles; in November 1797, seven dozen German almanacs and six English almanacs; in November 1799, six dozen German almanacs, one dozen English almanacs, three dozen (German) ABC books, a dozen German testaments, six English testaments, and six *Ready Reckoners.* Bookseller Godfrey Baker's invoices, LEL, roll 6: AS106, and roll 2: B1.

37. "Inventory and Amount of Store Goods Sold to Abraham Rex by Samuel Rex, June 1, 1807," HSI.

38. Armstrong was a basket maker or nail smith; his inventory (LEL, roll 9: AE1) includes "nailor's tools" and thirty-six coal baskets. His ethnicity is uncertain; he seems to have been bilingual, as he bought an English assistant book, but he was a member of the German Lutheran church. Brendle, *Brief History of Schaefferstown,* 19.

39. Among his English-language books, Rex sold "assistant books" and *Ready Reckoners,* handy books of conversion tables for businessmen. See, for example, Thomas Dilworth, *The Schoolmaster's Assistant* (Philadelphia: Joseph Crukshank, 1784); Daniel Fenning, *The Federal or New Ready Reckoner, and Traders' Useful Assistant* . . . (Chestnut Hill, Pa.: Samuel Sower, 1793); and Benjamin Workman, *The American Accountant or Schoolmasters' New Assistant* (Philadelphia: John M'Culloch for William Young, 1789).

40. Wilson's ethnicity is unknown. According to Brendle, *Brief History of Schaefferstown,* 25, an Anthony Wilson was an early resident of Schaefferstown. However, Rex usually reserved courtesy titles for the women from the iron furnaces.

41. James Jameson, *A Report of the Trial of James Jameson and James M'Gowan . . . December 1806, for the Murder of Jacob Eshelman . . . Likewise a Sketch of the Life of Jacob Eshelman, and an Accurate Account of the Life of James M'Gowan* (Harrisburg: Printed by John Wyeth, 1806). John Smith, whose family had been in Schaefferstown for several generations, was a weaver who worked in the traditional German style. Brendle, *Brief History of Schaefferstown*, 32, 172, 194.

42. Brown, *Knowledge Is Power*, 141.

43. Peters bought the book on November 1, 1804. Rex daybook 28, HSI.

44. On a visit to H & P Rice Booksellers in April 1795, Rex acquired one copy each of Blackstone's *Commentaries, Arabian Nights,* Boyle's *Voyages,* and *Cain and Abel,* and on September 1798 he bought *Flowers of History* and William Bartram's *Travels* from bookseller Robert Johnson. LEL, roll 6: AS106, and roll 2: B1. Blackstone refers to William Blackstone, *Commentaries on the Laws of England in Four Books.* Boyle's *Voyages* refers to William Rufus Chetwood, *The Voyages and Adventures of Captain Robert Boyle* (1730).

45. Eliza Parsons, *The Girl of the Mountains: A Novel* (Philadelphia: John Bioren and David Hogan, 1801).

46. The managers were Mr. Rhodes at Reading Furnace and Peter Leib, James Moore, and Hugh Gallagher at Cornwall; the ironmaster was George Ege. These loans appear in Rex daybook 1, HSI; daybook 25, LEL, roll 1: AB13; daybook 31, HSI; and daybook 34, LEL, roll 1: AB16.

47. The book's title shows how important it would have been to Rex and other justices of the peace: *Conductor Generalis, or the office, duty and authority of justices of the peace, high sheriffs, under-sheriffs, goalers, coroners, constables, jury men, over-seers of the poor, and also the office of clerks of assize and of the peace, &c. . . .* (Philadelphia: Printed and sold by Andrew Bradford, 1722).

48. The professionals in the community also borrowed *Girl of the Mountains, History of W. Montague, Beverige's Thoughts, History of Josephus,* and "a large book on Germany &c. . . . almost 200 years old." The loans are recorded in Rex daybooks 22, 40, 41, and 42.

49. This was almost certainly Henry Muhlenberg's German-English, English-German dictionary, printed by William Hamilton in Lancaster in 1812.

50. Stuart C. Sherman, "Leman Thomas Rede's *Bibliotheca Americana,*" *William and Mary Quarterly,* 3rd ser., 4 (July 1946): 348; Schoepf, *Travels in the Confederation,* 1:107, 104. Both quoted in Cazden, *Social History of the German Book Trade,* 17.

51. Carson, "Consumer Revolution in Colonial America," 672; Falk, "Constructing Identity with Belongings and Buildings," 21.

52. On German customs in high-style city homes, see Herman, *Town House,* 77–97. On Pennsylvania Germans' beds, food, furniture, and *Fraktur,* see Gehret and Keyser, *Homespun Textile Tradition;* Keyser, "Beds, Bedding, Bedsteads, and Sleep"; *Landis Valley Cookbook;* Weaver, *Pennsylvania Dutch Country Cooking* and *Sauerkraut Yankees;* Wenger, "Saffron Use Among Pennsylvania Germans"; Fabian, *Pennsylvania-German Decorated Chest;* and Weiser, "Fraktur." A photograph of the *Taufschein* commemorating Mary Rex's birth is in the Thomas R. Brendle Museum, Schaefferstown.

53. For Rex's expenditures in stocking the store, see figure 17.

54. Doerflinger, "Farmers and Dry Goods," 173, 178. See also Hersh and Hersh, *Cloth and Costume,* 55–80. For a glossary of textile terms, see Gehret, *Rural Pennsylvania Clothing,* 276–88.

55. Hood, "Material World of Cloth," 59, 64–65, and *Weaver's Craft,* 127; Shammas, "How Self-Sufficient Was Early America?" 253–58.

56. Gehret and Keyser, *Homespun Textile Tradition.*

57. Doerflinger, "Farmers and Dry Goods," 177.

58. Hood, *Weaver's Craft,* 127.

59. Rex daybook 18, HSI. Ellen J. Gehret estimates that a petticoat (skirt) and "shortgown" (blouse) would take about five yards of forty-five-inch-width fabric. Gehret, *Rural Pennsylvania Clothing,* 34. On textiles and clothing in this period, see also Hersh and Hersh, *Cloth and Costume;* Emerson, "Clothing the Pennsylvania Mennonite Woman."

60. Perkins, "Consumer Frontier," 508.

61. Stookey purchase, March 21, 1801, Rex daybook 15, LEL, roll 1: AB11; Shultz to Rex, May 18, 1801, LEL, roll 6: AS171.

62. Flower's purchase appears in Rex daybook 6, HSI.

63. Lewis, *Artisans in the North Carolina Backcountry*, 61.

64. Rex bought eighty-five hundred weavers' reeds from Jacob Harter in June 1799. Rex daybook 1, JDC. On weavers' reeds and brushes and the specialists who produced them, see Hood, *Weaver's Craft*, 96.

65. Dr. Jacob Grubb bought two dozen bottles of cordial in May 1802. Rex daybook 19, JDC.

66. Lewis, *Artisans in North Carolina Backcountry*, 60.

67. On mills and the toll or "custom" extracted by the miller, see Pendleton, *Oley Valley Heritage*, 38–40. Flour and grain were such an important part of the household economy that Henry Schaeffer left instructions in his will that his son Henry Jr. should take his stepmother's grain to the mill for grinding into flour. Schaeffer will, Dauphin County Courthouse, Harrisburg.

68. There were clockmakers in surrounding communities, including Lebanon, but if there were clockmakers in Heidelberg Township, either they did not sign their work or no examples of their work have survived.

69. Some storekeepers even took cash deposits, but there is no evidence of this practice in Rex's books. See Thorp, "Doing Business in the Backcountry," 392.

70. Gayda to Rex, December 20, 1799, LEL, roll 6: AS114; McClane (McClain) purchases, Rex daybook 10, LEL, roll 1: AB9.

71. February 3, 1798, Rex daybook 5, LEL, roll 1: AB7.

72. Larsen, "Profile of a Colonial Merchant," 282, quoted in Doerflinger, "Farmers and Dry Goods," 172.

73. The customers included Henry Schaeffer, four craftsmen, and two women; they may have used the books to record business and household accounts. Rex daybook 5, LEL, roll 1: AB6.

74. Rex daybook 21, JDC.

75. Rex daybook 19, JDC.

76. Fletcher to Rex, July 26, 1799, LEL, roll 7: TR8.

77. "Scheme of the Lottery" broadside, HSI.

78. Debit to Bombarger estate, August 13, 1803, Rex daybook 23, JDC. I have not found evidence outside of the Rex books of rice pudding being served at Pennsylvania German funerals. Raisin pie (often called funeral pie) is the dessert more commonly associated with these events.

79. Hubka, "Farm Family Mutuality," 13–23.

80. Debit to Widow McCalley's estate, October 26, 1805, Rex daybook 33, JDC.

81. Loan of bar glasses to Seyfert, March 21, 1800, Rex daybook 11, HSI; loan of greatcoat, April 7, 1802, Rex daybook 19, JDC; loan of pistol, December 31, 1802, Rex daybook 21, JDC.

82. *Landis Valley Cookbook*, 2.

83. These sales are shown in Rex daybook 11, HSI. Garret obtained a tavern license in 1799. Fox, "Our Old Taverns," 137.

84. On butchering, see *Landis Valley Cookbook*, 84–89.

85. Fletcher, *Pennsylvania Agriculture and Country Life*, 339–43, 353–56.

86. The sales to the innkeepers are listed in Rex daybook 8, JDC. Seyfert noted the date of the Cherry Fair and logged his credit sales that day in his tavern book. LEL, roll 7: GM6.

87. On the leisurely pace of business in early America, see Cole, "Tempo of Mercantile Life."

88. Doerflinger, "Farmers and Dry Goods," 172; Fanelli, "William Polk's General Store," 222.

89. Wood, *Conestoga Crossroads*, 95. Lewis Atherton found that despite laws to the contrary, southern storekeepers did "considerable" business on Sundays. Atherton, *Southern Country Store*, 67–68.

90. See Shoemaker, *Christmas in Pennsylvania*. On the increasing commercialism of the holiday, see Nissenbaum, *Battle for Christmas*, 132–75. Philadelphia stores were usually closed for Independence Day. On July 4, 1777, the city was illuminated in honor of the holiday; rioters broke a number of store windows to protest Quaker merchants' refusal to shut their stores. On

July 4, 1795, Elizabeth Drinker recorded that city newspapers called for a "fuss and do" in celebration. Drinker, *Diary of Elizabeth Drinker* (abridged version, 1994), 60, 151–52. See also Waldstreicher, *In the Midst of Perpetual Fetes,* 31–35.

91. Figures are based on a comparison of the customers in Rex's daybooks with the Heidelberg and Elizabeth Township property owners listed in USDT. The total of sixty-eight property owners and tenants in Schaefferstown excludes Rex. Frederick Bollman operated a tavern and store on Main Street in Myerstown, and Frantz Seibert had a small log "storehouse" in Newmanstown. Newmanstown also had three taverns, operated by Godfrey Kiener, Frederick Mattee, and John Meiser, who typically would have also sold some goods. USDT, Heidelberg Township, Dauphin County, schedule I.

92. Thorp describes this frontier model in "Doing Business in the Backcountry," 396. See Rothenberg, "Market and Massachusetts Farmers," 291–92, for an analysis of the distance over which farmers hauled goods to market; see Lemon, *Best Poor Man's Country,* 118–49, for a discussion of central-place theory and the placement of Pennsylvania market towns.

93. Sheetz's "black man" bought goods on January 10, 1800. Rex daybook 10, LEL, roll 1: AB9. On African Americans at the furnaces, see Chapter 3. Indian Kate's purchases appear in Rex daybook 12, JDC.

94. In 1791 and 1798, 10 percent of the transactions that Rex recorded in his daybooks involved sales to women. In 1806–7, 12 percent of sales were to women.

95. Perkins, "Consumer Frontier," 495–96; Thorp, "Doing Business in the Backcountry," 399; Kulikoff, *Tobacco and Slaves,* 178; McCurry, *Masters of Small Worlds,* 97; Bruegel, *Farm, Shop, Landing,* 53.

96. Cleary, "'She Will Be in the Shop.'"

97. Smith, "Food Rioters and the American Revolution."

98. On Pennsylvania German women, see Rush, *Account of the Manners of the German Inhabitants,* 66; Parsons, *Pennsylvania Dutch,* 222–26; Gibbons, *Pennsylvania Dutch and Other Essays,* 36–44; and Klees, *Pennsylvania Dutch,* 6, 201–2.

99. Rex daybook 4, LEL, roll 1: AB6.

100. August 30, 1822, Rex daybook 43, HSI.

101. Boydston, "Woman Who Wasn't There," and *Home and Work,* 36–42.

102. Estate papers of Christina Stickel (Stiegel) 1819, 1824–26; LEL, roll 10: SE14. Female seamstresses traditionally made women's clothing and men's shirts, while male tailors sewed other male garments. Widow Shreiner transaction, Rex daybook 8, JDC; Catherine Gass transaction, Rex daybook 20, HSI; sales of tow linen, Rex daybook 13, LEL, roll 1: AB10; and Rex daybooks 23 and 33, JDC.

103. See, for example, Rex daybook 38, LEL, roll 1: AB17, entry for October 9, 1806, when he credited Catherine Miller 2s. for digging potatoes.

104. Kelker to Rex, August 1798, LEL, roll 5: AS103.

105. Clark, *Roots of Rural Capitalism,* 164–67; Thorp, "Doing Business in the Backcountry," 399; Lewis, *Artisans in the North Carolina Backcountry,* 64.

106. Thorp, "Doing Business in the Backcountry," 405; Sweeney, "Gentlemen Farmers and Inland Merchants," 70; Wermuth, *Rip Van Winkle's Neighbors,* 94.

107. On this point, see Bushman, "Markets and Composite Farms," 362.

108. The commission references appear in Rex daybook or blotter, LEL, roll 1: AB2, and daybook 4, LEL, roll 1: AB6.

109. Rutman and Rutman make this observation about Virginia storekeepers in *Place in Time,* 229.

110. Folmer invoice, LEL, roll 6: AS104; Flower invoice, July 9, 1800, LEL, roll 2: B1. On November 1, 1804, John Flower made his mark in Rex's receipt book to acknowledge receipt of some cash that Rex had collected for him from a third party. Rex receipt book, LEL, roll 2: B1.

111. Folmer sold goods to the Kipplinger store in Jonestown and to Abraham Rex's store

in Mount Pleasant. Kipplinger store ledger, 1797–1799, Lebanon County Historical Society; Abraham Rex daybooks, passim, HSI.

112. I conclude that these businessmen (or their representatives) visited Rex rather than vice versa because Rex recorded the purchases in his daybook, not in his receipt book. In a typical transaction, Rex credited Albright & Lahn 18s. for thirty-six almanacs on November 8, 1793, and Demuth £5 16s. 3d. for sixty-two pounds of snuff on February 24, 1794. Rex daybook or blotter, May 21, 1793–March 1, 1795, LEL, roll 1: AB2. The Demuth family tobacco shop is still in operation at 114 East King Street, Lancaster.

113. Myrle Kline interview, quoted in Bergengren, "Transformations in the Houses of Schaefferstown," 528–29, 585.

114. Rex-Sweitzer nail account book, JDC. Sweitzer, who produced shoe, cask, lath, shingle, and saddler nails for Rex, came from a family of nail smiths. Samuel Rex bought nails in 1791 from Casper Sweitzer; Abraham Rex, while operating his store in Mt. Pleasant, bought nails from Leonard Sweitzer. Samuel Rex daybook 1, LEL, roll 1: AB2; Abraham Rex daybook 2 (Mount Pleasant), HSI.

115. If Sweitzer did have a shop, it was so small that the 1798 tax assessors did not bother with it. He was the occupant of Widow Fidler's 18 x 16-foot, one-story log house, and the house was in "bad order," suggesting that Sweitzer truly was down on his luck. USDT, Heidelberg Township, Dauphin County, schedule I.

116. In November 1800 Michael Grabill sold Rex "sundry nailsmith tools now in the possession of John Sweitzer . . . the said Samuel Rex Esquire to take the aforesaid nailsmith tools into his immediate possession." Grabill legal document, November 13, 1800, LEL, roll 9: TR141.

117. Ege had a slitting mill capable of producing the iron rods at his Charming Forge complex.

118. Rex daybook 10, LEL, roll 1: AB9.

119. These credits and debits appear in Rex ledger 5, HSI.

120. Brendle describes Moore's hotel in *Brief History of Schaefferstown*, 33; Moore's purchases appear in Rex daybook 22, HSI.

121. Mabel Haag, interview by author, July 2001, Schaefferstown.

122. "Ramblings in Winter," *Family Magazine* 1 (1836): 264, quoted in Weaver, *Pennsylvania Dutch Cooking*, 131.

123. Tinkcom, "Sir Augustus in Pennsylvania," 383.

124. On December 8, 1801, Rex credited Philip Boyer 6s. for "killing the hogs bought of Benjamin Louser." Rex daybook 18, HSI. Boyer was a carpenter who supplemented his regular work with butchering.

125. Waggoner and Moore's land holdings are listed in USDT, Heidelberg Township, Dauphin County, schedule II.

126. Sowers, *Colonial Taxes*, 101–6; USDT, Heidelberg Township, Dauphin County, schedule II.

127. My thanks to J. Ritchie Garrison and Rosalind Remer for their suggestions about Rex's whiskey purchases and concealing transactions.

128. Entry for September 1, 1802, Rex daybook 20, HSI.

129. These transactions appear in Rex daybook 15, LEL, roll 1: AB11. Thomas typically would have kept one-tenth of each bushel (measured in his toll box as the grain came into the mill) as his compensation for milling the wheat. This means that Rex paid him with six bushels of wheat. Pendleton, *Oley Valley Heritage*, 38–40. For more on Dubs & Earl, see Chapter 4.

130. On the flaxseed trade, see Doerflinger, *Vigorous Spirit of Enterprise*, 103–4.

131. In November 1805, for example, Rex delivered $100 to Grabill, "which sum he rec'd for me of Mr. John Kapp in Phila. on account of oil sold for me." Rex receipt book, HSI.

132. Rex daybook 4, LEL, roll 1: AB6; Rex daybook 17, LEL, roll 1: AB11.

133. Jensen, *Loosening the Bonds*, 85–87.

134. Samuel Rex's purchases and store credits are shown in Abraham Rex ledger 3, HSI.

135. Rex probate inventory, LEL, roll 9: RE5. Calculations based on Lemon, "Household Consumption in Eighteenth-Century America," 63.

136. On storekeepers and butter, see Danhof, *Change in Agriculture: The Northern United States,* 40. Although Rex might have stored butter in crocks, his sales receipts show that he delivered it to Philadelphia in kegs or tubs, so logic suggests the procedure described here. Rex's branding iron, pictured in LEL, roll 13: P4, is still in the family's possession, according to Robert Frey, who tried unsuccessfully to buy it. Frey, telephone conversation with author, January 1999.

137. Philadelphia law required that exported butter be "sufficiently" salted and packed in fifty-pound white oak kegs. Rex's barrels varied in weight from fifty to one hundred pounds, so city buyers would have had to repack his butter if they chose to export it. Mease, *Picture of Philadelphia,* 62.

138. Jensen, *Loosening the Bonds,* 109; Oakes, "Ticklish Business," 204.

139. Jensen, *Loosening the Bonds,* 82–83.

140. Rex daybook 41, HSI.

141. Garret's log house was "old and in bad order," but his 50 x 25-foot stone and log barn was in good condition, and he also owned a still house with two stills. USDT, Heidelberg Township, Dauphin County, schedules I and II.

142. Chalfint bought rags in 1806 and 1807. Other rag buyers included John Longreen (1795–98) and William Salenheimer and Enoch Collar (in 1799). Rex specifically identified Chalfint and Collar as papermakers; Salenheimer may have worked for Collar. Rex daybooks, passim.

143. Jensen, *Loosening the Bonds,* 83.

144. Roeber, "'Whatever Is Not English Among Us,'" 257, 264.

145. De Cunzo, "Culture Broker Revisited," 185–86.

146. Nobles, "Rise of Merchants," 5.

147. On November 19, 1798, Rex debited Elizabeth Furnace for "2 pair hose (delv Fredk Johnston) per Mr. Fletchers werbel order." Rex daybook 6, HSI.

148. Thanks to Christine L. Mason of the Lebanon County Historical Society for locating the translation of *Kump. Stick-Feiss* reference, Rex's letter of November 28, 1822, LEL, roll 5: AS28.

149. The Rexes were sponsors in April 1793 for Johannes, son of blacksmith John Neip and his wife; in September 1795 for Anne Marie, daughter of Nicholas and Catherine Swanger; and, in January 1803 for Samuel, son of Philip and Eva Boyer. Brendle, *Brief History of Schaefferstown,* 108, 110, 116.

150. Lard correction, daybook 40, LEL, roll 1: AB19. The Becker and Kramer transactions are listed in their accounts in Rex ledger 5, HSI. The Ellinger credit appears in Rex daybook 28, HSI.

151. Roop indenture, Lebanon County Historical Society; Rex legal summons, LEL, roll 6: AS155. The indenture also required that Rex supply a new "freedom suit" at the end of the nine years, but Roop apparently was not apprenticed the full time and did not get his new clothes.

152. Power of attorney from William Reilly to Samuel Rex, December 30, 1830, deed book D, p. 640, Lebanon County Courthouse. See Chapter 5 for more on Valentine's debt.

CHAPTER 3

1. Grubb's letter to Rex can be found in 1802, HSI Archives.

2. William Penn, *Some Account of the Province of Pennsylvania* (London, 1681), 5, quoted in Bining, *Pennsylvania Iron Manufacture,* 14.

3. In addition to the ore deposits at Cornwall, there were many small veins throughout the region, but by the early twentieth century ore production in the Lake Superior area surpassed Cornwall. Bining, *Pennsylvania Iron Manufacture,* 48, 57–59; Miller, *Rise of an Iron Community,* 80–81; Eggert, *Iron Industry in Pennsylvania,* 2.

4. Bining, *Pennsylvania Iron Manufacture,* 14–18; Eggert, *Iron Industry in Pennsylvania,* 19–21.

5. Hopewell Furnace, Elverson, Berks County, is not to be confused with Hopewell Forge in Lancaster County.

6. Arbitration settlement, Schaeffer and Gemberling, LEL, roll 7: TR15.

7. Zerbe, *Annals of Shaefferstown*, 297.

8. Brooke Family Papers, Berks County Historical Society, Reading, Pennsylvania, quoted in Walker, *Hopewell Village*, 210.

9. Noble, *Touch of Time*, 4–10; Miller, *Rise of an Iron Community*, 12, 88; Bining, *Pennsylvania Iron Manufacture*, 20–21.

10. Dibert, *Iron, Independence and Inheritance*, 55. The last of the Grubb family, Daisy Elizabeth Brooke Grubb, died in 1936; she sold her interest in the Cornwall Mines to the Pennsylvania Steel Company in 1902. The mines were later purchased by Bethlehem Steel Corporation. Bernard, "History of Grubb Family," typescript, Lebanon County Historical Society, n.d., 7.

11. Another Reading (or Redding) Furnace operated in Chester County from 1736 to 1778; see Cremers, *Reading Furnace, 1736*, 1–2. To add to the confusion, Berkshire Furnace was first called Roxborough. John Patton renamed it Berkshire when he bought it in 1764; Ege changed the name to Reading sometime after he bought it in 1788; and a later owner renamed it Robesonia Furnace. These changes are described in Ibach, *Hub of the Tulpehocken*, 58–59.

12. Grittinger, "Cornwall Furnace and the Cornwall Ore Banks," 36; Schoepf, *Travels in the Confederation*, 1:202. Stiegel, who lived "in a very ostentatious manner," went deeply into debt to build his glassworks at Manheim, Pennsylvania. When he was unable to pay his creditors, he was sent to prison. Released by a special act of the state assembly, he died in 1785 in such obscurity that even his burial place is unknown. Bining, *Pennsylvania Iron Manufacture*, 127–29.

13. Wallace, *Rockdale*, 44.

14. Eggert, *Iron Industry in Pennsylvania*, 17–19.

15. Coleman started William at Speedwell in 1797; in 1801 he made him manager of Cornwall and put James in charge of Speedwell. Noble, *Touch of Time*, 9–10.

16. This causes some confusion in interpreting Rex's documents. Rex variously listed furnace and forge purchases in the name of the facility, in the name of the ironmaster/owner, or in the name of the superintendent or clerk of the site.

17. Boyd to Rex, December 12, 1795, LEL, roll 6: AS121.

18. Bining, *Pennsylvania Iron Manufacture*, 126.

19. Beck, "Cannon Hill and the Hessian Ditch," 30–31.

20. Carnegie rose from poverty to become one of the richest businessmen of his era, with an annual income of $25 million; he owned mansions in Pittsburgh and New York City and a forty-thousand-acre estate in Scotland. Lichtenstein et al., *Who Built America?* 39–41.

21. USDT, Warwick and Elizabeth townships, Lancaster County; Bernard, "History of Grubb Family," 4.

22. USDT, Lebanon Township, Dauphin County; Noble, *Touch of Time*, 10.

23. For popular articles on the mansion at Charming Forge, see Creznic, "Charming Forge"; and Myers, "Forging a Link with History."

24. Lichtenstein et al., *Who Built America?* 125–29.

25. Bining, *Pennsylvania Iron Manufacture*, 112; Walker, *Hopewell Village*, 185–205; Miller, *Rise of an Iron Community*, 101.

26. Mount Hope workers were able to take payments in cash. Mount Hope Furnace journals, 1797–1800, microfilm, roll 130, Hopewell National Historic Site, Elverson, Pennsylvania (hereafter HNHS).

27. USDT, Warwick and Elizabeth townships, Lancaster County, and Lebanon Township, Dauphin County.

28. Walker, *Hopewell Village*, 99–119; Miller, *Rise of an Iron Community*, 91.

29. Rudolph Kelker, for example, lived in a furnished house at Cornwall. His probate inventory, taken in June 1801, shows that the only furniture he owned was a desk, clock, and bookcase. Kelker will and inventory, Dauphin County Courthouse, Harrisburg.

30. Schoepf, *Travels in the Confederation*, 1:200.

31. Mount Hope Furnace ledger, 1799, microfilm, roll 123, HNHS; Cornwall Furnace accounts,

quoted in Miller, *Rise of an Iron Community,* 98–99. On wages, see also Walker, *Hopewell Village,* 261–63, 313–15.

32. Mount Hope Furnace journal, 1797–1800, microfilm, roll 130, HNHS. Clearly not all jobs at the iron site were directly involved in iron production, but for the purposes of this study I refer to anyone employed by the ironmasters as an ironworker.

33. Bezís-Selfa, "Tale of Two Ironworks," 105–11.

34. On worker diversity, see Bining, *Pennsylvania Iron Manufacture,* 96.

35. Ironmasters used other forms of unfree labor in addition to slaves. They contracted with indentured servants, usually German and British, and during the Revolution they hired Hessian prisoners of war. Ibid., 97–102; Walker, *Hopewell Village,* 304–17; Miller, *Rise of an Iron Community,* 15–17, 92–93.

36. Miller, *Rise of an Iron Community,* 16, 93. The law, enacted on March 1, 1780, gradually abolished slavery in Pennsylvania by declaring children born of slaves after the law's passage to be free, although they had to remain servants until they reached age twenty-eight. The law further required that slave owners register their slaves or they would be automatically freed; slaves who were registered remained slaves for life unless specifically manumitted by their owners.

37. *Heads of Families at the First Census,* 95.

38. USDT, Lebanon Township, Dauphin County.

39. *Heads of Families at the First Census,* 43; Jackson, Moore, and Teeples, *Pennsylvania 1800 Census Index,* 431; Myers, "Forging a Link," 49.

40. Grubb's men who came to the store included "Negro Casteel," "Negro Mark," "Negro Jack," "Negro Joseph," Henry Clemons ("Mr. Grubb's black man"), and a man known in Rex's books as the "black 'ostler.'" For more information on Coleman, Grubb, Ege, and other slave owners in Pennsylvania, including the names of many slaves registered after the passage of the emancipation law, see Afrolumens Project, "Central Pennsylvania African American History for Everyone," http://www.afrolumens.org/slavery, last updated October 16, 2006.

41. Perkins, "Consumer Frontier," 496–97.

42. Unsigned note to Rex, June 14, 1806, LEL, roll 6: AS162; Willson to Rex, March 5, 1801, LEL, roll 5: AS79. Walker records similar instances of African American teamsters delivering large amounts of cash to Robert Coleman from the ironmaster at Hopewell Village. Walker, *Hopewell Village,* 314.

43. Both transactions appear in Rex daybook 9, HSI. Rex does not say whether Clemons or his employer paid for the tailoring.

44. On the agency of slaves and free men of color at southern ironworks, see Bezís-Selfa, "Tale of Two Ironworks."

45. Entry for March 19, 1791, Berkshire Furnace ledger, Pennsylvania State Archives, Harrisburg.

46. Bining, *Pennsylvania Iron Manufacture,* 107–8.

47. Miller, *Rise of an Iron Community,* 94; Walker, *Hopewell Village,* 230–31.

48. Eggert, *Iron Industry in Pennsylvania,* 3.

49. Miller, *Rise of an Iron Community,* 88; Silverman, "Blast from the Past," 20; Bining, *Pennsylvania Iron Manufacture,* 26; Eggert, *Iron Industry in Pennsylvania,* 16.

50. Walker, *Hopewell Village,* 395–419.

51. June 17, 1799, purchase, Rex daybook 8, JDC; August 19, 1799, purchase, Rex daybook 9, HSI.

52. Purchases by Casper Sieger, Henry Clemons, Alexander Stevenson, Henry Shreader, and John Burnside, October 7, 1799, Rex daybook 9, HSI. It is not clear whether the men were buying cloth for their own clothing or filling orders given to them by wives and daughters, but their purchases also included buttons, silk twist, and thread.

53. July 21, 1800, Rex daybook 12, JDC.

54. Rex daybook 14, JDC.

NOTES TO PAGES 93-98

55. Long sale of lard, December 1, 1801, Rex daybook 18, HSI. Long purchases, August 9, 1802, Rex daybook 20, HSI.

56. Nantz transaction, May 5, 1800, Rex daybook 11, HSI; Crass soap sales, July 25, 1806, Rex daybook 37, HSI. Crass's family's position at the furnace is unknown, but Rex gave her the courtesy title of "Miss."

57. Mount Hope records show purchases from Shanahan & Smith in Philadelphia, as well as from local storekeepers Jacob and John Frey, George Shenberger, and Heintzelman & Metzler, the firm operated by Henry Grubb's illegitimate nephew. Mount Hope Furnace journal, 1797–1800, microfilm, roll 130, HNHS.

58. Debit to Thomas Wilson's account, June 22, 1797, ibid.

59. "Henry B. Grubb Dr to Samuel Rex," statement of account, March 1799, HSI.

60. As indicated above, Mount Hope did do business on occasion with Heintzelman. I am grateful to James A. Dibert for his comments on this chapter, and especially for the information about the tie between Grubb and Heintzelman. See Dibert, *Iron, Independence and Inheritance,* 19, 53, 58; Heiges, "General S. P. Heintzelman Visits His Hometown"; and Hostetter, "Major General Samuel Peter Heintzelman."

61. Kelker bridle purchase, December 15, 1800, Rex daybook 14, JDC; Eaton saddle and bridle purchase, May 13, 1805, Rex daybook 31, HSI; cheese purchase, May 20, 1806, Rex daybook 36, HSI.

62. Rex obtained a steelyard from Christian Seiler for David Eaton and some stove pipe from Philip Brecht for William Coleman, and sold both at cost. "Stilyard" purchase, December 18, 1801, Rex daybook 18, HSI; stovepipe purchase, December 4, 1805, Rex daybook 34, LEL, roll 1: AB16.

63. Rex bought coal baskets for 32½d. and charged the ironmasters 36d. See April 27, 1797, Rex daybook 3, JDC, and ledger 5, HSI, for Kramer's credits for baskets. For Rex's sales of baskets to the ironmasters, see transactions on March 26, 1798, daybook 5, LEL, roll 1: AB6, and October 31 and November 6, 1798, Rex daybook 6, HSI.

64. Miller, *Rise of an Iron Community,* 16; Kemper, *American Charcoal Making,* 24.

65. Irwin to Rex, August 12, 1798, LEL, roll 5: AS79.

66. Rex's predecessor, Lewis Kreider, performed the same service. Kreider account, Berkshire Furnace ledger, 1791, Pennsylvania State Archives, Harrisburg.

67. February 21, March 2, and October 24, 1791, Rex daybook or blotter, JDC; corresponding debits to Montgomery and Atkinson and credits for Rex appear in entries for February, March, and October, Berkshire Furnace ledger, 1791, Pennsylvania State Archives, Harrisburg.

68. Rex daybook 35, HSI.

69. Stuart to Rex, LEL, roll 6: AS197.

70. In a typical transaction, on November 11, 1805, James Willson (of Berkshire/Reading Furnace) sold Rex nine kegs of hog lard totaling 450 pounds and at the same time bought two more new kegs. Rex daybook 33, JDC.

71. Mount Hope Furnace journal, 1797–1800, microfilm, roll 130, HNHS.

72. October 21, 1796, Rex daybook 3, JDC.

73. Boyd to Rex, December 4 and 12, 1795, LEL, roll 6: AS121.

74. Fletcher to Rex, December 13, 1799, LEL, roll 5: AS10.

75. December 11, 1801, Rex daybook 18, HSI.

76. Erpff loan, December 14, 1800, Rex daybook 14, JDC.

77. On the economic repercussions of the war, see Walton and Rockoff, *History of the American Economy,* 150–56.

78. January 28, 1804, Rex daybook 25, LEL, roll 1: AB13.

79. Rex daybooks 25 and 26, LEL, roll 1: AB13, AB14.

80. Ledger sheet, HSI; Fletcher to Rex, December 18, 1799, LEL, roll 6: AS109.

81. Coleman to Rex, December 13, 1801, LEL, roll 5: AS3.

82. Boyd to Rex, December 14, 1797, LEL, roll 6: AS154.

83. November 24, 1800, Rex daybook 14, JDC.

84. Grubb loan, August 11, 1800, Rex daybook 12, JDC; Coleman loan, April 4, 1806, Rex daybook 35, HSI; Grubb to Rex, March 22, 1801, HSI.

85. Fletcher loan, May 17, 1800, Rex daybook 11, HSI.

86. Moore to Rex, December 11, 1801, LEL, roll 2: BI.

87. Isaac Funston to Rex, December 4, 1805, LEL, roll 9: TR125.

88. John Peters, Jacob Frolick, and John Lemons brought in the orders. Rex daybook or blotter, 1791, JDC.

89. Ibid.

90. Rex daybook 15, LEL, roll 1: AB11.

91. Rex daybook 7, LEL, roll 1: AB8.

92. James Willson to Rex, December 27, 1815; private collection of Catherine Bucher Eckert.

93. Fletcher to Rex, December 15, 1800, January 1, 1807, LEL, roll 6: AS79, AS196.

94. Fletcher to Rex, December 18, 1799, LEL, roll 6: AS109.

95. Brendle, *Brief History of Schaefferstown,* 19, 157, 170.

96. The identity of the boy's mother is a mystery, and family histories do not mention the child. See, for example, Kelker, *Genealogical Record of the Family of Koelliker,* 73–74. Although Kelker discharged his duty to his son during his lifetime, he bequeathed the boy only £200 and left the bulk of his estate to his parents. Rudolph Kelker will, Dauphin County Courthouse, Harrisburg.

97. Signage, Saugus Ironworks National Historic Site, Saugus, Massachusetts. Bining estimates that iron bars weighed twenty-three pounds each, but Rex's iron bars weighed forty pounds apiece. Bining, *Pennsylvania Iron Manufacture,* 73.

98. April 7, 1801, Rex daybook 15, LEL, roll 1: AB11; Kurtz to Rex, roll 2: BI.

99. Rex daybook 28, HSI.

100. Rex daybook 8, JDC.

101. January 26, 1799, Rex daybook 7, LEL, roll 1: AB8.

102. Boyer's purchases appear in Rex daybooks 19 and 21, JDC, and daybook 22, HSI.

103. February 1, 1802, Rex daybook 18, HSI.

104. October 19, 1798, Rex daybook 9, HSI.

105. Rex daybook 22, HSI.

106. March 16, 1799, Rex daybook 7, LEL, roll 1: AB8.

107. Paskoff, *Industrial Evolution,* 47.

108. Thorp, "Doing Business in the Backcountry," 402.

109. Rex sent 11 kegs of butter, 1 tierce of tallow, 34 pounds of beeswax, 515 pounds of ham, and 23 bars of iron to Thomas Miller, merchant of Philadelphia, according to his memorandum dated 1791 (no month or day), LEL, roll 2: BI.

110. Paskoff, *Industrial Evolution,* 55.

111. The iron prices are shown in Rex's daybook or blotter, 1791, JDC.

112. Darroch to Rex, LEL, roll 6: AS105.

113. Lane to Rex, LEL, roll 6: AS202.

114. For the wages Rex paid for hauling iron, see entry for May 16, 1806, Rex daybook 36, HSI. Rex and his business associates expressed the weight of iron with three digits separated by periods, denoting its weight it hundredweights, quarters of hundredweights (28 pounds), and pounds (e.g., when Rex sent his 23 bars of iron to Philadelphia in 1791 he listed their weight as 9.0.0.)

115. Rex daybook 9, HSI; Rex daybook 10, LEL, roll 1: AB9.

116. May 10, 1800, Rex daybook 11, HSI.

117. Pennsylvania iron producers formed their first cartel in 1774; it lasted until April 1775. Paskoff, *Industrial Evolution,* 67–69; Eggert, *Iron Industry in Pennsylvania,* 25.

118. On city merchants' lack of profits on some deals, see Jensen, *Maritime Commerce of Colonial Philadelphia,* 94–95.

119. There is no way of telling what percentage of Rex's sales were cash, since he almost never recorded these transactions.

120. Clerks at city firms and iron furnaces typically used a much more complicated set of books, including cash books and letter books, while farmers often used only a daybook. On period bookkeeping, see Dilworth, *Young Book-Keeper's Assistant;* Bruchey, *Robert Oliver and Mercantile Bookkeeping;* and Chandler, *Visible Hand,* 38.

121. Thorp, "Doing Business in the Backcountry," 405; Sweeney, "Gentlemen Farmers and Inland Merchants," 70; Wermuth, *Rip Van Winkle's Neighbors,* 95–96.

122. Rex daybook or blotter, 1791, JDC; Rex daybook 24, HSI.

123. Rex to Barr, June 23, 1801, LEL, roll 5: AS4.

124. McClafferty to "Saml Wrecks," November 21, 1801, LEL, roll 6: AS206.

125. This was standard procedure for businessmen at the time. See Pendleton, *Oley Valley Heritage,* 47; Schweitzer, *Custom and Contract,* 142–45.

126. Anonymous justice of the peace book, Myerstown, 1807, JDC.

127. Henry Schaeffer to Constable M. Meyer, March 3, 1798, LEL, roll 6: AS134.

128. Rex ledger 8, LEL, roll 2: AB22; loose ledger sheets, Schuylkill Forge, August 18, 1820, LEL, roll 6: AS176. Ege still owed the debt when Rex died in 1835; Rex's executor sold the debt at the estate sale. Entry in Rex's daybook 43 (used by the executor for estate entries after Rex's death), HSI.

129. On merchants' anxieties, see Ditz, "Shipwrecked; or, Masculinity Imperiled."

130. Leib to Rex, January 27, 1801, LEL, roll 6: AS203. Rose blankets were decorated on each corner with embroidered patterns resembling compass points called "compass roses." Hersh and Hersh, *Cloth and Costume,* 88.

131. Leib could not pay Rex, so his employer, George Ege, assumed the debt, thus adding to his own financial difficulties.

CHAPTER 4

1. These sales appear in Rex daybook 9, HSI.

2. Fries, *Urban Idea in Colonial America,* 90.

3. Cole, "Tempo of Mercantile Life," 288.

4. Lindstrom, *Economic Development in the Philadelphia Region,* 93–95; Dauer, "Colonial Philadelphia's Interregional Transportation System," 2; Bushman, "Shopping and Advertising in Colonial America," 234.

5. Schoepf, *Travels in the Confederation,* 1:112.

6. James Lemon found that horse-drawn wagons could travel about thirty miles a day under favorable conditions, and at least four horses were needed to draw a wagon with a capacity of one ton. Lemon, *Best Poor Man's Country,* 29, 165. Paul Paskoff notes, however, that twenty miles a day is a more realistic figure, and even this meant driving from dawn till after dark. Paskoff, *Industrial Evolution,* 45. On wagon travel, see also Fletcher, *Pennsylvania Agriculture and Country Life,* 259–60.

7. Schoepf, *Travels in the Confederation,* 1:104; Cazenove, *Cazenove Journal,* 84.

8. Faris, *Old Roads Out of Philadelphia,* 123.

9. The number of merchants is based on Doerflinger's estimate that there were 440 merchants in 1791. Doerflinger, *Vigorous Spirit of Enterprise,* 17–18.

10. Schoepf, *Travels in the Confederation,* 1:112.

11. "Letters of Phineas Bond, British Consul at Philadelphia . . . ," *Annual Report of the American Historical Association for the Year 1896,* 2 vols. (Washington, D.C., 1897), 1:568, quoted in Nash, *Forging Freedom,* 73.

12. On city life in this era, see Miller, "Federal City"; Riley, "Philadelphia, the Nation's Capital"; Thompson, *Rum Punch and Revolution;* and Warner, *Private City,* 3–19.

13. Ricketts's attraction was commonly known as Ricketts' Circus; prior to 1795 it was on the outskirts of the city, but in 1795 Ricketts opened a new building, ninety-seven feet in diameter, at Sixth and Chestnut streets; it seated more than twelve hundred people. The circus burned in December 1799. See Eberlein and Hubbard, *Diary of Independence Hall*, 336; Riley, "Philadelphia, the Nation's Capital," 377; and Webster, *Philadelphia Preserved*, 57. On Peale's museum, see Brigham, *Public Culture in the Early Republic*. In 1795 Jacob Hiltzheimer viewed an elephant on the south side of High between Third and Fourth streets; two years later, on his way to the statehouse, he paid twenty-five cents to see a lion. Hiltzheimer, *Diary of Jacob Hiltzheimer*, 225, 250.

14. Billy Smith assesses the grim life that working-class Philadelphians faced in *The "Lower Sort."* On the yellow fever epidemic, see Miller, "Federal City," 180–88; Riley, "Philadelphia, the Nation's Capital," 357–63.

15. Swank, "Germanic Fragment," 3–11; on redemptioners, see also Salinger, *"To Serve Well and Faithfully."*

16. On African American and French immigration following the French Revolution and the slave uprising in Saint Dominique, see Nash, *Forging Freedom*, 73, 140.

17. Schweitzer, "Spatial Organization of Philadelphia," 39.

18. See, for example, Warner, *Private City*, 14.

19. Schweitzer, "Spatial Organization of Philadelphia," 34–38.

20. Warner, *Private City*, 14, 56. St. Mery, *St. Mery's American Journey*, 264.

21. By the mid-eighteenth century, the area along the Delaware was lined with warehouses and other structures related to maritime and commercial uses. Some structures survived until the 1960s, when all buildings between the river and the east side of Front Street were demolished to make way for Interstate Route 95. Webster, *Philadelphia Preserved*, 39.

22. For the occupations of street residents, see Stafford, *Philadelphia Directory for 1801*, 9–16. This directory is particularly useful for understanding residential patterns because it is arranged by street rather than alphabetically.

23. Salinger, "Spaces, Inside and Outside," 3–4.

24. Descriptions of buildings in this chapter come from USDT, Philadelphia County.

25. On combination shops and dwellings, see Herman, *Town Houses*, 105–9.

26. Klepp and Branson, "Working Woman," 156.

27. Webster, *Philadelphia Preserved*, 39.

28. Philadelphia direct tax assessors in 1798 listed commercial buildings on a separate schedule, as they were taxed at a lower rate than residences. Dual-purpose structures, such as stores combined with living quarters, were included on the same list as private residences and therefore taxed at the higher rate.

29. *Pennsylvania Gazette*, March 24, 1798, Accessible Archives, item 69896.

30. St. Mery, *St. Mery's American Journey*, 176.

31. Adam Zantzinger cash book, 1796–97, Cumberland County Historical Society, Carlisle, Pennsylvania; advertisements for Wetherill and Poultney, *Pennsylvania Gazette*, April 24, 1766, April 14, 1773, and May 2, 1792; Coates ad (shown in figure 16), Historical Society of Pennsylvania, Harrisburg.

32. Charles Coxe's store room was lined with cedar, according to his ad in the *Pennsylvania Gazette*, March 5, 1767. Cited in Wainwright, *Colonial Grandeur in Philadelphia*, 6.

33. Boehm, who was identified in his will as a "merchant," died in November 1790, leaving an estate worth £7,080. Will book W, p. 13, Philadelphia County, microfilm, JDC. Boehm's net worth indicates that he was far below the wealthiest of the city's merchants, whose estates Doerflinger estimated ranged between £15,000 and £35,000 in value. Doerflinger, *Vigorous Spirit of Enterprise*, 26.

34. For a close reading of the interior of a country store with an eye to accessibility, service, and security, see Taylor, "'Where Humbler Shop-Men from the Crowd Retreat,'" 47.

35. Doerflinger, *Vigorous Spirit of Enterprise*, 17.

36. Martin to Rex, November 26, 1795, LEL, roll 2: B1.

37. For an example of family employment as a career path, see Tooker, *Nathan Trotter,* 9. On merchants' apprentices, see Guffin, "'Satisfaction of Arriving to a Good Market'"; and Tolles, *Meeting House and Counting House,* 93–94.

38. Cleary, "'She Will Be in the Shop.'"

39. Klepp and Branson, "Working Woman," 173.

40. Conrad Beates sold tobacco to Rex in 1797 and 1798; after 1799 the receipts bear Barbara's name. The other widowed shop owners with whom Rex did business were Elizabeth Cottringer and Catherine Wood.

41. Rex receipt book, HSI.

42. Eldredge to Rex, December 22, 1801, LEL, roll 5: AS2.

43. Eldredge to Rex, March 5, 1802, LEL, roll 6: AS139.

44. Guffin, "Richard Vaux," 7.

45. Miller to Rex, April 13, 1791, LEL, roll 6: AS104.

46. John Rex to Samuel Rex, October 2, 1791, LEL, roll 5: AS101.

47. John Rex to Samuel Rex, June 14, 1792, LEL, roll 6: AS118.

48. John Rex to Samuel Rex, February 9, 1794, LEL, roll 6: AS158.

49. "Invoice of Sundry Goods . . . ," LEL, roll 1: AB1.

50. This summary is based on the Philadelphia receipts, LEL, roll 2: B1, roll 6: AS107, and Rex's receipt book, HSI.

51. Changes in handwriting and sometimes language in Rex's daybooks show his absences from the store on such trips. Whoever kept store while he was away on the November 1799 trip wrote the entries in German.

52. Nottnagle and Montmollen are noteworthy for being the only merchants Rex visited who still owned slaves in 1798. The partners paid one dollar tax on their two slaves; USDT, Chestnut Ward, Philadelphia County, schedule C.

53. Rex's receipt book shows that he paid the firms £18 10s. 7d. and £40 13s. 7d., respectively, but no bills survive to show when he made the purchases or what he bought.

54. Eldredge was acting as an intermediary between Rex and Lane, who occasionally bought iron from Rex. The nature of this particular deal is not known.

55. Bartram, Evans, and Weiser, *Journey from Pennsylvania to Onondaga,* 107.

56. *The North-American and West-Indian Gazetteer: Containing an Authentic Description of the Colonies in That Part of the Globe* (London: G. Robinson, 1776).

57. Rush, *Account of the Manners of the German Inhabitants,* 67–68.

58. Cazenove, *Cazenove Journal,* 84.

59. Fletcher, *Pennsylvania Agriculture and Country Life,* 473–74; Sachse, *Wayside Inns on the Lancaster Roadside,* 92, 106–7; and Schoepf, *Travels in the Confederation,* 1:104.

60. Cazenove found this was true of farmers in Kutztown. Cazenove, *Cazenove Journal,* 32.

61. Thorp, "Doing Business in the Backcountry," 400–401.

62. Tooker, *Nathan Trotter,* 120.

63. Zerbe, *Annals of Shaefferstown,* 297.

64. Toward the end of his life, Peter Moore (1765–1827) also built canal boats in Schaefferstown and hauled them by horse and wagon about seven miles to the Union Canal. Huber, *Schaefferstown,* 56–57.

65. On July 2, 1802, Rex credited John Weaver £11 5s. for hauling goods to and from Philadelphia and debited his account for the £1 2s. 6d. that Rex had already paid "his [Weaver's] man Jacob Snyder" in Philadelphia. In other words, it seems that both men worked, and Weaver received the payment. Rex daybook 20, HSI. Jacob Snyder may be the same man who later was a tenant on one of Rex's plantations; see Chapter 5.

66. On May 5, 1803, Rex hired Nicholas Swanger, Peter Prussman, and John Stover to haul the materials. Rex daybook 22, HSI.

67. October 1, 1804, Rex daybook 28, HSI.

68. Darroch reported the receipt of the money and the shipment of goods per "Mr. Grabill" in a note to Rex, June 20, 1792, LEL, roll 5: AS17.

69. Rex daybook beginning May 21, 1792, LEL, roll 1: AB2.

70. These transactions are shown in Rex daybook 3, September 24, 1796, JDC (payment to Thomas), and daybook 19, June 18, 1802, JDC (payment to Klein).

71. Memo, "Sent Mr. Thomas Miller . . . per Alexander Montgomery," LEL, roll 2: B1.

72. Wistar & Cooke to Rex, "twelve month" (December) 5, 1794, LEL, roll 2: B1.

73. Darroch to Rex, December 15, 1791, LEL, roll 5: AS79.

74. Rex receipt book, LEL, roll 5: AS80.

75. Rex daybook 8, August 9, 1799, JDC.

76. The rate for four horses and a wagon on the Lancaster Turnpike varied according to the width of the vehicle's wheels; for wagons with wheels less than four inches in breadth, the toll was one-eighth dollar per horse. Sachse, *Wayside Inns on the Lancaster Roadside,* 127–28.

77. Rex daybook 28, HSI.

78. Dubs to Rex, September 1, 1802, HSI.

79. Nicholas Swanger and Henry Strock, for example, occasionally drove for the ironmasters in addition to carrying cargoes for Rex. Berkshire Furnace accounts, 1789–91, Pennsylvania State Archives, Harrisburg.

80. Darroch to Rex, December 20, 1792, LEL, roll 5: AS15.

81. Abbot & Simpson advertisement, *Pennsylvania Gazette,* November 30, 1796; Daniel Drinker advertisement, *Pennsylvania Gazette,* November 5, 1767.

82. Zantzinger cash book, Cumberland County Historical Society.

83. Bevan advertisement, October 24, 1771, *Pennsylvania Gazette,* Accessible Archives, item 499811.

84. J. Dull for Eldredge, undated, LEL, roll 6: AS192.

85. Baker to Rex, January 28, 1795, LEL, roll 6: AS106.

86. MacFarlane, *History of Early Chestnut Hill,* 13–20.

87. Sachse, *Wayside Inns on the Lancaster Roadside,* 124–26.

88. Rex bought tobacco, molasses, and other unspecified goods from Wilmington merchants Israel Brown, Jacob Creeman, William Hemphill, and Rumsey and Broom on October 9 and 10, 1793. Rex receipt book, HSI.

89. The Newman credit appears in Rex ledger 5, HSI.

90. Eldredge to Rex, LEL, roll 6: AS209.

91. Cooke to Rex, LEL, roll 6: AS205.

92. On May 6, 1791, Rex purchased more than £5 worth of goods at the city auction, and on May 24, 1797, he bought fifty-two gallons of oil at the wharf. LEL, roll 6: AS104, A106. Goods could be had very cheap at auction, but sometimes the auction crowds were rowdy. Trautman, "Pennsylvania Through a German's Eyes," 45.

93. The term "agent" is my own, designating a merchant with whom Rex enjoyed a regular business relationship. On agents and factors among the international merchant community, see Hancock, *Citizens of the World,* 124–28. Hancock explains that "factors" did not have the same liability for lawsuits that agents did. Factors "traded in their own names, possessed the goods, and usually did not reveal the names of the people for whom they were acting."

94. Rex's earliest agents were wet goods merchants Thomas Miller (1790–91) and Henry Darroch (1790–93); in 1795 he dealt with Dubs & Marquedant, William Clark, and John Martin.

95. Eldredge's brokerage of iron is apparent in a letter from William Lane to Rex, June 3, 1801, LEL, roll 6: AS202.

96. Doerflinger, *Vigorous Spirit of Enterprise,* 92.

97. Rex receipt book, HSI.

98. On this point, see Doerflinger, *Vigorous Spirit of Enterprise,* 98.

99. Dubs & Earl to Rex, October 13, 1802, LEL, roll 6: AS120.

100. Eldredge to Rex, May 16, 1800, LEL, roll 6: AS108.

101. Dubs to Rex, September 1, 1802, HSI.

102. Dubs & Earl to Rex, July 26, 1798, LEL, roll 6: AS119.

103. Eldredge to Rex, July 31, 1799, LEL, roll 2: B1.

104. Dubs & Earl to Rex, March 30, 1801, LEL, roll 7: TR6.

105. Wood, *Conestoga Crossroads*, 103; Doerflinger, *Vigorous Spirit of Enterprise*, 59.

106. Doerflinger, *Vigorous Spirit of Enterprise*, 92.

107. The discounting practice is explained in Tooker, *Nathan Trotter*, 140–42. Trotter continued to discount bills well into the 1800s.

108. It is impossible to calculate precisely the percentage of Rex's cash and credit purchases over the years. There are few bills extant for 1801 and later, and his receipt book, the source of information about his buying from 1801 to 1807, shows only his cash payments.

109. Miller to Rex April 13, 1791, LEL, roll 6: AS104.

110. Schlatter to Rex, November 6, 1800, LEL, roll 6: AS193.

111. Eldredge to Rex, December 22, 1801, LEL, roll 5: AS2.

112. Dorsey to Rex, 1st month (January) 28, 1795, LEL, roll 7: TR113.

113. Wistar to Rex, December 9, 1797, LEL, roll 2: B1. In addition, the error emphasizes that city merchants dealt with a number of rural storekeepers in many small towns in southeastern Pennsylvania and illustrates the multiplicity of networks throughout the countryside.

114. The same was true in the revolutionary era. Doerflinger, *Vigorous Spirit of Enterprise*, 135.

115. Ibid., 18.

CHAPTER 5

1. Samuel and Abraham eventually settled for £675 12s. 3d. "Inventory and Amounts of Store Goods June 1, 1807," HSI. This large listing did not include all of Samuel Rex's stock; he retained some to sell or use later and sold some at a public auction. Samuel Rex ledger 7, LEL, roll 2: AB21.

2. Abraham recorded payments to Dietrich Goshert and George Burkholder for hauling his goods to Schaefferstown. Abraham Rex ledger 1 (Mount Pleasant), HSI.

3. Brendle, *Brief History of Schaefferstown*, 73–74.

4. Dublin, "Rural Putting-Out Work"; Henretta, "Transition to Capitalism in America." On businessmen and manufacturing, see Dalzell, *Enterprising Elite*.

5. On this point, see Appleby, "Commercial Farming and the 'Agrarian Myth,'" 838.

6. On gentleman farmers, see Fletcher, *Pennsylvania Agriculture and Country Life*, 126–27; Sweeney, "Gentleman Farmers and Inland Merchants." Rex's farmers were tenants who rented the farms and paid the taxes on the property (though he reimbursed them for tax payments). On tenants and cottagers, see Clemens and Simler, "Rural Labor and the Farm Household," 112.

7. In 1798 Henry Mock's farm was only sixty acres, but he must have acquired more land or a different farm altogether, for Abraham Rex recorded that his half of the property was seventy acres. LEL, roll 5: AS50.

8. Deed book P, p. 87, Lebanon County Courthouse.

9. Rex estate papers, LEL, roll 9: RE5; "Administrative Account of Abraham Rex," HSI.

10. Theodorus Dodendorff rented the Hocker farm and harvested more than 349 bushels of grain in 1823, but Rex did not record what share of Dodendorff's harvest he took for rent. Samuel Rex daybooks 42 and 43, HSI.

11. On agricultural improvers, see Henretta, "Transition to Capitalism in America," and Bushman, "Opening the American Countryside," 219, 228, 247–49.

12. Rex's father supposedly introduced Germantown farmers to the idea of using plaster of paris as fertilizer. MacFarlane, *History of Early Chestnut Hill*, 53. In July 1816 Rex credited Charles Francis with hauling ten barrels of flour to Philadelphia and bringing back 1.5 tons of plaster. Rex daybook 42, HSI. In March 1819 Rex noted that he sent tenant Henry Kessler two

bushels of clover seed; he furnished one bushel but charged the other to Kessler's account. The following year Rex sent Kessler another bushel of clover seed and a ton of plaster of paris. Rex daybook 42, HSI.

13. Samuel Rex daybook 42, HSI.

14. On farm exchanges, see Sweeney, "Gentlemen Farmers and Inland Merchants," and Clemens, "Rural Culture and the Farm Economy."

15. Fletcher, *Pennsylvania Agriculture and Country Life*, 313–21; Stommel and Stommel, *Volcano Weather*; Harrington, *Year Without a Summer?*

16. May 17, 1817, Samuel Rex daybook 42, HSI.

17. Samuel Rex daybook 42, HSI.

18. Samuel's sales appear in Abraham Rex's Schaefferstown ledgers 3, 4, and 5, HSI.

19. Rex ledger 8, LEL, roll 2: AB22.

20. Long debt, March 1, 1816; Howser debt, April 23, 1819, Rex daybook 42, HSI.

21. "A List of Amount of Bonds, Notes, &c due to Samuel Rex by Sundry Persons, taken by said Samuel Rex January 1834," HSI.

22. Gass was married to Rex's sister-in-law, Catherine Valentine. Rex estate papers, LEL, roll 9: RE5; "Administrative Account of Abraham Rex," HSI.

23. "List of Amount of Bonds, Notes, &c," HSI. Rex's lists for 1835 and 1830 appear in LEL, roll 6: AS148 and AS149, respectively.

24. Samuel Rex will, will book B, p. 333, Lebanon County Courthouse; LEL, roll 6: AS128.

25. Cazenove, *Cazenove Journal*, 31, 36. Portions of the early checkerboard exterior treatment are still visible inside the attic of the stone lean-to of the Gemberling-Rex House.

26. On painting and refinement, see Bushman, *Refinement of America*, 134, 257–58.

27. For more on the remodeling of the house, see Wenger, "Reading the Gemberling-Rex House."

28. Bergengren, "Transformations in the Houses of Schaefferstown," 258.

29. Ibid., 284. I am indebted to Charles Bergengren for his suggestion to me that the country builder worked from a verbal description.

30. On other Pennsylvania Germans whose homes combined elements of urban and German style, see Herman, *Town House*, 77–97.

31. Rex probate inventory, LEL, roll 9: RE5. On parlors as expressions of gentility, see Bushman, *Refinement of America*, 273–79.

32. These loans were made on October 19, 1812, October 4 and 28, 1813, and November 24, 1814. Rex daybook 42, HSI.

33. Though Samuel never encountered legal sanctions for his estate management, his brother was not so fortunate. When Abraham settled Samuel's estate in 1835, an orphan's court judge ordered Abraham to pay himself less in fees and charge himself more for interest owed to his brother's estate. Samuel Rex estate papers, LEL, roll 9: RE5; "Administrative Account of Abraham Rex," HSI.

34. Croll, *Ancient and Historic Landmarks*, 117. Rex received £25 and Valentine inherited Erpff's house and corner cupboard, though he had to pay the estate £200 for the property, which Erpff valued at £500. In addition, under the terms of the will, half of the remaining estate went to the church, while the other half was divided among Rex, Valentine, and eight other beneficiaries. Erpff will, Dauphin County Courthouse, Harrisburg; LEL, roll 9: EE1.

35. "Notice to Berks County constable to jail Henry Valentine," LEL, roll 12: L17; broadside advertising sale of Henry Valentine's goods, LEL, roll 13: N9.

36. Transfer of Henry Schaeffer Jr.'s goods to A. Rex and J. Bomberger, 1816, LEL, roll 7: TR16. Other documents on Henry Schaeffer Jr. appear in roll 5: AS98.

37. Coleman (no first name given) to unnamed recipient, October 10, 1823, LEL, roll 5: AS79.

38. Bockius to Rex, November 2, 1823, LEL, roll 5: AS79.

39. Minute book, Berks and Dauphin Turnpike Road Company, 1816–19, Pennsylvania State Archives, Harrisburg.

40. "Parish Register, 1764–1834, St. Luke Evangelical Lutheran Church, Schaefferstown, Pa.," typescript, 219, 226–27. Rex's relative by marriage, Jacob Gass, succeeded him as treasurer; Abraham Rex took over from Gass in 1819.

41. Ibid., 219; "A List for to Collect Oats of Sundry Members of the Lutheran Congregation in the Town of Heidelberg for the Use of Parson Beates as a Present," April 4, 1817, HSI.

42. Rex daybook, LEL, roll 1: AB2

43. Rex daybook 4, LEL, roll 1: AB6. "Doctor Kill or Cure" bought nails, a coffee pot, whiskey, a half quire of paper, a plate, some butter, and 6d. worth of cheese.

44. Beers, *Biographical Annals of Lebanon County*, 1:72.

45. July 28, 1822, Rex daybook 42, HSI.

46. Samuel Rex to "Dear Brother," November 28, 1822, LEL, roll 5: AS28.

47. William Valentine "commenced going to school to Samuel Emison" in November 1832; Michael Valentine "came to stay awhile with Samuel Rex" in January 1832; along with Levi Garret, he began school on January 23, 1832. In November 1833 Lewis Heldt came to Rex "to stay with him for some time and to go to school in the winter." In March 1834 Rex paid tuition to schoolmaster Philip White for Lewis Heldt, Mary Bellman, and Samuel Birehin; in November 1834 William Reilly (Michael Valentine's grandson) came to Rex and "commenced going to school." Rex daybook 42, HSI. Baptismal records show that Lewis Heldt and Abraham Kaley were both fourteen years old when they stayed with Rex. Brendle, *Brief History of Schaefferstown*, 162, 133.

48. Entry for November 19, 1832, Rex daybook 43, HSI.

49. Rex to Frederick Saylor, August 17, 1833, LEL, roll 5: AS60.

50. The gifts are described in Rex daybook 43, HSI.

51. A. S. Brendle described Rex as an "adoptive father" to Margaret Valentine Mace. Brendle, *Brief History of Schaefferstown*, 69. Rex's papers show that he treated both nieces equally well. Polly Bucher was the wife of Dr. Christian Bucher; the couple's portraits, painted by Jacob Maentel in the 1830s, are pictured in Hollander, *American Radiance*, 42–43.

52. Power of attorney, December 23, 1830, deed book A, p. 713, Lebanon County Courthouse.

53. Enoch Rex to Samuel Rex, LEL, roll 5: AS79. Rex was not alone in worrying about Bockius; his mother, Anna Rex, placed the same restriction on Catherine's inheritance in her will, dated August 10, 1819. Will book 8, p. 389, Philadelphia County, microfilm, JDC.

54. There is no evidence in his daybooks that Rex advanced money to Bockius, who was the son either of Catherine and John Bockius or of Samuel's sister Margaret and her husband, Joseph Bockius. Bockius to Rex, LEL, roll 5: AS79.

55. Rush, *Letters of Benjamin Rush*, 1:426.

56. Deed, March 4, 1806, Samuel and Anna Maria Rex to Jacob Gass, HSI.

57. Mary's work in the store before she married Samuel is mentioned in letters from John Rex to Samuel Rex, July 17, 1791, LEL, roll 6: AS188, and October 2, 1791, roll 5: AS101.

58. Samuel Rex to "Dear Wife," LEL, roll 6: AS113.

59. The Rexes owned a sausage stuffer, snitz (apple slice) dryer, dough trough, milk pans, butter churn, quilting frame, spinning and wool wheels, and two reels.

60. Samuel Rex, Enoch and Elizabeth's son, was baptized September 10, 1802, and Anna Maria Rex, John and Margaret's daughter, was baptized August 22, 1807. Baptism records of St. Michael's Church, Germantown Historical Society, Germantown.

61. Among Rex's papers is a bill for the repair of his "carriage" in 1807, but by the time of his death he owned only the sleigh and a gig (a one-person conveyance); the sidesaddle is also listed in his probate inventory. LEL, roll 9: RE5.

62. March 30, 1822, Rex daybook 43, HSI.

63. Samuel Rex to Margaret Rex Bockius, November 6, 1832, LEL, roll 5: AS60. Mary had died just a few days earlier, on November 2.

64. Rex to Frederick Saylor, August 17, 1833, LEL, roll 5: AS60.

65. Abraham Rex, Samuel's executor, used Samuel's last daybook to record the funeral and estate expenses. Rex daybook 43, HSI.

66. Samuel Rex inventory, LEL, roll 9: RE5. Rex bequeathed the house to Abraham, with the stipulation that Abraham pay £500 for it. Abraham turned the house over to his daughter and son-in-law, Polly (Maria) and Peter Zimmerman, who were living in the property in 1859 when Abraham sold it to Polly for one dollar. Deed, Abraham and Elizabeth Rex to Polly Zimmerman, September 30, 1859, recorded January 12, 1928, deed book N, vol. 6, p. 34, Lebanon County Courthouse. Like the Buchers, the Zimmermans also had their portraits painted by Maentel; these watercolors remained in the Rex house until the mid-twentieth century and are also a promised gift of Ralph Esmerian to the American Folk Art Museum. The paintings are pictured in Hollander, *American Radiance,* 40–41.

67. Rex owned two shares in Eva Stroam's dower. When John Stroam, Eva's husband, died intestate, leaving her with six children, George Hocker bought the Stroam plantation, including the obligation to pay the widow's thirds and to divide the dower among her children when she died. In 1812 Samuel Rex bought the Stroam/Hocker property, including the responsibility to pay the widow's thirds, at sheriff's sale. In 1818 Rex purchased two shares in the dower from Eva's sons Michael and John. Deed book A, p. 713; deed book C, p. 671; deed book E, p. 568; and deed book P, p. 87, Lebanon County Courthouse. Rex's periodic payments to Eva Stroam for her widow's dower are shown in his receipt book, 1802–34, LEL, roll 5: AS80.

68. Samuel Rex estate papers, LEL, roll 9: RE5; "Administrative Account of Abraham Rex," HSI.

69. Doerflinger, *Vigorous Spirit of Enterprise,* 26; Blumin, *Emergence of the Middle Class,* 118.

70. Abraham Rex-Hagy lease, LEL, roll 12: L3.

71. Jacob Hagy, who sold the store to Abraham, reportedly built the first hotel in Schoeneck in 1792 and kept "a small place of merchandise" there. Ellis and Evans, *History of Lancaster County,* 723. Samuel and Mary Rex stood as godparents for Abraham and Elizabeth's children, Mary and Samuel Schaeffer, when they were baptized at Schoeneck. Rex family genealogy, LEL, roll 8: TR44.

72. In July 1802 Samuel sold Abraham a dozen butter kegs and twenty-five pounds of rice; later that month Samuel went to Philadelphia and purchased $500 worth of goods for Abraham. Samuel Rex daybook 20, HSI.

73. Abraham Rex ledger 1 (Mount Pleasant), HSI.

74. In December 1803 Abraham Rex sold eleven hogs totaling 1,862 pounds to the Colemans for Elizabeth Furnace; in December 1804 he sold another 5,600 pounds of pork to the Colemans and 4,136 pounds of meat to George Ege at Reading Furnace. Abraham Rex daybook 1 (Mount Pleasant), JDC.

75. Abraham's purchases in Philadelphia appear in his receipt book, HSI.

76. Abraham Rex daybook 1 (Mount Pleasant), JDC.

77. Abraham filled sixteen daybooks while he was in Mount Pleasant. When he moved to Schaefferstown he began a new set of daybooks, and he eventually filled another eighty-three volumes, but he kept on using the same "bar book" he had begun in Mount Pleasant, indicating that he gave out far less credit in the bar than he did in the store.

78. Abraham bought the property on March 31, 1814, from Peter Leydich, who had purchased it from Samuel Rex in 1805. "Brief of Title to Lot #17 in Schaefferstown, Lebanon County, Pennsylvania," HSI. The exact date on which Abraham moved his business is unknown. He did not renumber his store daybooks when he moved.

79. Abraham Rex ledger 5 (Schaefferstown), HSI.

80. For a more detailed description of the building, see Bergengren, "Transformations in the Houses of Schaefferstown," 90, 152, 180–81, 510. Abraham and Elizabeth's children are listed in Appendix A.

81. Abraham Rex daybook 64, HSI.

82. Abraham Rex daybook 77 (Schaefferstown), HSI; Abraham Rex Sr. to Abraham Rex Jr., May 14, 1833, LEL, roll 5: AS94.

83. *Lebanon Daily News,* centennial ed., September 30, 1972, J8.

84. May 22, 1809, Abraham Rex daybook 9 (Schaefferstown), HSI. On changes in banking,

see Walton and Rockoff, *History of the American Economy*, 260–61; Gilje, "Rise of Capitalism in the Early Republic," 2–5.

85. This brief sketch of Samuel S. and Abraham Jr. is drawn from their letters, LEL, roll 5: AS94. Their store account book with Elizabeth Furnace is in the Pennsylvania State Archives in Harrisburg; the list of the store inventory they purchased from their father is in the HSI archives.

86. Deed, George and Catharine Fessler to Abraham Rex, April 1, 1834, Lebanon County Historical Society. The house stayed in the hands of Rex's descendents until the mid-twentieth century.

87. John Ermentrout to A. Rex, November 13, 1838, LEL, roll 5: AS 94.

88. On silkworms and railroads, see the correspondence between S. S. Rex and Abraham Rex Jr., May 1839, LEL, roll 5: AS96.

89. Brendle, *Brief History of Schaefferstown*, 81. Correspondence between the Rex brothers reveals that they did not entirely trust Weigley and that they resented him for gaining his father-in-law's confidence and ultimately taking over the family store. LEL, roll 5: AS36.

90. "Brief of Title to Lot #17 in Schaefferstown, Lebanon County, Pennsylvania," HSI.

91. Miller recorded his name and position as clerk inside the front cover of one of Abraham Rex's daybooks. As for earlier storekeepers, business served as a springboard for advancement for Miller and Lauser. Both were justices of the peace, and Lauser went on to serve as a Lebanon County judge. Brendle, *Brief History of Schaefferstown*, 71. See also Wenger, "Brief History of Storekeeping in Schaefferstown."

92. Brendle, *Brief History of Schaefferstown*, 81–82. Weigley's son Rex took over the store, and, after 1887 Rex sold the business to his brother William, who resided in Philadelphia. William hired Aaron Zug to run the store while Milton Hartman operated the post office in the same building. In 1903 Hartman took over the store in partnership with Harry Umberger, and in 1940 Umberger became the sole owner. Store history, Umberger's Store advertising card, 1976, HSI. The Umberger family operated the store into the 1980s.

93. "Suburban Residence," *Godey's Lady's Book and Magazine*, April 1875, 386. The mansion is also pictured in Egle, *History of the Counties of Dauphin and Lebanon*, 200.

94. Bergengren interprets the mansion differently. He stresses that although the exterior was quite different, the interior design, with its closed floor plan, resembled earlier Schaefferstown houses. Bergengren, "Transformations in the Houses of Schaefferstown," 552–53.

EPILOGUE

1. Brendle, *Brief History of Schaefferstown*, 73; Beers, *Biographical Annals of Lebanon County*, 1:72. Previous owners claimed that the building is haunted; see Tom Epler, "Innkeepers Looking for New Haunts," *Lebanon Daily News*, February 14, 1999, 11A.

2. Sellers, *Market Revolution*, 5, 16.

APPENDIX A

1. Schutte, "George Rex (1682–1772)," 243–44.

2. Ibid., 247; Rex family Bible, Germantown Historical Society, Germantown; Brendle, *Brief History of Schaefferstown*, 172, 176. Dates in brackets indicate discrepancies between the sources.

3. Schutte, "George Rex (1682–1772)," 257; Brendle, *Brief History of Schaefferstown*, 221.

4. Brendle, *Brief History of Schaefferstown*, 172, 174, 176, 207–8; Vallentine, "Vallentine Family History," typescript, 1980, Lebanon County Historical Society, 46–53.

5. Brendle, *Brief History of Schaefferstown*, 209; Vallentine, "Valentine Family History," 53–54.

BIBLIOGRAPHY

PRIMARY SOURCES

Manuscripts

Cumberland County Historical Society, Carlisle, Pennsylvania
  Susannah Ross Thompson daybook, Carlisle, 1792–95
  Adam Zantzinger cash book, Philadelphia, 1796–97
Hagley Museum and Library, Wilmington, Delaware
  Jeremiah Brown daybook and ledgers, Little Britain, Pennsylvania, 1796–1820
Historic Schaefferstown, Inc., Schaefferstown, Pennsylvania (HSI)
  Philip Erpff receipt book, Schaefferstown, 1774–98
  Samuel and Abraham Rex daybooks, ledgers, and other papers, 1789–1835
Historical Society of Pennsylvania, Philadelphia, Pennsylvania
  Cornwall Furnace ledgers, 1789–91, 1794–99, 1804–22
  John M. Price letter book, Philadelphia, 1794–96
Hopewell Furnace National Historic Site, Library and Archives, Elverson, Pennsylvania
  Mount Hope Furnace ledgers and journals, Manheim, 1797–1819, microfilm
Lebanon County Historical Society, Lebanon, Pennsylvania
  D. R. Bernard, "History of Grubb Family, Lebanon Co., Penna," typescript, n.d.
  Kipplinger store ledger, Jonestown, 1797–99
  Leon E. Lewis Collection, 14 rolls microfilm (duplicate at Winterthur Library, Winterthur, Delaware) (LEL)
  "Records of Christ Lutheran, Stouchburg"
  John F. Valentine, "The Valentine Family History," typescript, 1980
Lebanon Valley College, Bishop Library, Rare Book Room, Annville, Pennsylvania
  William Louer tavern ledger, Hummelstown, 1802–4
Pennsylvania State Archives, Harrisburg, Pennsylvania
  Berks and Dauphin Turnpike Road Company, minute book, 1816–20
  Berkshire Furnace ledgers, Robesonia, 1789–91, 1791–94
  Dauphin County tavern license petitions, microfilm
  Elizabeth Furnace daybook, Brickerville, 1764
  Rex Store (Brickerville) accounts with Elizabeth Furnace, 1833
St. Luke Evangelical Lutheran Church, Schaefferstown, Pennsylvania
  Parish register, 1763–1834, typescript
University of Delaware Center for Historic Architecture and Design
  U.S. direct tax returns (USDT), 1798, Dauphin, Lancaster, Philadelphia counties, microfilm
A. R. Wentz Library, Gettysburg Theological Seminary, Gettysburg, Pennsylvania
  Records and documents from St. Luke Lutheran Church, Schaefferstown
Henry Francis du Pont Winterthur Library, Winterthur, Delaware
  Joseph Downs Collection of Manuscripts and Printed Ephemera (JDC)

Joshua Fisher & Sons ledger, microfilm
Leon E. Lewis Collection, 14 rolls microfilm (duplicate at Lebanon County Historical Society)
Anthony Seyfert tavern book, 1799
Justice of the Peace Book, Myerstown, 1797
Samuel and Abraham Rex daybooks, 1790–1818

Newspapers

Lancaster Journal, 1796–98, microfilm, Lancaster County Historical Society
Lebanon Daily News, centennial edition, 1972
Pennsylvania Gazette, 1761–98
    Accessible Archives CD-ROM edition of *Pennsylvania Gazette*
    Accessible Archives, http://www.accessible.com/
    Pennsylvania Gazette, bound, Morris Library, University of Delaware
Poulson's American Daily Advertiser, March 4, 1801

Printed Primary Sources

Account Book of a Country Storekeeper in the 18th Century at Poughkeepsie. Poughkeepsie: Vassar Bros. Institute, 1911.
Bartram, John, Lewis Evans, and Conrad Weiser. *A Journey from Pennsylvania to Onondaga in 1743.* Barre, Mass.: Imprint Society, 1973.
Beers, J. H. *Biographical Annals of Lebanon County, Pennsylvania, Containing Sketches of Prominent and Representative Citizens and of Many of the Early Settled Families.* 2 vols. 1904. Reprint, Bowie, Md.: Heritage Books, 1993.
Biddle, Clement, ed. *The Philadelphia Directory.* Philadelphia, 1791.
Brissot de Warville, Jacques-Pierre. *New Travels in the United States of America, Performed in 1788.* 1792. Reprint, New York: Augustus M. Kelley, 1970.
Cazenove, Theophile. *Cazenove Journal, 1794: A Record of the Journey of Theophile Cazenove Through New Jersey and Pennsylvania.* Edited by Rayner Wickersham Kelsey. Haverford, Pa.: Pennsylvania History Press, 1922.
Croll, P. C. *Ancient and Historic Landmarks in the Lebanon Valley.* Philadelphia: Lutheran Publishing Society, 1895.
Day, Sherman. *Historical Collections of the State of Pennsylvania Containing a Copious Selection of the Most Interesting Facts, Traditions, Biographical Sketches, Anecdotes, etc. Relating to History and Antiquities Both General and Local with Topographical Description of Every County and all the Large Towns in the State.* Philadelphia: George W. Gorton, 1843.
Dilworth, Thomas. *The Young Book-Keeper's Assistant.* Philadelphia: Printed by B. Johnson, [1794].
Drinker, Elizabeth. *The Diary of Elizabeth Drinker: The Life Cycle of an Eighteenth-Century Woman.* Edited by Elaine Forman Crane. Boston: Northeastern University Press, 1991; abridged version, 1994.
Egle, William Henry, ed. *Pennsylvania Archives.* Series 3:17. Harrisburg, Pa.: William Stanley Ray, State Printer, 1897.
Fox, Priscilla Stanley. "Our Old Taverns." *Papers of Lebanon County Historical Society* 10 (1931): 117–58.
Graydon, Alexander. *Memoirs of a Life, Chiefly Passed in Pennsylvania.* Harrisburg, Pa.: John Wyeth, 1811.

Heads of Families at the First Census of the United States Taken in the Year 1790: Pennsylvania. Washington, D.C.: U.S. Government Printing Office, 1908.

Hiltzheimer, Jacob. *Extracts from the Diary of Jacob Hiltzheimer of Philadelphia, 1765–1798.* Edited by Jacob Cox Parsons. Philadelphia: William F. Fell, 1893.

Hocker, Edwin. *Genealogical Data Relating to the German Settlers of Pennsylvania and Adjacent Territory from Advertisements in German Newspapers Published in Germantown and Philadelphia.* Baltimore: Genealogical Publishing Co., 1980.

Jackson, Ronald Vern, Richard Allen Moore, and Gary Ronald Teeples. *Pennsylvania 1800 Census Index.* Vol. 1. Bountiful, Utah: Accelerated Index Systems, 1972.

La Rochefoucauld-Liancourt, François Alexandre Frédéric, duc de. *Travels Through the United States of North America, the Country of the Iroquois, and Upper Canada in the Years 1795, 1796, and 1797.* 2nd ed. 4 vols. London: T. Gillet for R. Phillips, 1800.

Mair, John. *Book-Keeping Methodized.* Edinburgh, 1765.

Mease, James. *The Picture of Philadelphia.* Philadelphia: B. & T. Kite, 1811.

Morgan, George H. *Centennial: The Settlement, Formation and Progress of Dauphin County, Pennsylvania, from 1785 to 1876.* Harrisburg, Pa.: Telegraph Steam Book and Job Printing House, 1877.

M'Robert, Patrick. *A Tour Through Part of the North Provinces of America: Being a Series of Letters Wrote on the Spot in the Years 1774, & 1775.* Edinburgh: Printed for the Author, 1776. Offprint from *Pennsylvania Magazine of History and Biography* (April 1935). Philadelphia: Historical Society of Pennsylvania, 1935.

Muhlenberg, Henry Melchior. *The Journals of Henry Melchior Muhlenberg.* Translated by Theodore G. Tappert and John W. Doberstein. 2 vols. Philadelphia: Evangelical Lutheran Ministerium, Muhlenberg Press, 1958.

Robinson, James. *Philadelphia City and County Register for 1803.* Philadelphia: William M. Woodward, 1803.

Rush, Benjamin. *An Account of the Manners of the German Inhabitants of Pennsylvania.* Introduction and annotations by Theodore E. Schmauk. Part 21 of *Pennsylvania: The German Influence in its Settlement and Development: A Narrative and Critical History.* Lancaster, Pa.: Pennsylvania German Society, 1910.

———. *Letters of Benjamin Rush.* Edited by L. H. Butterfield. 2 vols. Princeton: Princeton University Press, 1951.

Sachse, Julius Friedrich. *A Photographic Ramble in the Millbach Valley (Lebanon County, Penna.).* Philadelphia: Alfred J. Ferris, 1896.

Schoepf, Johann David. *Travels in the Confederation, 1783–1784.* 2 vols. Translated and edited by Alfred J. Morrison. Philadelphia: William J. Campbell, 1911.

Scott, Joseph. *A Geographical Dictionary of the United States of North America, Containing a General Description of Each State, with a Succinct Account of Indiana, and Upper and Lower Louisiana Territories.* Philadelphia: Archibald Bartram for Thomas Armstrong, Proprietor, 1805.

Shea, John H. *Bookkeeping by Single and Double Entry.* Baltimore, 1841.

Sowers, Gladys Bucher. *Colonial Taxes, Heidelberg Township, Lancaster County, Pennsylvania, 1751–1783 (now Lebanon County).* Morgantown, Pa.: Masthof Press, 2004.

Stafford, Cornelius William. *Philadelphia Directory for 1799.* Philadelphia: William M. Woodward, 1799.

———. *Philadelphia Directory for 1801.* Philadelphia: William M. Woodward, 1801.

Stephens, Thomas. *Philadelphia Directory for 1796.* Philadelphia: William M. Woodward, 1796.

St. Mery, Moreau de. *Moreau de St. Mery's American Journey, 1793–1798.* Translated and edited by Kenneth Roberts and Anna M. Roberts. Garden City, N.Y.: Doubleday, 1947.

"Suburban Residence." *Godey's Lady's Book and Magazine* 90 (April 1875): 386.

Tinkcom, Harry M. "Sir Augustus in Pennsylvania: The Travels and Observations of Sir Augustus Foster in Early Nineteenth-Century Pennsylvania." *Pennsylvania Magazine of History and Biography* 75 (1951): 369–99.

Trautman, Frederic. "Pennsylvania Through a German's Eyes: The Travel of Ludwig Gall, 1819–1820." *Pennsylvania Magazine of History and Biography* 105 (January 1981): 35–65.

Weiser, Frederick S., and Larry M. Neff. *Records of Purchases of the King George Hotel, Schaefferstown, Lebanon County, Pennsylvania, 1762–1773.* Birdsboro, Pa.: Pennsylvania German Society, 1987.

SECONDARY SOURCES

Appleby, Joyce. *Capitalism and a New Social Order: The Republican Vision of the 1790s.* New York: New York University Press, 1984.

————. "Commercial Farming and the 'Agrarian Myth' in the Early Republic." *Journal of American History* 68 (March 1982): 833–49.

————. "The Vexed Story of Capitalism Told by American Historians." *Journal of the Early Republic* 21 (spring 2001): 1–18.

Atherton, Lewis. *The Southern Country Store, 1800–1860.* New York: Greenwood Press, 1949.

Barron, Hal S. "Reaping What Has Been Sown: The Current State of Rural History." In *After the Backcountry: Rural Life in the Great Valley of Virginia, 1800–1900,* ed. Kenneth E. Koons and Warren R. Hofstra, 287–92. Knoxville: University of Tennessee Press, 2000.

Bashman, Leslie Debra. "The Sugartown Store: A Study in Community, Commerce, and Preservation." Master's thesis, University of Delaware, 1992.

Beck, Herbert H. "Cannon Hill and the Hessian Ditch with Personal Reminiscences of the Furnace Hills." *Papers of Lancaster County Historical Society* 44 (1940): 21–39.

Becker, Laura Leff. "The American Revolution as a Community Experience: A Case Study of Reading, Pennsylvania." Ph.D. diss., University of Pennsylvania, 1978.

————. "Diversity and Its Significance in an Eighteenth-Century Pennsylvania Town." In *Friends and Neighbors: Group Life in America's First Plural Society,* ed. Michael Zuckerman, 196–221. Philadelphia: Temple University Press, 1982.

————. "The People and the System: Legal Activities in a Colonial Pennsylvania Town." *Pennsylvania Magazine of History and Biography* 105 (April 1981): 134–55.

Beers, J. H. *Biographical Annals of Lebanon County, Pennsylvania, Containing Sketches of Prominent and Representative Citizens and of Many of the Early Settled Families.* 2 vols. 1904. Reprint, Bowie, Md.: Heritage Books, 1993.

Bender, Thomas. *Community and Social Change in America.* New Brunswick: Rutgers University Press, 1978.

Benes, Peter, ed. *The Farm.* Dublin Seminar for New England Folklife Annual Proceedings, 1986. Boston: Boston University, 1988.

Berg, Harry D. "The Organization of Business in Colonial Philadelphia." *Pennsylvania History* 10 (July 1943): 157–77.

Bergengren, Charles Lang. "The Cycle of Transformations in the Houses of Schaefferstown, Pennsylvania." Ph.D. diss., University of Pennsylvania, 1988.

————. "From Lovers to Murderers: The Etiquette of Entry and the Social Implications of House Form." *Winterthur Portfolio* 29 (Fall 1994): 43–72.

Bezanson, Anne, Robert Gray, and Miriam Hussey. *Wholesale Prices in Philadelphia, 1784–1861.* Philadelphia: University of Pennsylvania Press, 1936.

Bezís-Selfa, John. "A Tale of Two Ironworks: Slavery, Free Labor, Work, and Resistance in the Early Republic." *William and Mary Quarterly,* 3d ser., 56 (October 1999): 677–700.

Bining, Arthur. *Pennsylvania Iron Manufacture in the Eighteenth Century.* Harrisburg, Pa.: Pennsylvania Historical and Museum Commission, 1938; 1973.

Blumin, Stuart M. *The Emergence of the Middle Class: Social Experience in the American City, 1760–1900.* Cambridge: Cambridge University Press, 1989.

Bodle, Wayne. "Themes and Directions in Middle Colonies Historiography, 1980–1994." *William and Mary Quarterly,* 3d ser., 51 (July 1994): 355–88.

Boydston, Jeanne. *Home and Work: Housework, Wages, and the Ideology of Labor in the Early Republic.* New York: Oxford University Press, 1990.

———. "The Woman Who Wasn't There: Women's Market Labor and the Transition to Capitalism in the United States." *Journal of the Early Republic* 16 (Summer 1996): 183–206.

Boyer, Paul, and Stephen Nissenbaum. *Salem Possessed: The Social Origins of Witchcraft.* Cambridge: Harvard University Press, 1974.

Breen, T. H. "'Baubles of Britain': The American and Consumer Revolutions of the Eighteenth Century." *Past and Present* 119 (May 1988): 73–104.

———. "An Empire of Goods: The Anglicization of Colonial America, 1690–1776." *Journal of British Studies* 25 (October 1986): 467–99.

Brendle, A. S. *A Brief History of Schaefferstown.* 1901. Reprint, with index, Schaefferstown, Pa.: Historic Schaefferstown, Inc., 1979.

Brener, David A. "Lancaster's First Jewish Community, 1714–1804: The Era of Joseph Simon." *Journal of the Lancaster County Historical Society* 80 (Michelmas 1976): 211–322.

Bridenbaugh, Carl. *The Colonial Craftsman.* New York: New York University Press, 1950.

Brigham, David R. *Public Culture in the Early Republic: Peale's Museum and Its Audience.* Washington, D.C.: Smithsonian Institution Press, 1995

Brown, Donald R. *Lebanon County: A Post Card History.* Lebanon, Pa.: Lebanon County Historical Society, 1992.

Brown, Richard D. *Knowledge Is Power: The Diffusion of Information in Early America, 1700–1865.* New York: Oxford University Press, 1989.

Bruchey, Stuart W. *Robert Oliver and Mercantile Bookkeeping in the Early Nineteenth Century.* New York: Arno Press, 1976.

Bruegel, Martin. *Farm, Shop, Landing: The Rise of a Market Society in the Hudson Valley, 1780–1860.* Durham: Duke University Press, 2002.

Bushman, Richard Lyman. "Markets and Composite Farms in Early America." *William and Mary Quarterly,* 3d ser., 55 (July 1998): 351–74.

———. "Opening the American Countryside." In *The Transformation of Early American History: Society, Authority, and Ideology,* ed. James Henretta, Michael Kammer, and Stanley Katz, 239–56. New York: Knopf, 1991.

———. *The Refinement of America: Persons, Houses, Cities.* New York: Vintage Books, 1993.

———. "Shopping and Advertising in Colonial America." In *Of Consuming Interests: The Style of Life in the Eighteenth Century,* ed. Cary Carson, Ronald Hoffman, and Peter J. Albert, 233–51. Charlottesville: University Press of Virginia for the U.S. Capitol Historical Society, 1994.

Carmean, Edna J., ed. *Lebanon County, Pennsylvania—A History.* Lebanon, Pa.: Lebanon Historical Society, 1976.

Carson, Cary. "Consumer Revolution in Colonial America: Why Demand?" In *Of Consuming Interests: The Style of Life in the Eighteenth Century*, ed. Cary Carson, Ronald Hoffman, and Peter J. Albert, 483–697. Charlottesville: University Press of Virginia for the U.S. Capitol Historical Society, 1994.

Carson, Cary, Ronald Hoffman, and Peter J. Albert, eds. *Of Consuming Interests: The Style of Life in the Eighteenth Century.* Charlottesville: University Press of Virginia for the U.S. Capitol Historical Society, 1994.

Carson, Gerald. *The Old Country Store.* New York: Oxford University Press, 1954.

Cazden, Robert E. *A Social History of the German Book Trade in America to the Civil War.* Columbia, S.C.: Camden House, 1984.

Chandler, Alfred D., Jr. *The Visible Hand: The Managerial Revolution in American Business.* Cambridge: Belknap Press of Harvard University Press, 1977.

Clark, Christopher. "The Consequences of the Market Revolution in the North." In *The Market Revolution in America: Social, Political, and Religious Expressions, 1800–1880*, ed. Melvyn Stokes and Stephen Conway, 23–42. Charlottesville: University Press of Virginia, 1996.

———. "Economics and Culture: Opening Up the Rural History of the Early American Northeast." *American Quarterly* 43 (June 1991): 279–301.

———. "Household Economy, Market Exchange, and the Rise of Capitalism in the Connecticut Valley, 1800–1860." *Journal of Social History* 13 (Winter 1979): 168–89.

———. *The Roots of Rural Capitalism: Western Massachusetts, 1780–1860.* Ithaca: Cornell University Press, 1990.

Clark, Thomas D. *Pills, Plows, and Petticoats: The Southern Country Store.* 1944. Reprint, Norman: University of Oklahoma Press, 1974.

Cleary, Patricia. "'She Will Be in the Shop': Women's Sphere of Trade in Eighteenth-Century Philadelphia and New York." *Pennsylvania Magazine of History and Biography* 119 (July 1995): 181–202.

Clemens, Paul G. E. "Rural Culture and the Farm Economy in Late Eighteenth-Century New Jersey." Foreword to Peter O. Wacker and Paul G. E. Clemens, *Land Use in Early New Jersey: A Historical Geography.* Newark: New Jersey Historical Society, 1995.

Clemens, Paul G. E., and Lucy Simler. "Rural Labor and the Farm Household in Chester County, Pennsylvania." In *Work and Labor in Early America*, ed. Stephen Innes, 106–43. Chapel Hill: University of North Carolina Press for the Institute of Early American History and Culture, 1988.

Cole, Arthur H. "The Tempo of Mercantile Life in Colonial America." *Business History Review* 33 (Autumn 1959): 277–99.

Comprehensive Plan, Heidelberg Township, Lebanon County, Pa. Schaefferstown, Pa.: Heidelberg Township Board of Supervisors, 2000.

Conroy, David W. *In Public Houses: Drink and the Revolution of Authority in Colonial Massachusetts.* Chapel Hill: University of North Carolina Press for the Institute of Early American History and Culture, 1995.

Contosta, David R. *Suburb in the City: Chestnut Hill, Philadelphia, 1850–1990.* Columbus: Ohio State University Press, 1992.

Cox, Harold. "Pennsylvania Gubernatorial Election Returns, 1799." *Pennsylvania Election Statistics, 1789–2004.* Wilkes University Election Statistics Project. http://staffweb.wilkes.edu/harold.cox/index.html.

———. "Pennsylvania Gubernatorial Election Returns, 1800." *Pennsylvania Election Statistics, 1789–2004.* Wilkes University Election Statistics Project. http://staffweb.wilkes.edu/harold.cox/index.html.

Cremers, Estelle. *Reading Furnace, 1736.* Elverson, Pa: Redding Furnace Press, 1986.

Creznic, Jean. "Charming Forge." *Early American Homes* (June 1998): 20–31.

Dalzell, Robert F., Jr. *Enterprising Elite: The Boston Associates and the World They Made.* Cambridge: Harvard University Press, 1987.

Danhof, Clarence H. *Change in Agriculture: The Northern United States, 1820–1870.* Cambridge: Harvard University Press, 1969.

Dauer, David E. "Colonial Philadelphia's Interregional Transportation System: An Overview." Working Paper, Regional Economic History Research Center. Greenville, Del.: Eleutherian Mills-Hagley Foundation, 1979.

De Cunzo, Lu Ann. "The Culture Broker Revisited: Historical Archaeological Perspectives on Merchants in Delaware, 1760–1815." *North American Archaeologist* 16 (1995): 181–222.

De Cunzo, Lu Ann, Angela Hoseth, Jay Hodny, JoAnn E. Jamison, Wade P. Catts, and David C. Bachman. *Final Archaeological Investigations at the John Darrach Store Site, Delaware Route 6—Woodland Beach Road, Smyrna Section, Delaware Route 1 Corridor, Kent County, Delaware.* Delaware Department of Transportation Archaeology, Series no. 93. Newark: University of Delaware Department of Anthropology, Center for Archaeological Research, 1992.

Dibert, James A. *Iron, Independence and Inheritance: The Story of Curttis and Peter Grubb.* Cornwall, Pa.: Cornwall Furnace Associates, 2000.

Ditz, Toby L. "Mercantile Correspondence and the Experience of Risk." Paper presented at the Delaware Seminar in Art, History, and Material Culture, University of Delaware, Newark, April 16, 1997.

———. "Shipwrecked; or, Masculinity Imperiled: Mercantile Representations of Failure and the Gendered Self in Eighteenth-Century Philadelphia." *Journal of American History* 81 (June 1994): 51–80.

Dobb, Maurice. *Studies in the Development of Capitalism.* Rev. ed. New York: International Publishers, 1963.

Doerflinger, Thomas M. "Farmers and Dry Goods in the Philadelphia Market Area, 1750–1800." In *The Economy of Early America: The Revolutionary Period, 1763–1790,* ed. Ronald Hoffman, John J. McCusker, Russell R. Menard, and Peter J. Albert, 167–95. Charlottesville: University Press of Virginia for the United States Capitol Historical Society, 1988.

———. *A Vigorous Spirit of Enterprise: Merchants and Economic Development in Revolutionary Philadelphia.* New York: W. W. Norton, 1987.

Downs, Joseph. *The House of the Miller at Millbach: The Architecture, Arts, and Crafts of the Pennsylvania Germans.* Philadelphia: Pennsylvania Museum of Art, 1929.

Dublin, Thomas. "Rural Putting-Out Work in Early Nineteenth-Century New England: Women and the Transition to Capitalism in the Countryside." *New England Quarterly* 64 (December 1991): 531–73.

Dunn, Richard S., and Mary Maples Dunn, eds. *The World of William Penn.* Philadelphia: University of Pennsylvania Press, 1986.

Eberlein, Harold Donaldson, and Cortlandt Van Dyke Hubbard. *Diary of Independence Hall.* Philadelphia: J. B. Lippincott, 1948.

———. *Portrait of a Colonial City: Philadelphia, 1670–1838.* Philadelphia: J. B. Lippincott, 1939.

Eggert, Gerald G. *The Iron Industry in Pennsylvania.* Pennsylvania History Studies 25. Middletown, Pa.: Pennsylvania Historical Association, 1994.

Egle, William Henry. *History of the Counties of Dauphin and Lebanon in the Commonwealth of Pennsylvania: Biographical and Genealogical.* 1883. Reprint, Salem, Mass.: Higginson Book Company, 1991.

Ellis, Franklin, and Samuel Evans. *The History of Lancaster County, Pennsylvania, with Biographical Sketches of Many of Its Pioneers and Prominent Men.* Philadelphia: Everts & Peck, 1883.

Ellis, Richard E., et al. "A Symposium on Charles Sellers, *The Market Revolution: Jacksonian America, 1815–1846.*" *Journal of the Early Republic* 12 (Winter 1992): 445–76.

Emerson, Catherine L. West. "Clothing the Pennsylvania Mennonite Woman in the Eighteenth Century. *Pennsylvania Mennonite Heritage* (April 1997): 2–19.

Engel, Katherine Carté. "The Strangers' Store: Moral Capitalism in Moravian Bethlehem, 1753–1775." *Early American Studies* 1 (January 2003): 90–126.

Fabian, Monroe. *The Pennsylvania-German Decorated Chest.* 1978. Reprint, Atglen, Pa.: Schiffer Publishing, 2004.

Falk, Cynthia G. *Architecture and Artifacts of the Pennsylvania Germans: Constructing Identity in Early America.* University Park: Pennsylvania State University Press, 2008.

———. "Constructing Identity with Belongings and Buildings: Pennsylvania Germans in the New Nation." Ph.D. diss., University of Delaware, 2000.

Fanelli, Doris D. "William Polk's General Store in Saint George's, Delaware." *Delaware History* 19 (1981): 212–28.

Faris, John T. *Old Roads Out of Philadelphia.* Philadelphia: J. B. Lippincott, 1917.

Fletcher, Stevenson Whitcomb. *Pennsylvania Agriculture and Country Life, 1640–1840.* Harrisburg, Pa.: Pennsylvania Historical and Museum Commission, 1950.

Fogleman, Aaron Spencer. *Hopeful Journeys: German Immigration, Settlement, and Political Culture in Colonial America, 1717–1775.* Philadelphia: University of Pennsylvania Press, 1996.

Foreman, Benno M. "German Influences in Pennsylvania Furniture." In Scott T. Swank, et al., *Arts of the Pennsylvania Germans,* 102–70. New York: W. W. Norton, for the Henry Francis du Pont Winterthur Museum, 1983.

Frick, William K. *Henry Melchior Muhlenberg, Patriarch of the Lutheran Church in America.* Philadelphia: Lutheran Publication Society, 1902.

Friend, Craig T. "Merchants and Markethouses: Reflections on Moral Economy in Early Kentucky." *Journal of the Early Republic* 17 (Winter 1997): 553–75.

Fries, Sylvia. *The Urban Idea in Colonial America.* Philadelphia: Temple University Press, 1977.

Garrison, J. Ritchie. "Battalion Day: Militia Exercise and Frolic in Pennsylvania Before the Civil War." *Pennsylvania Folklife* 26 (1976–77): 2–12.

Garvan, Beatrice B. *The Pennsylvania German Collection.* Handbooks in American Art, no. 2. Philadelphia: Philadelphia Museum of Art, 1982.

Garvan, Beatrice B., and Charles F. Hummel. *The Pennsylvania Germans: A Celebration of Their Arts, 1683–1850.* Philadelphia: Philadelphia Museum of Art, 1982.

Gehret, Ellen J. *Rural Pennsylvania Clothing.* York, Pa.: George Shumway, 1976.

Gehret, Ellen J., and Alan G. Keyser. *The Homespun Textile Tradition of the Pennsylvania Germans.* Harrisburg: Pennsylvania Historical and Museum Commission, 1976.

Gibbons, Phebe Earle. *Pennsylvania Dutch and Other Essays.* Philadelphia: J. B. Lippincott, 1882.

Gilje, Paul A. "The Rise of Capitalism in the Early Republic." In *Wages of Independence: Capitalism in the Early American Republic,* ed. Paul A. Gilje, 1–22. Madison, Wis.: Madison House, 1997.

Gillett, Mary C. *The Army Medical Department, 1775–1818.* Washington, D.C.: U.S. Army, Center of Military History, 1981.

Glatfelter, Charles H. *The Pennsylvania Germans: A Brief Account of Their Influence on Pennsylvania.* Pennsylvania History Studies 20. University Park: Pennsylvania Historical Association, 1990.

Grittinger, Henry C. "Cornwall Furnace and the Cornwall Ore Banks, or Mine Hills Situate at Cornwall, Lebanon County, Penna." *Papers of the Lebanon County Historical Society* 2 (1901): 1–54.

———. "The Iron Industries of Lebanon County." *Papers of the Lebanon County Historical Society* 3 (1905).

Guffin, Robert A., Jr. "'The Satisfaction of Arriving to a Good Market': Richard Vaux and the Eighteenth-Century World of Trade." Master's thesis, University of Delaware, 1991.

Guice, Julia Cook. *Frederick Stump: The Rest of the Story.* Biloxi, Miss., 1991.

Hahn, Steven, and Jonathan Prude, eds. *The Countryside in the Age of Capitalist Transformation: Essays in the Social History of Rural America.* Chapel Hill: University of North Carolina Press, 1985.

Hammond, Bray. *Banks and Politics in America.* Princeton: Princeton University Press, 1937.

Hancock, David. *Citizens of the World: London Merchants and the Integration of the British Atlantic Community, 1735–1785.* Cambridge: Cambridge University Press, 1995.

Harrington, C. R., ed. *The Year Without a Summer? World Climate in 1816.* Ottawa: Canadian Museum of Nature, 1992.

Hays, Jo N. "Overlapping Hinterlands: York, Philadelphia, and Baltimore, 1800–1850." *Pennsylvania Magazine of History and Biography* 116 (July 1992): 295–321.

Heiges, George L. "General S. P. Heintzelman Visits His Hometown of Manheim." *Journal of the Lancaster County Historical Society* 68 (1964): 68–109.

Henretta, James A. "Families and Farms: *Mentalité* in Pre-Industrial America." *William and Mary Quarterly,* 3d ser., 35 (January 1978): 3–32.

———. "The 'Market' in the Early Republic." *Journal of the Early Republic* 18 (Summer 1998): 289–304.

———. "The Transition to Capitalism in America." In *The Transformation of Early American History: Society, Authority, and Ideology,* ed. James A. Henretta, Michael Kammer, and Stanley Katz, 218–38. New York: Knopf, 1991.

Henretta, James A., Michael Kammer, and Stanley Katz, eds. *The Transformation of Early American History: Society, Authority, and Ideology.* New York: Knopf, 1991.

Herman, Bernard L. *Town House: Architecture and Material Life in the Early American City, 1780–1830.* Chapel Hill: University of North Carolina Press for the Omohundro Institute of Early American History and Culture, 2005.

Hersh, Tandy, and Charles Hersh. *Cloth and Costume, 1750 to 1800: Cumberland County, Pennsylvania.* Carlisle, Pa.: Cumberland County Historical Society, 1995.

Hess, Clarke. *Mennonite Arts.* Atglen, Pa.: Schiffer Publishing, 2002.

Higginbotham, Sanford W. *The Keystone in the Democratic Arch: Pennsylvania Politics, 1800–1816.* Harrisburg: Pennsylvania Historical and Museum Commission, 1952.

Historic Philadelphia from the Founding Until the Early Nineteenth Century: Papers Dealing with Its People and Buildings, with an Illustrative Map. Philadelphia: America Philosophical Society, 1953.

History of St. Paul's Church, Schaefferstown, Pa., 1765–1965. Schaefferstown: St. Paul's Church Council, 1965.

Hollander, Stacy C. *American Radiance: The Ralph Esmerian Gift to the American Folk Art Museum.* New York: American Folk Art Museum in association with Harry N. Abrams, Inc., 2001.

Hood, Adrienne D. "The Gender Division of Labor in the Production of Textiles in Eighteenth-Century Rural Pennsylvania (Rethinking the New England Model)." *Journal of Social History* 27 (Spring 1994): 537–61.

———."The Material World of Cloth: Production and Use in Eighteenth-Century Rural Pennsylvania." *William and Mary Quarterly,* 3d ser., 53 (January 1996): 43–66.

———. *The Weaver's Craft: Cloth, Commerce, and Industry in Early Pennsylvania.* Philadelphia: University of Pennsylvania Press, 2003.

Hoover, E. Eileen. "Questions Regarding the Early History of Schaefferstown." *Historic Schaefferstown Record* 7 (December 1973): 46–53.

Hostetter, A. K. "Major General Samuel Peter Heintzelman." *Papers Read Before the Lancaster County Historical Society* 17 (1913): 56–78.

Huber, Charles. *Schaefferstown, Pennsylvania, 1763–1963.* Schaefferstown, Pa.: Schaefferstown Bicentennial Committee, 1963.

Hubka, Thomas C. "Farm Family Mutuality: The Mid-Nineteenth-Century Maine Farm Neighborhood." In *The Farm,* Dublin Seminar for New England Folklife Annual Proceedings, 1986, ed. Peter Benes, 13–23. Boston: Boston University, 1988.

Hutchins, Catherine, ed. *Everyday Life in the Early Republic.* Winterthur, Pa.: Henry Francis du Pont Winterthur Museum, 1994.

Ibach, Earl W. *The Hub of the Tulpehocken.* Lebanon, Pa.: Boyer Printing Co., 1975.

Innes, Stephen, ed. *Work and Labor in Early America.* Chapel Hill: University of North Carolina Press, for the Institute of Early American History and Culture, 1988.

Jackson, Joseph. *Market Street: The Most Historic Highway in America.* Philadelphia: Joseph Jackson, 1918.

Jaffee, David. "Peddlers of Progress and the Transformation of the Rural North, 1760–1860." *Journal of American History* 78 (September 1991): 511–35.

Jenkins, Charles F. *Guidebook to Historic Germantown.* Germantown, Pa.: Prepared for the Site & Relic Society, 1902; 1973.

Jensen, Arthur L. *The Maritime Commerce of Colonial Philadelphia.* Madison: State Historical Society of Wisconsin for the Department of History, University of Wisconsin, 1963.

Jensen, Joan M. *Loosening the Bonds: Mid-Atlantic Farm Women, 1750–1850.* New Haven: Yale University Press, 1986.

Jensen, Merrill. *The New Nation: A History of the United States During the Confederation, 1781–1789.* New York: Knopf, 1950.

Johnson, Laurence A. *Over the Counter and on the Shelf.* New York: Bonanza Books, 1961.

Kelker, Rudolph F. *Genealogical Record of the Family of Koelliker of Herrliburg, District Meilen, Canton Zurich, Switzerland.* Harrisburg, Pa.: Lane S. Hart, 1883.

Kemper, Jackson III. *American Charcoal Making in the Era of the Cold-Blast Furnace.* Elverson, Pa.: Hopewell Furnace National Historic Site, 1941.

Keyser, Alan G. "Beds, Bedding, Bedsteads, and Sleep." *Der Reggeboge* 12 (1978): 1–28.

———."Gardens and Gardening Among the Pennsylvania Germans." *Pennsylvania Folklife* 20 (Spring 1971): 2–15.

Klees, Fredric. *The Pennsylvania Dutch.* New York: Macmillan, 1950.

Klepp, Susan E., and Susan Branson. "A Working Woman: The Autobiography of Ann Baker Carson." In *Life in Early Philadelphia: Documents from the Revolutionary and Early National Periods,* ed. Billy G. Smith, 155–74. University Park: Pennsylvania State University Press, 1995.

Kline, Myrle Mann. *Education in Heidelberg Township, ? to 1962.* Manuscript. 1976.

Knauff, James Owen, Jr. *Social Conditions Among the Pennsylvania Germans in the Eighteenth*

Century as Revealed in German Newspapers Published in America. Lancaster: Pennsylvania German Society, 1922.

Koons, Kenneth E., and Warren R. Hofstra. *After the Backcountry: Rural Life in the Great Valley of Virginia, 1800–1900*. Knoxville: University of Tennessee Press, 2000.

Kulikoff, Allan. *The Agrarian Origins of American Capitalism*. Charlottesville: University Press of Virginia, 1992.

———. "Households and Markets: Toward a New Synthesis of American Agrarian History." *William and Mary Quarterly*, 3d ser., 50 (April 1993): 342–55.

———. *Tobacco and Slaves: The Development of Southern Cultures in the Chesapeake, 1680– 1800*. Chapel Hill: University of North Carolina Press, for the Institute of Early American History and Culture, 1986.

———. "The Transition to Capitalism in Rural America." *William and Mary Quarterly*, 3d ser., 46 (January 1989): 120–44.

Lamoreaux, Naomi R. "Accounting for Capitalism in Early American History: Farmers, Merchants, Manufacturers, and Their Economic Worlds." Paper presented at the annual meeting of the Society for Historians of the Early Republic, Lexington, Kentucky, July 16, 1999.

———. "Rethinking the Transition to Capitalism in the Early American Northeast." *Journal of American History* 90 (September 2003): 437–61.

Landis Valley Cookbook: Pennsylvania German Food and Traditions. Lancaster: Pennsylvania Historical and Museum Commission and Landis Valley Associates, 1999.

Larkin, Jack. *The Reshaping of Everyday Life, 1790–1840*. New York: Harper & Row, 1988.

Larsen, Grace Hutchinson. "Profile of a Colonial Merchant: Thomas Clifford of Pre-Revolutionary Philadelphia." Ph.D. diss., Columbia University, 1995.

Lemon, James T. *The Best Poor Man's Country: A Geographical Study of Early Southeastern Pennsylvania*. Baltimore: Johns Hopkins University Press, 1972.

———. "Household Consumption in Eighteenth-Century America." *Agricultural History* 41 (January 1967): 59–79.

Lewis, Johanna Miller. *Artisans in the North Carolina Backcountry*. Lexington: University Press of Kentucky, 1995.

Lichtenstein, Nelson, et al. *Who Built America? Working People and the Nation's Economy, Politics, Culture, and Society*. American Social History Project, vol. 2. New York: Worth Publishers, 2000.

Lindstrom, Diane. *Economic Development in the Philadelphia Region, 1810–1850*. New York: Columbia University Press, 1978.

Livingood, James Weston. *The Philadelphia-Baltimore Trade Rivalry, 1780–1860*. 1947. Reprint, New York: Arno Press, 1970.

Lockridge, Kenneth A. *A New England Town: The First Hundred Years*. New York: W. W. Norton, 1970; 1985.

Long, Amos. "The General Store." *Pennsylvania Folklife* 39 (Spring 1990): 98–116.

Loose, Jack W. W. "Charcoal Furnace and Forge Industries." *Early Manufacturing in Lancaster County: Papers of the Lancaster County Historical Society* 59 (1956): 168–80.

MacFarlane, John J. *History of Early Chestnut Hill*. Philadelphia: City Historical Society, 1927.

Mancall, Peter C. *Valley of Opportunity: Economic Culture Along the Upper Susquehanna, 1700–1800*. Ithaca: Cornell University Press, 1991.

Martin, Ann Smart. "Buying into the World of Goods: Eighteenth-Century Consumerism and the Retail Trade from London to the Virginia Frontier." Ph.D. diss., College of William and Mary, 1993.

———. "Makers, Buyers, and Users: Consumerism as a Material Culture Framework." *Winterthur Portfolio* 28 (Summer–Autumn 1993): 141–57.

Martin, Margaret E. *Merchants and Trade of Connecticut River Valley, 1750–1820.* Smith College Studies in History 24. Northampton, Mass.: Smith College, Department of History, 1939.

Matson, Cathy. "Making Waves or All Washed Up: Thinking About Commerce in the Early American Republic." Paper presented at the History Workshop in Technology, Society, and Culture, University of Delaware, Newark, February 16, 1999.

———. *Merchants and Empire: Trading in Colonial New York.* Baltimore: Johns Hopkins University Press, 1998.

Mays, George. *"Battalion" or Training Days at Schaefferstown in the Olden Time.* Paper of Lebanon County Historical Society. Lebanon, Pa.: Courier Print, 1899.

———. *The Jewish Colony at Tower Hill: Schaefferstown, Lebanon Co., Pennsylvania.* Philadelphia, 1905.

McCoy, Drew R. *The Elusive Republic: Political Economy in Jeffersonian America.* New York: W. W. Norton, 1982.

McCurry, Stephanie. *Masters of Small Worlds: Yeoman Households, Gender Relations, and the Political Culture of the Antebellum South Low Country.* New York: Oxford University Press, 1995.

McCusker, John J. *Money and Exchange in Europe and America, 1660–1775.* New York: W. W. Norton, 1982.

McMurry, Sally. *Transforming Rural Life: Dairying Families and Agricultural Change, 1820–1885.* Baltimore: Johns Hopkins University Press, 1995.

Merrill, Michael. "Cash Is Good to Eat: Self-Sufficiency and Exchange in the Rural Economy of the United States." *Radical History Review* 4 (Winter 1977): 42–71.

———. "Putting 'Capitalism' in Its Place: A Review of Recent Literature." *William and Mary Quarterly,* 3d ser., 52 (April 1995): 315–26.

Meyer, David R. *The Roots of American Industrialization.* Baltimore: Johns Hopkins University Press, 2003.

Miller, Daniel. *Early German American Newspapers.* Pennsylvania: The German Influence in Its Settlement and Development; A Narrative and Critical History, no. 22. Lancaster: Pennsylvania German Society, 1911.

Miller, Frederic K. *The Rise of an Iron Community: An Economic History of Lebanon County, Pennsylvania, from 1740 to 1865.* Lebanon, Pa.: Lebanon County Historical Society, 1950.

Miller, Richard G. "The Federal City, 1783–1800." In *Philadelphia: A 300-Year History,* ed. Russel F. Weigley, 155–207. New York: W. W. Norton, 1982.

Mitchell, Robert D. *Commercialism and Frontier: Perspectives on the Early Shenandoah Valley.* Charlottesville: University Press of Virginia, 1977.

Montgomery, Morton L. *Historical and Biographical Annals of Berks County, Pennsylvania.* 2 vols. Chicago: J. H. Beers & Co., 1909.

Mui, Hoh-Cheung, and Lorna H. Mui. *Shops and Shopkeeping in Eighteenth-Century England.* Montreal: McGill-Queen's University Press, 1989.

Mutch, Robert E. "Yeoman and Merchant in Pre-Industrial America: Eighteenth-Century Massachusetts as a Case Study." *Societas* 7 (Autumn 1977): 279–302.

Myers, Lori. "Forging a Link with History." *Central PA,* October 2000, 43–49.

Myerstown, Pennsylvania, 1768–1968. Myerstown, Pa.: Bicentennial Committee, 1968.

Nash, Gary B. *Forging Freedom: The Formation of Philadelphia's Black Community, 1720–1840.* Cambridge: Harvard University Press, 1988.

Nettels, Curtis. P. *The Emergence of a National Economy, 1775–1815*. New York: Holt, Rine-hart, Winston, 1962.

Newman, Paul Douglas. *Fries's Rebellion: The Enduring Struggle for the American Revolution*. Philadelphia: University of Pennsylvania Press, 2004.

Nissenbaum, Stephen. *The Battle for Christmas*. New York: Alfred A. Knopf, 1996.

Noble, Richard E. *The Touch of Time: Robert Habersham Coleman, 1856–1930*. Lebanon, Pa.: Lebanon County Historical Society, 1983.

Nobles, Gregory. "The Rise of Merchants in Rural Market Towns: A Case Study of Eighteenth-Century Northampton, Massachusetts." *Journal of Social History* 24 (Fall 1990): 5–23.

Nolt, Steven M. *Foreigners in Their Own Land: Pennsylvania Germans in the Early Republic*. Pennsylvania German History and Culture Series, no. 2. University Park: Pennsylvania State University Press, 2002.

Oakes, Elinor F. "A Ticklish Business: Dairying in New England and Pennsylvania, 1750–1812." *Pennsylvania History* 47 (July 1980): 195–212.

Oblinger, Carl. *Cornwall: The People and Culture of an Industrial Camelot*. Harrisburg: Pennsylvania Historic and Museum Commission, 1984.

Osterud, Nancy Grey. "Gender and the Transition to Capitalism in Rural America." *Agricultural History* 67 (Spring 1993): 14–29.

Papenfuse, Edward C. *In Pursuit of Profit: The Annapolis Merchants in the Era of the American Revolution, 1763–1805*. Baltimore: Johns Hopkins University Press, 1975.

Parsons, William T. *The Pennsylvania Dutch: A Persistent Minority*. Boston: Twayne Publishers, 1976.

Paskoff, Paul F. *Industrial Evolution: Organization, Structure, and Growth of the Pennsylvania Iron Industry, 1750–1860*. Baltimore: Johns Hopkins University Press, 1983.

Pencak, William. *Jews and Gentiles in Early America, 1654–1800*. Ann Arbor: University of Michigan Press, 2005.

Pendleton, Philip E. *Oley Valley Heritage: The Colonial Years, 1700–1775*. Birdsboro: Pennsylvania German Society, and Oley, Pa: Oley Valley Heritage Association, 1994.

Perkins, Edwin J. "The Entrepreneurial Spirit in Colonial America: The Foundations of Modern Business History." *Business History Review* 43 (Spring 1989): 160–86.

Perkins, Elizabeth A. "The Consumer Frontier: Household Consumption in Early Kentucky." *Journal of American History* 78 (September 1991): 486–510.

Plummer, Wilbur C. "Consumer Credit in Colonial Philadelphia." *Pennsylvania Magazine of History and Biography* 66 (October 1942): 385–409.

Pruitt, Bettye Hobbs. "Self-Sufficiency and the Agricultural Economy of Eighteenth-Century Massachusetts." *William and Mary Quarterly*, 3d ser., 41 (July 1984): 333–64.

Quimby, Ian M. G. *The Craftsman in Early America*. New York: W. W. Norton, for the Henry Francis du Pont Winterthur Museum, 1984.

Rechcige, Miloslav Jr. "The Demuth Genealogy Revisited: A Moravian Brethren Family from Czechoslovakia." *Journal of Lancaster County Historical Society* 92 (1989–90): 55–68.

Reist, John R. *History of St. Luke's Lutheran Church, Schaefferstown, PA, Sesqui-Centennial, 1765–1915*. Schaefferstown, Pa.: Published by Request of Church Council, 1915.

Remer, Rosalind. *Printers and Men of Capital: Philadelphia Book Publishers in the New Republic*. Philadelphia: University of Pennsylvania Press, 1996.

Rice, William S. "Mount Hope Furnace: An Early Landmark." *American-German Review* (1951): 28–29.

Richman, Irwin. *Pennsylvania German Arts: More than Hearts, Parrots, and Tulips.* Atglen, Pa.: Schiffer Publishing, 2001.

Riley, Edward. "Philadelphia, the Nation's Capital, 1790–1800." *Pennsylvania History* 20 (October 1953): 357–79.

Ritter, Abraham. *Philadelphia and Her Merchants.* Philadelphia, 1860.

Roach, Hannah Benner. *The Back Part of Germantown: A Reconstruction.* Philadelphia: Genealogical Society of Pennsylvania, 2001.

Roeber, A. G. "'The Origin of Whatever Is Not English Among Us': The Dutch-Speaking and the German-Speaking Peoples of British America." In *Strangers Within the Realm: Cultural Margins of the First British Empire,* ed. Bernard Bailyn and Philip D. Morgan, 220–83. Chapel Hill: University of North Carolina Press for the Institute of Early American History and Culture, 1991.

———. *Palatines and Property: German Lutherans in Colonial British America.* Baltimore: Johns Hopkins University Press, 1993; 1998.

Rothenberg, Winifred B. "The Emergence of Farm Labor Markets and the Transformation of the Rural Economy, Massachusetts, 1750–1855." *Journal of Economic History* 48 (September 1988): 537–66.

———. *From Market Places to a Market Economy: The Transformation of Rural Massachusetts, 1750 to 1850.* Chicago: University of Chicago Press, 1992.

———. "The Invention of American Capitalism: The Economy of New England in the Federal Period." In *Engines of Enterprise: An Economic History of New England,* ed. Peter Temin, 68–108. Cambridge: Harvard University Press, 2000.

———. "The Market and Massachusetts Farmers, 1750–1855." *Journal of Economic History* 41 (June 1981): 283–314.

Rutman, Darret B. "The Social Web: A Prospectus for the Study of the Early American Community." In *Insights and Parallels: Problems and Issues of American Social History,* ed. William L. O'Neill, 57–89. Minneapolis: Burgess Printing, 1973.

Rutman, Darret B., and Anita H. Rutman. *A Place in Time: Middlesex County, Virginia, 1650–1750.* New York: W. W. Norton, 1984.

Sachse, Julius F. *The Wayside Inns on the Lancaster Roadside Between Philadelphia and Lancaster.* 2d ed. Lancaster, Pa.: New Era Printing Co., 1915.

Salinger, Sharon V. "Spaces, Inside and Outside, in Eighteenth-Century Philadelphia." *Journal of Interdisciplinary History* 26 (Summer 1995): 1–31.

———. *"To Serve Well and Faithfully": Labor and Indentured Servants in Pennsylvania, 1682–1800.* Cambridge: Cambridge University Press, 1987.

Salinger, Sharon V., and Charles Wetherell. "Wealth and Renting in Prerevolutionary Philadelphia." *Journal of American History* 71 (March 1985): 826–40.

Schantz, F. J. F. *The Domestic Life and Characteristics of the Pennsylvania-German Pioneer.* Lancaster: Pennsylvania German Society, 1900.

Schlereth, Thomas J. "Country Stores, County Fairs, and Mail-Order Catalogues: Consumption in Rural America." In *Consuming Visions: Accumulation and Display of Goods in America, 1880–1920,* ed. Simon J. Bronner, 339–75. New York: W. W. Norton, 1989.

Schmauk, Theodore E. *The Early Churches of Lebanon County.* Publication of the Lebanon Historical Society. Lebanon, Pa.: Century Printing Co., 1902.

Schutte, Doris Rex. "George Rex (1682–1772) of Germantown, Pennsylvania." *National Genealogical Society Quarterly* 68 (December 1980): 243–58.

Schweitzer, Mary M. *Custom and Contract: Household, Government, and the Economy in Colonial Pennsylvania.* New York: Columbia University Press, 1987.

―――. "Spatial Organization of Federalist Philadelphia." *Journal of Interdisciplinary History* 24 (Summer 1993): 31–57.

Schwind, Arlene Palmer. "Pennsylvania German Earthenware." In Scott T. Swank, et al., *Arts of the Pennsylvania Germans*, 171–99. New York: W. W. Norton, for the Henry Francis du Pont Winterthur Museum, 1983.

Sellers, Charles. *The Market Revolution: Jacksonian America, 1815–1846*. New York: Oxford University Press, 1991.

Shammas, Carole. "How Self-Sufficient Was Early America?" *Journal of Interdisciplinary History* 13 (Autumn 1982): 244–73.

―――. *The Pre-Industrial Consumer in England and America*. Oxford: Clarendon Press, 1990.

―――. "The Space Problem in Early United States Cities." *William and Mary Quarterly*, 3d ser., 57 (July 2000): 505–42.

Shoemaker, Alfred L. *Christmas in Pennsylvania*. 1959. Reprint, with introduction and new foreword and afterword by Don Yoder. Mechanicsburg, Pa.: Stackpole Books, 1999.

Siegel, Adrienne, ed. *Philadelphia: A Chronological and Documentary History, 1615–1970*. Dobbs Ferry, N.Y.: Oceana Publications, 1975.

Silverman, Sharon Hernes. "A Blast from the Past: Cornwall Iron Furnace." *Pennsylvania Heritage* (Spring 1988): 20–31.

Simler, Lucy. "The Township: The Community of the Rural Pennsylvanian." *Pennsylvania Magazine of History and Biography* 106 (January 1982): 41–68.

Simpson, Henry. *The Lives of Eminent Philadelphians, Now Deceased*. Philadelphia: William Brotherhead, 1859.

Smart, Ann Morgan. "The Urban/Rural Dichotomy of Status Consumption: Tidewater Virginia, 1815." Master's thesis, College of William and Mary, 1986.

Smith, Barbara Clark. "Food Rioters and the American Revolution." *William and Mary Quarterly*, 3d ser., 51 (January 1994): 3–38.

Smith, Billy G. *The "Lower Sort": Philadelphia's Laboring People, 1750–1800*. Ithaca: Cornell University Press, 1990.

Stern, Malcolm H. "Two Jewish Functionaries in Colonial Pennsylvania." *American Jewish Historical Quarterly* 57 (1967): 27–51.

Stokes, Melvyn, and Stephen Conway. *The Market Revolution in America: Social Political, and Religious Expressions, 1800–1880*. Charlottesville: University Press of Virginia, 1996.

Stommel, Henry M., and Elizabeth Stommel. *Volcano Weather: The Story of 1816, the Year Without a Summer*. Newport, R.I.: Seven Seas Press, 1983.

Stoudt, John Joseph. *Sunbonnets and Shoofly Pies: A Pennsylvania Dutch Cultural History*. New York: Castle Books, 1973.

Strattan, Richard. "History of the Cornwall Ore Bank Company: Part I, Historical Background." *Cornwall Ledger* 9 (May 1998): 1–2.

―――. "The Iron Industry in the Schaefferstown Area." *Historic Schaefferstown Record* 29 (1996).

Swank, Scott T. "The Architectural Landscape." In Scott T. Swank et al., *Arts of the Pennsylvania Germans*, 20–34. New York: W. W. Norton for the Henry Francis du Pont Winterthur Museum, 1983.

―――. "The Germanic Fragment." In Scott T. Swank et al., *Arts of the Pennsylvania Germans*, 3–19. New York: W. W. Norton for the Henry Francis du Pont Winterthur Museum, 1983.

Swank, Scott T., et al. *Arts of the Pennsylvania Germans*. New York: W. W. Norton for the Henry Francis du Pont Winterthur Museum, 1983.

Sweeney, Kevin M. "Gentlemen Farmers and Inland Merchants: The Williams Family and

Commercial Agriculture in Pre-Revolutionary Western Massachusetts." In *The Farm*, Dublin Seminar for New England Folklife Annual Proceedings, 1986, ed. Peter Benes, 6–73. Boston: Boston University, 1988.

Taylor, Charles Rogers. *The Transportation Revolution, 1815–1860*. New York: Rinehart, 1951.

Taylor, Susan Leigh. "'Where Humbler Shop-Men from the Crowd Retreat': Gable Front Stores and the Early Commercial Landscape of Rural Delaware." Master's thesis, University of Delaware, 1997.

Thompson, Peter. *Rum Punch and Revolution: Taverngoing and Public Life in Eighteenth-Century Philadelphia*. Philadelphia: University of Pennsylvania Press, 1999.

Thornton, Tamara Plakins. *Handwriting in America: A Cultural History*. New Haven: Yale University Press, 1996.

Thorp, Daniel B. "Doing Business in the Backcountry: Retail Trade in Colonial Rowan County, North Carolina." *William and Mary Quarterly*, 3d ser., 48 (July 1991): 387–408.

Tinkcom, Harry Marlin. *The Republicans and Federalists in Pennsylvania, 1790–1801: A Study in National Stimulus and Local Response*. Harrisburg, Pa.: Pennsylvania Historical and Museum Commission, 1950.

Tolles, Frederick Barnes. *Meeting House and Counting House: The Quaker Merchants of Colonial Philadelphia, 1682–1763*. Chapel Hill: University of North Carolina Press, for the Institute of Early American History and Culture, 1948.

Tönnies, Ferdinand. *Fundamental Concepts of Sociology (Gemeinschaft und Gesellschaft)*. Translated and supplemented by Charles Loomis. New York: American Book Co., 1940.

Tooker, Elva. *Nathan Trotter, Philadelphia Merchant, 1787–1853*. Harvard Studies in Business History 19. Cambridge: Harvard University Press, 1955.

Ulrich, Laurel Thatcher. "Martha Ballard and Her Girls: Women's Work in Eighteenth-Century Maine." In *Work and Labor in Early America*, ed. Stephen Innes, 70–105. Chapel Hill: University of North Carolina Press for the Institute of Early American History and Culture, 1988.

———. "Wheels, Looms, and the Gender Division of Labor in Eighteenth-Century New England." *William and Mary Quarterly*, 3d ser., 55 (January 1998): 3–38.

Vickers, Daniel. "Competency and Competition: Economic Culture in Early America." *William and Mary Quarterly*, 3d ser., 47 (January 1990): 3–29.

Wainwright, Nicholas. *Colonial Grandeur in Philadelphia: The House and Furniture of General John Cadwalader*. Philadelphia: Historical Society of Pennsylvania, 1964.

Waldstreicher, David. *In the Midst of Perpetual Fetes: The Making of American Nationalism, 1776–1820*. Chapel Hill: University of North Carolina Press, 1997.

Walker, Joseph E. *Hopewell Village: The Dynamics of a Nineteenth-Century Iron-Making Community*. Philadelphia: University of Pennsylvania Press, 1966.

Wallace, Anthony F. C. *Rockdale: The Growth of an American Village in the Early Industrial Revolution*. New York: Knopf, 1978.

Walton, Gary M., and Hugh Rockoff. *History of the American Economy*. 8th ed. Fort Worth: Dryden Press, 1998.

Walzer, John F. "Colonial Philadelphia and Its Backcountry." *Winterthur Portfolio* 7 (1972): 161–74.

Warner, Sam Bass, Jr. *The Private City: Philadelphia in Three Periods of Its Growth*. Philadelphia: University of Pennsylvania Press, 1968.

Weaver, William Woys. *Pennsylvania Dutch Cooking*. New York: Abbeville Press, 1993.

———. *Sauerkraut Yankees: Pennsylvania Dutch Foods and Foodways*. 2d ed. Mechanicsburg, Pa.: Stackpole Books, 2002.

Webster, Richard J. *Philadelphia Preserved: Catalog of the Historic American Buildings Survey.* Philadelphia: Temple University Press, 1976.

Weiser, Frederick S. "Fraktur." In Scott T. Swank, et al. *Arts of the Pennsylvania Germans,* 230–64. New York: W. W. Norton for the Henry Francis du Pont Winterthur Museum, 1983.

Wenger, Diane E. "A Brief History of Storekeeping in Schaefferstown." *Historic Schaefferstown Record* 33 (November 2000).

———. "Creating Networks: The Country Storekeeper and the Mid-Atlantic Economy." Ph.D. diss., University of Delaware, 2001.

———. "Delivering the Goods: The Country Storekeeper and Inland Commerce in the Mid-Atlantic." *Pennsylvania Magazine of History and Biography* 129 (January 2005): 45–72.

———. "Reading the Gemberling-Rex House: The Historical Evidence." *Pennsylvania History* 75 (Winter 2008): 67–85.

———. "Saffron Use Among Pennsylvania Germans: A History and Ethnography." *Der Reggeboge* 36 (2002): 3–20.

———. "Samuel Rex's Store, Heidelberg, Pa.: An Early 19th-Century Business, Its Proprietor, and Its Customers." Master's thesis, Pennsylvania State University at Harrisburg, 1994.

Wermuth, Thomas S. *Rip Van Winkle's Neighbors: The Transformation of Rural Society in the Hudson River Valley.* Albany: State University of New York Press, 2001.

Wesson, Kenneth R. "The Southern Country Store Revisited: A Test Case." *Alabama Historical Quarterly* 42 (Fall–Winter 1980): 157–66.

Whisker, James Biser. *Pennsylvania Potters, 1660–1900.* Lewiston, N.Y.: Edwin Mellen Press, 1993.

Wilentz, Sean. "Society, Politics, and the Market Revolution, 1815–1848." In *The New American History,* ed. Eric Foner, 51–71. Philadelphia: Temple University Press, 1990.

Winpenny, Thomas R. *Bending Is Not Breaking: Adaptation and Persistence Among 19th-Century Lancaster Artisans.* Lanham, Md.: University Press of America, 1990.

Wolf, Stephanie Grauman. "Artisans and the Occupational Structure of an Industrial Town: 18th-Century Germantown, Pennsylvania." Working Paper, Regional Economic History Research Center. Greenville, Del.: Eleutherian Mills-Hagley Foundation, 1977.

———. *Urban Village: Population, Community, and Family Structure in Germantown, Pennsylvania, 1683–1800.* Princeton: Princeton University Press, 1976.

Wood, Gordon S. "The Significance of the Early Republic." *Journal of the Early Republic* 8 (Spring 1988): 1–20.

Wood, Jerome H., Jr. *Conestoga Crossroads: Lancaster, Pa., 1730–1790.* Harrisburg: Pennsylvania Historical and Museum Commission, 1979.

Yeakel, Rubin. *Jacob Albright and His Co-Laborers.* Cleveland: Publishing House of the Evangelical Association, 1883.

Zerbe, Charles M. *Annals of Shaefferstown with Some Reference to the Early Jewish Community.* Lebanon: Lebanon County Historical Society, 1908.

INDEX

CPSIA information can be obtained at www.ICGtesting.com
Printed in the USA
BVOW082218061112

304850BV00001B/14/P